Public
Speaking
as a
Liberal Art

--•◀ *Second Edition* ▶•--

Public Speaking as a Liberal Art

--◦▪{ *Second Edition* }▪◦--

JOHN F. WILSON

HERBERT H. LEHMAN COLLEGE
THE CITY UNIVERSITY OF NEW YORK

CARROLL C. ARNOLD

PENNSYLVANIA STATE UNIVERSITY

ALLYN AND BACON, INC.,
BOSTON

Library of Congress Catalog Card Number 68-19715

PRINTED IN THE UNITED STATES OF AMERICA

Third printing . . . . April, 1969

Preface

In revising *Public Speaking as a Liberal Art* we have weighed again all that was said in the first edition, tried to say it better, introduced new topics where experience showed they were needed, and updated evidence from recent research to increase the book's usefulness. Our revision has been complete though not dramatic. We have preserved the spirit and substance of the earlier edition for we are committed to both by the lessons of study and experience. We offer what we hope is a better though not basically different treatment of public speaking as a humane and liberating art.

We hold that public speaking is an art because it is principled human behavior of considerable expressive and social consequence. We hold that it is a *liberal* art when comprehensively studied in theory and use. The art comprises the choices men have as social beings related by speaking and listening; disciplined exertion of social force is its end. We have revised, as we originally wrote, in the belief that modern college students will speak in public and pass judgment on public speeches. The understanding with which they speak and the competence with which they judge seem to us important, if it is important that liberally educated men and women shall know themselves, their potentialities, and their human environment.

No one entirely understands the acts of making and responding to speech. Philosophers, teachers, literary men, statesmen, scientists, and generations of students have probed these distinctively human experiences without fully penetrating their nature. This book tries to explain one aspect of these experiences insofar as our limited understandings allow. The exposition is traditional in that it rests on knowledge and hypotheses developed over many centuries. It is modern in that empirical evidence undergirds much that is said.

The plan of this revision essentially duplicates that of the first edition. We seek to present an organized body of theory to be contemplated, evaluated, and practically applied. We emphasize the demands that are imposed on speakers because primary effects of public speech emerge from dynamic interactions among speaker, audience, material, and occasion. We retain our original emphasis on the nature and problems of public speaking in general, treating secondarily the variations from general practice that speaking to inform, inquire, reinforce, persuade, and entertain require. For this reason a special index is provided to assist those who prefer to emphasize the forms or types of speeches.

Two features of our plan require prefatory explanation. First, we frequently open topics for study with historical reviews and with alternative definitions of relevant concepts and terms. We hope thereby to suggest that public speaking is not a skill learned by rule but an exercise of judgment that can be no better than the speaker's understanding of the nature of communicative acts. We hope students and teachers will find it intellectually exciting to analyze why some men have thought more wisely than others about human communication. There is, we think, much to be learned about public speaking from examining and accounting for conflicting declarations about "the way things are." Such reflection liberates men from the mistakes of their forebears and from mindless dependence on definitions and rules.

Second, we have chosen to omit such topics as group discussion, debating, and broadcasting in order to present a unified, relatively brief, but thorough book. We have tried, however, to treat fundamental problems of theory and practice in such ways that those who choose to introduce additional material will find what we have said of public speaking a sound foundation on which to rest consideration of other modes of oral discourse.

No book is published without the contributions and assistance of others. Most of what is worthy here we have learned from our students, our colleagues, and our teachers. We are particularly indebted to those who helped prepare the first edition: Professor Edelwina C. Legaspi and Nancy Wolfers, Assistant Editor, Allyn and Bacon, Inc., who lent valuable editorial assistance; Bie Arnold, who prepared the final manuscript; Barbara L. Rowan, who read proof; and Wayne A. Barcomb,

Executive Editor, Allyn and Bacon, Inc., who provided valuable suggestions and encouragement. In preparing this second edition we add to these: Jon Verplanck, Associate Editor and Beverly Malatesta, Assistant Editor, Allyn and Bacon, Inc., and Janet Koltun, who performed editorial tasks with insight and understanding, and Professor Joseph A. De Vito, Hunter College, City University of New York, who aided in the final stages of preparation. In revising we also incurred a special debt to Professor Marie B. Carr, San Jose State College and Professor R. Victor Harnack, University of Illinois at Chicago Circle. We have leaned heavily on their incisive criticism of the first edition, always reserving the privilege of erring on our own account.

J.F.W.
C.C.A.

Contents

Contents

Public
Speaking
as a
Liberal Art

--◦◀ *Second Edition* ▶◦--

The Art of
Public Speaking

We ought, therefore, to think of the art of discourse just as we think of the other arts, and not to form opposite judgments about similar things, nor show ourselves intolerant toward that power, which, of all the faculties which belong to the nature of man, is the source of most of our blessings. For in the other powers which we possess . . . we are in no respect superior to other living creatures; nay, we are inferior to many in swiftness and in strength and in other resources; but, because there has been implanted in us the power to persuade each other and to make clear to each other whatever we desire, not only have we escaped the life of the wild beasts, but we have come together and founded cities and made laws and invented arts; and generally speaking, there is no institution devised by man which the power of speech has not helped us to establish.

Isocrates, "Antidosis"[1]

It is difficult to picture a world of silence—a world in which there is no human speech. Yet, most of us take for granted our ability to communicate with others. We have been talking for years, but few pause to consider what it is we do when we talk or why we talk. We are scarcely aware that approximately 75 per cent of a normal day is spent listening and speaking. Probably about one-third of

---

[1] Reprinted by permission of the publishers and the Loeb Classical Library from Isocrates, "Antidosis," trans. by George Norlin in *Isocrates* (Cambridge, Mass.: Harvard University Press, 1956), II, p. 327.

our time is spent associating with others through the medium of speech.[2]

Speech is learned quite by chance from those around us; from our friends, our parents, our teachers, and our religious leaders. Some of us learn to speak well because our models are good; some of us develop poor speech habits because our models are bad. Even those of us who have accidentally learned to speak well can improve our ability to express thoughts and feelings.

Most of us take speech so much for granted that only when it is defective or breaks down do we accord it attention. We pity the deaf and the mute, or the boy who stutters, or the girl who lisps. Indeed, "communication breakdown" has become one of the great tragic themes of our time. The physiological breakdown of communication is vividly portrayed in the writings of Helen Keller. Breakdown due to psychological difficulties is exemplified in Herman Melville's *Billy Budd* and in Robert Anderson's *Tea and Sympathy*. Too often we must experience a crisis in spoken communication before we attend to speech, but we do not wait for a breakdown in our writing abilities before trying to learn to write properly. It is sensible to consider human speech at least as seriously as any other communicative behavior.

Many misconceptions concern speech and public speaking. First is the idea that good speech cannot be learned, that it is inherited or just "rubs off on you." While it is true that a good environment aids good speech, the number of improved speakers, the last-day speeches delivered in a public speaking course compared to the first, the letters from graduates of such courses, all testify that one can learn to speak better.

Second, the idea exists that if you have something to say you don't have to worry about how to say it. The content of the message will insure its understandable delivery. Professorial lectures poorly organized, delivered with blurred articulation and

---

[2] The most reliable estimate we have on this matter is somewhat dated. This estimate claimed that 45 per cent of our time is spent listening, 30 per cent in speaking, 16 per cent in reading, and 9 per cent in writing. Paul T. Rankin, "The Importance of Listening Ability," *English Journal* (College Edition), XXVII (Oct. 1928), 623–630.

inadequate volume, and directed to the trees outside the class-room window eloquently refute the content-is-enough allegation of people who regard studying speech as something unworthy of their time.

Equally unfounded is a third misconception: that no content is needed. The purveyors of hot air who believe, "It isn't what you say, it's the way you say it," tread on dangerous ground. These Willy Lomans of the world will eventually find, as he did, that verbal tricks won't do. Empty phrases reflecting empty minds are not strengthened by dulcet tone or sweeping gesture. The discerning listener will see the emptiness. The exhibitionist who speaks primarily to be admired has forgotten the true functions of speech.

A fourth misconception goes hand-in-hand with the third. It is that all courses in speech are primarily concerned with manipulation of the body and the voice, with how to pound the lectern and sound the "O." While it is true that there are courses in voice and in a few of our universities there are courses in bodily action, these courses deal with components of speech but represent only facets of the experiences that are speech. Courses in public speaking, essentially courses in speech composition, do consider the voice as a transmitting medium for the ideas; but considerations of articulation and enunciation, of quality and rate of utterance, are incidental to the broader task of preparing ideas for public reception. Attention is also paid to gesture in public speaking courses, but only as it gives meaning to ideas by punctuating and reinforcing them. Those who think that to study speech is to study only the physiological transmission of ideas are simply misinformed.

Speech as a Liberal Study

With major misconceptions swept away, we are ready to approach speech as a liberal study. We say *as a liberal study* for while it is true that public speaking is a tool leading to success in legislatures, law courts, classrooms, pulpits, engineering laboratories, and market places, it is even more true that to understand the nature of public speaking is to understand man in all these settings. To study speech in general or public speaking in particular is to explore highly intricate processes by which man apprehends truths about himself and his environment. To say that speech is a tool that yields power and success is of less consequence than to say study of it yields insight into the nature of man through examining an ever-present facet of his behavior. A study of speaking man and his works entails discrimination in observing and producing action and reaction. It requires one to learn much about how ideas become meaningful through the selective, sifting, and structuring processes that govern thought's emergence from the human mind. The study of man speaking explores systems of symbolization—verbal, vocal, gestural—that regulate the significance of uttered thought. To study man's speech frees the mind from parochial concentration upon self, for this study not only proclaims with Socrates, "Know thyself," but admonishes, likewise, "Know others!" So, while it is not deplorable to learn to give public speeches for the sake of future careers, it is more important to learn through speaking and studying speech making how it is that mind links to mind through speech, regardless of your position or your profession.

In this book we are not concerned with examining human speech in all its aspects; our attention will focus on that speech usually called public speaking. In every modern era of Western civilization, some have insisted that public speech depends upon practiced skill far more than upon understanding. We think this view ignores a most important fact about the creation of anything that has impact upon the minds of men. Whether the created thing is a painting, a musical score, a poem, an essay, a speech, or any other artistic work capable of influence, someone purposefully *selected* what he would work with, gave it distinctive form or shape, and released it in a particular manner calculated to influence the rest of mankind. Significant works of fine art do not happen by setting monkeys to work on typewriters, canvases, or clavichords; significant works of art come into being when an artist, both skilled and sensitive, successfully matches idea, medium, and purpose, utilizing all relevant resources to endow ideas with just the qualities his purpose requires. This is precisely the achievement of the ideal public speaker. He is an artist, a good one if he understands enough about the world in which he lives to distinguish a significant from an insignificant idea, if he understands the full range of resources and limitations embodied in his medium—human speech—and if he can bring those resources to bear upon his ideas and hence endow them with the qualities his social purposes require. Practice without understanding will never bring him to this achivement except by sheer, unrepeatable accident. This is the sense in which we choose to call public speaking an art. We do not suggest that every intelligent and understanding person can by thought and diligence become a Daniel Webster, a Clarence Darrow, or a Franklin D. Roosevelt. We do insist, however, that disciplined study helps one to apply such principles as these men successfully used in shaping our society. Such experience will, at the least, produce knowledge of self and of others; at best it will produce the sensitivity and skill essential to artistic use of speech in formal communication. But it matters *how* one thinks about speech.

Some who write about public speaking focus almost entirely on personality and the persuasive elements emanating from character, making the study of public speaking exclusively speaker-centered. Others focus on ideas and their symbolization, on the mental processes, avowing that the study of public speaking ought to be speech-centered or message-centered. Still others emphasize motivation and adaptation, claiming that the study should be audience-centered. Though such emphases can be justified, each is partial. The study of public speaking as a liberal art ought to be *all* of these. It can and should be man-centered. A liberal view of the public speaker acknowledges him as a complete man—versatile and potentially artistic—projecting himself as a thinking, feeling being. It is a view that reveals him as man relating personal experience to the diverse experience of others, projecting and reinforcing his meaning through voice and gesture. So understood, the public speaker becomes Emerson's "man thinking" under the influence of nature, drawing not only upon minds of the past but upon the lessons of action as well. Such is the speaker of whom we shall think in the chapters that follow.

Wisely conducted, the study of public speaking can and should correlate with other liberal studies. In deciding what to say in practice speeches you will need to draw upon other subjects such as history, government, and literature. In deciding how to speak reasonably and systematically you will need to call upon your experience with practices in thinking acquired through the study of philosophy, the physical sciences, and mathematics. You may assimilate what you learned in literature, English composition, linguistics, and foreign languages as you select word symbols to convey your messages. The process of voicing your thoughts may make you see special meanings in physics, music, or acoustical engineering. The management of your body to reinforce your ideas may prompt you to bring to bear knowledge acquired in biology, physiology, physical education, and dance. Public speaking is an eclectic art, the resources of which are as varied as man's shared knowledge.

We have been treating public speaking as a liberal *art*. In a sense it may be viewed as a liberal *science*. In science one must not merely contemplate subject matter. Scientific processes must be directly explored. Theories must be tested in the laboratory and the methods of scientific exploration must be mastered. Without such direct learning through personal experience scientific education is nowadays thought to be incomplete. As has already been hinted, any thoroughgoing study of public speaking involves similar practical, personal experience with the art. You will therefore be wise to consider each speech you give as an experiment in human relations. You will gain from asking yourself: "Given a particular body of material, a particular speaker, and a particular audience, all existing in particular moments of time, what effects or reactions will occur when a given set of ideas is presented in a particular order and reinforced with a particular set of vocal and gestural behavior?" You will find, of course, that you are dealing with an experimental setting in which there are many variables. A change of word, the fact that the audience has lived a day longer, the temporary effect of a cold—dozens of variables mean that no speaking situation can be duplicated perfectly. Even so, a scientific, objective attitude toward the experimentation that goes on in the speech laboratory, the classroom, can enable you to acquire sound generalizations about human communication. You will establish no universal laws through observing speech making with a scientific detachment, but you will be able to see more clearly the choices men make in order to be understood as they intend.

Public speaking as an academic study is a crossroads of the arts and sciences. It is a hybrid art, run through with the strands of other studies. It is a social art using speech as its medium, thought and feeling as its content, and influence upon the experience of others as its end. To understand its processes requires reflection and experimentation: study of the constituents of the art and practice to discover their potentialities.

What Is Speech?

Public speaking falls within the broader phenomenon, speech. To understand the distinctive nature of public speaking one needs to consider what is meant by that very common term: *speech.*

Speech has been viewed and defined from diverse vantage points and by diverse methods. Gray and Wise have examined speech in their book, *The Bases of Speech*, from nine different points of view: the social, physical, physiological, neurological, phonetic, linguistic, psychological, genetic, and semantic.[3] Speech has also been defined by synonym, analytic dissection, function, and description. Speech has been broken down into its parts; it has been diagrammed and charted. There has been little agreement on any single definition, but by placing several kinds of definition side by side we may gain insight into the nature of speech. Realizing that no one definition achieves perfection, let

---

[3] See Giles W. Gray and Claude M. Wise, *The Bases of Speech*, 3rd ed. (New York: Harper & Brothers, 1959).

us examine some useful definitions with an eye to constructing one of our own.

If we were to define speech by synonym, we would use such terms as "oral communication and expression," "orally verbalized thought," "spoken rhetoric and poetic," or "oral discourse." We might simply call speech "talk." Yet, not everyone would agree that these labels were entirely accurate since it might be argued that all speech is not "talk" and that not all speech is oral. If gesture and pantomime and silent but visible signals are to be included among the ways the human organism expresses meanings and elicits responses, some of our synonyms would have to be rejected as too confining.

Some have defined speech by breaking it down into its elements. Borchers and Wise did so from an almost exclusively physical point of view when they wrote, "Speech is a code of audible signs made with the muscles and other tissues producing voice, and of visible signs made with other muscles and tissues of the body, both codes being used for the purpose of communication."[4] Charles Henry Woolbert, who wrote a good deal about speech in the 1920's, identified mental as well as physical components of speech. He said:

> A man speaking is four things, all of them needed in revealing his mind to others. First he is a will, an intention, a meaning which he wishes others to have, a thought; second, he is a user of language, molding thought and feeling into words; third, he is a thing to be heard, carrying his purpose and words to others through voice; and last, he is a thing to be seen, shown to the sight, a being of action to be noted and read through the eye.[5]

Woolbert suggested that these "Four Phases of Speech" (thought, language, voice, and bodily action) be studied in reverse order. Some speech textbooks and some speech courses are organized in this pattern with the result that thought is examined last and is

---

[4] Gladys L. Borchers and Claude M. Wise, *Modern Speech* (New York: Harcourt, Brace, 1947), p. 2.

[5] C. H. Woolbert, *The Fundamentals of Speech* (New York: Harper & Brothers, 1920), p. 3.

consequently too often de-emphasized in study. In the two definitions we have just cited the authors seem to be attempting to answer the question, "What is speech made of?"

Elwood Murray defines speech by highlighting its function. He says speech is the chief means by which we carry on personal adjustments and social relations. He sees in every speech act "phonetic skills," "semantic skills," and "social skills."

> The emphasis to be presented here is that the essence of speech is in its social aspect . . . the most important means of carrying on human relations. To improve speech, therefore, is to improve effectiveness in human relations. . . . *Speech is defined as a tool of social adjustment, which reflects the efficient personality, and as a psychological and sociological technique of modifying human behavior by means of body, voice, thought and language.*[6]

We see in this definition a tentative answer to the question, "What is speech good for?"

Speech has also been defined by describing or charting the cycle of sequential actions and reactions that takes place when we speak. Alan H. Monroe characterized this chain of events by calling it the "circular response."

> An idea forms in the speaker's mind where it is translated into language symbols; reacting to impulses from the nervous system, the muscles used in speech convert these language symbols into audible speech; the sounds are carried as wave patterns in the air until they strike the eardrums of the listener; as nerve impulses, they travel to the brain, where they again become language symbols which convey meaning to the listener's mind; the listener reacts to what he has heard; the speaker observes this reaction and responds to it.[7]

Monroe, through description, provides an answer to the question, "What happens when we speak?"

Weaver and Ness suggest another answer by identifying and

---

[6] Elwood Murray, *The Speech Personality*, rev. ed. (Chicago: Lippincott, 1944), pp. 3, 10.

[7] *Principles and Types of Speech*, 3rd ed. (Chicago: Scott, Foresman, 1949), pp. 28–29.

diagramming the sender, receiver, and message as the basic elements of a speaking event. They tell us that when we speak a phenomenon called "feedback" occurs. "Feedback" here means that audience reactions or cues stimulate the speaker's subsequent actions and reactions. Weaver and Ness go on to compare speakers to self-regulating machines like thermostatically controlled heating systems, radar-directed missiles, and automatic chemical plants.[8]

While it is certainly helpful to trace the path of action and reaction in the speech act, we must note that while speech is not just a one-way process, neither is it just a two-way process. In most of the descriptive constructs available to us, no account is taken of the fact that during the speech act the speaker not only stimulates and is stimulated by others but he also stimulates himself. Wendell Johnson explored this aspect of reaction in his book entitled *Your Most Enchanted Listener*. There he explained that that listener is you![9]

A group of educators, whose specialties varied from public address to drama and radio, agreed at a workshop meeting of the Speech Association of the Eastern States in 1952 on a definition of speech for purposes of discussion.[10] This definition read: "Speech is the process by which ideas and feelings are transmitted through the integration of words, voice, and action."[11] We agree substantially with this general definition, though we realize the values of other definitions emphasizing physiological or physical, sociological or psychological aspects of speech. If we choose to look at speech as a phenomenon consisting of substance, process, and function, we arrive at this definition: *Speech is thought conceived, transmitted, and expressed by brain, voice, and body,*

---

[8] See Andrew T. Weaver and Ordean G. Ness, *An Introduction to Public Speaking* (New York: Odyssey Press, 1961), pp. 4, 10.

[9] See Wendell Johnson, *Your Most Enchanted Listener* (New York: Harper & Brothers, 1956), especially pp. 23–29.

[10] Members of this group were: Carroll C. Arnold, J. Calvin Callaghan, Giraud Chester, Donald L. Clark, Martin T. Cobin, John Crawford, Magdalene Kramer, Orvin P. Larson, James M. Mullendore, Loretta Wagner Smith, Walter H. Stainton, and Buell B. Whitehill, Jr.

[11] From the unpublished proceedings of a Speech Association of the Eastern States workshop, 1952, "Excerpts from Findings," mimeographed.

producing stimuli for auditors and for the speaker himself, and influencing subsequent thoughts, feelings, and actions.

Public Speaking and Related
Forms of Speech

What distinguishes public speaking from other forms also falling under the labels and definitions applied to speech? Specifically, how does public speaking differ from conversation, reading aloud, or acting, all of which are also forms of speech?

PUBLIC SPEAKING AND CONVERSATION

Public speaking differs from conversation in that public speaking is usually directed at more listeners than is most conversation. In most instances you will be addressing more people when giving a public speech than in daily exchanges with friends.

Sometimes public speech evolves in the course of conversation. You may be talking with one or two friends and find that you have attracted the attention of others who were passing by. They stop to listen. You find that instead of exchanging ideas with one or two persons you are propounding your views to a dozen or more who respond by listening rather than by talking. As interest and intensity mount you draw apart from the group and stand above them on a box, a chair, or staircase so that they may better see you and hear what you have to say. Conversation has enlarged; it has become public speech.

A second difference between conversation and public speaking is now readily observable. You do most of the talking. *Public speaking is relatively uninterrupted discourse.* This does not mean there are no one-sided conversations. Many conversations with your dogmatic elders are *almost* speeches directed at you. A professor or an advising father, such as Polonius, may brook little interruption. But, he is still not delivering a public speech. What he says is meant for one set of ears and one set only. It is private discourse. Private discourse is at least susceptible to interruption and to give and take. Applause, laughter, and the lustily shouted "Amen, Brother!" of the revival meeting are interruptions, but in most instances such interjections account for a small percentage of the total time of a public speech. The primary burden for directing the flow of stimulation falls more exclusively on the public speaker than on the conversationalist.

In addition to the usual presence of more auditors and the relative continuity of discourse, public speaking requires intensified volume of voice and bodily action. The larger the audience the greater the physical demands. You must make yourself easily seen and easily heard. Before a small, intimate audience gestures can be more subtle and voice less forceful than when you appear before a large assembly.

Finally, public speaking is prepared utterance while most conversation is not. It is true that rare individuals, like Oscar Wilde, have prepared conversations for the salon, but this is the exception rather than the rule. It is also true that some impromptu speeches are delivered "off the cuff." Yet most public speaking engagements occur only after prior notice. Hence, planning, ranging from careful thinking to writing out the utterance, marks most successful public speaking performances.

These readily observable differences which usually prevail do not mean that good public speaking is totally unlike good conversation. Good public speaking has many of the features of good conversation. Directness, spontaneity, animation, and emphasis are characteristics of both these activities. To be successful in either, you must look the audience in the eye and adapt to the listeners and to the occasion as you go. Such adaptation often means incorporating phrasings and examples not previously anticipated. Furthermore, you will succeed best in both public speaking and conversation if your body and voice are ready to respond to your material, your audience, and the occasion. Visual and vocal activity ought to compel the listener to attend to what you say and realize the importance of your ideas. In these ways public speaking and conversation are similar, but while it is easy to say, "Be conversational" when presenting a public speech, being conversational is not the whole answer. It is more to the point to say, "Adapt those characteristics of conversation suitable to the moment." Conversationality in public speaking results from control and modification of elements to be found in conversation. To speak on a public platform in exactly the way you would speak in situations calling for private, reciprocal communication, or to reproduce conversation on the platform for other than illustrative purposes is likely to prove ineffectual.

PUBLIC SPEAKING AND ORAL READING

Public speaking differs from oral reading in the material presented, the purposes of the presentation, and the process of preparation. The oral reader, unless he is reading his own composition, acts as an interpreter of someone else's ideas. He must discover the author's intellectual and emotional meanings, and transmit them to the audience. This position calls for different imaginative capacity from that required of a public speaker, especially the extemporaneous speaker. Moreover, the two modes of speaking involve different processes of selectivity. The oral reader has had the ideas and words selected for him; he must exercise selectivity in deciding about emphasis and his modes of transmission. The public speaker selects his own ideas and the symbols for those ideas; then he chooses how to emphasize and transmit them. Sometimes the reader must become someone other than himself; he must impersonate another. At other times the oral reader remains himself but suggests the character of some other person. Most often, he merely reveals himself and the meanings he has discovered in what he reads. In the last of these circumstances, he and a public speaker may have the same purpose.

The reader's purpose may or may not be rhetorical. He may read to provide information, to instruct, to persuade, or to entertain his audience. His purposes, like those of the public speaker, may be distinctly utilitarian, aimed at useful, practical ends. On the other hand, his purpose may be largely aesthetic; he may seek a response to the beauty of his material. Such a response is often sought when literary works—short stories, drama, portions of novels, or pieces of poetry—are read aloud to an audience. A good public speaker seldom invites primarily aesthetic responses. While he may evoke feelings and engender emotional responses, his aim is seldom to focus attention upon the universality or the poetic quality of his message.

Unless the reader reads a speech he has composed himself, his preparation of materials and his oral rehearsal will differ markedly from the procedures he follows to ready a speech for public presentation. Preparation of a selection for oral reading involves research to discover the author's true meaning and the selection's emotional content. The reader searches through his selection many times, sometimes word by word, to make sure that he discovers the meanings intended. He may also read other selections by the same author, or what has been written about the author, to gain further insight into the material he is preparing. A public speaker reading his own speech knows the meanings he intends to convey, for he invented them. He obviously knows the author more intimately than anyone else. But if he reads a speech by some other person, he follows the same procedures in preparation as the oral interpreter.

Speakers who read their own speeches or deliver them from memory are really practicing a kind of oral reading—one which differs from reading someone else's prose or poetry and from extemporaneous speaking. Manuscript speakers and memorizers preserve pre-set wordings; they do not symbolize their ideas afresh as they speak. They have no need to put sentences together or to devise wordings and phrasings at the time of utterance as do extemporaneous speakers. Those who read or memorize their own ideas do not have the special problems of discovering meaning and emotional content which face most oral interpreters.

It is increasingly common for speakers to read their own speeches, but it is increasingly rare for speakers to deliver speeches from memory. Those who read their speeches usually do so because they have not had time to gain command of their ideas or because they lack confidence in their control over them. Before the advent of disc and tape recording, speakers memorized or read for a reason that no longer applies: to assure accurate reproduction of their speeches in print. With modern means of recording this concern for faithful reportage is no longer very important; nonetheless, in some settings such as dedications, anniversaries, commencements, and important state occasions, tradition still prompts speakers to write out and read their messages. Except in this latter circumstance, it is debatable whether tradition serves the cause of effective communication.

PUBLIC SPEAKING AND ACTING

Public speaking differs from acting in that the speaker rarely reveals any character or personality traits other than his own. In contrast, the actor must create a character for his audience. There are other differences. The public speaker usually works alone; the actor most often works with a group and so must accommodate his behavior to ensemble communication. Except on television, the public speaker does not ordinarily use scenery, costume, or make-up to help him communicate; an actor does. The speaker may occasionally have special lighting and platform decorations to reinforce his message; but if he is competent, he must be able to succeed without these aids. Furthermore, the public speaker deals only with his own composition while the actor, like the oral reader, has all the problems of interpreting the words of another. The actor serves as a sort of middleman for the playwright and reveals the intentions of a director. Thus, the purposes of the actor are at once like and unlike those of the public speaker. Perhaps this is why some speakers need to be warned *not* to act; some temptation to do so is always present. The actor may seek utilitarian responses or he may seek aesthetic responses, depending upon his material; but the public speaker's concerns should always be primarily with utilitarian responses.

The Demands of Public Speaking

In distinguishing public speaking from other forms of speech we may say: *Public speaking is that form of speech which is relatively uninterrupted, which involves more than two persons, and in which the communicator invents and symbolizes his own ideas in order to elicit primarily utilitarian rather than aesthetic responses.*

Public speaking is an audience-centered, problem-solving, non-exhibitionistic art wherein time-tested principles are applied to specific situations.

Public speaking is adaptive in nature. The study of man speaking in public is a study of adaptation. Such study calls upon us to perceive a series of interactive relationships and to integrate them as harmoniously as possible. Diagrammed, these relationships indicate the various connections between the components of public speaking situations.

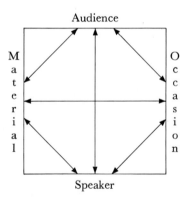

Given these relationships, here are the questions a speaker must seek to answer in preparing for a public engagement:

1. What is my relationship to the audience?
2. What is the audience's relationship to me?
3. What is the relationship between the audience and occasion?

4. What effect does the occasion, the particular circumstance in which the speech is to be delivered, have upon the audience?

5. What influence does the audience exert upon my material, upon what I have to say?

6. What is the relationship of my speech content, my material, to the audience?

7. What is my relationship to my material? What do I as a person bring to my material to determine its final substance and form?

8. What effect does my material (my subject choice, the facts, opinions, and illustrations) have upon me as a person?

9. What is my connection with the occasion?

10. What is the effect of the occasion upon me as a speaker?

11. What influence does the occasion have upon my materials, upon what I intend to say?

12. What does the content of my speech do to modify the nature of the occasion?

Exploration of these twelve questions constitutes the work of a would-be public speaker. Given a particular situation, you must seek to answer each of these questions. Answers to some will be hard to come by. Indeed, in some cases, you may be unable to provide even probable answers. In some situations some questions will be more important than others. Sometimes the best you will be able to do is to formulate some educated guesses. Given the information available to you, it is your duty to calculate the probable answers to as many questions as you can. Should you ignore a crucial question or arrive at answers which prove to be in error, you may fail to achieve your purpose, to elicit the response you seek, or to achieve the degree of adaptation necessary to insure success.

We believe that the study of speech is a man-centered activity of which public speaking is but one branch, which has as its main concern the eliciting of utilitarian responses. In order to study man speaking we must know not only the responses he seeks, we must know what aspects of the speech situation he must satisfy in order to elicit the responses he wants. Demands are made upon the public speaker by each major element of the speaking situation. As public speaker you must meet the demands of the audience at almost every turn if you are to gain the reactions you desire. You must so fashion your communication that it meets demands inherent in the speech material itself. Next, you must meet certain demands which your own organism makes upon the message. And lastly, you must meet demands made by the physical space-time setting which constitutes the occasion. Thus it is that as a public speaker you must consider data concerning the audience, yourself, the content, and the occasion. Failure to consider all four of these components and their interrelationships can easily cause failure in communication.

It is our purpose in this book to look at public speaking largely as a process of acceding to and satisfying the demands of audience, content, self, and occasion. Our approach will be to explore speech preparation and delivery by inquiring into the probable demands imposed upon you during each phase of the communicative experience.

After some initial background which will serve as a context for study and for your first performances, we shall devote the remainder of this book to discussion of five general aspects of speech making, often called the "classical canons of rhetoric." We shall first examine the problems of *invention*, considering the nature of audiences and the means by which ideas for speeches may be discovered and sifted. Next we shall consider the *disposition* of materials selected for inclusion in a speech—the principles according to which they may be assembled and structured. Our third and fourth considerations will concern the symbolization of ideas—*style*, and *delivery* of the finished speech. What ancient writers called *memoria* or command of the entire speech as planned and composed will be discussed at various points in the chapters that follow, since many of the decisions that speakers make during discovery, disposition, and symbolization of ideas have direct bearing on ability to retain command over the speech until delivery is completed. In considering each of these five major aspects of public speaking we shall seek to determine what demands you must meet and the reasons they must be met if you are to be understood as you intend.

The "demand" approach may seem too practical to some; yet we feel that it is essential for comprehensive understanding of man communicating formally and orally. Intellectual and social adaptation for the purpose of gaining and giving responses is the central feature of speaking-listening man. What to do to achieve a desired response is and has been the chief concern of every public speaker in every age; modulation of his own responses in the face of purposive adaptation is the chief concern of every listener. Adaptation, then, is inevitably a very practical matter. This is why we shall focus in succeeding chapters upon the demands under which each speaker inevitably works and to which he must adjust if he is to effect those responses he seeks.

In this chapter we have taken notice of the pervasiveness of speech as human experience. Despite misconceptions, public speaking is not fundamentally different from man's other arts. Like most arts and all sciences, it cannot be fully commanded without direct experience in using principles and processes. Artistic achievement requires that the resources peculiar to speech making must serve the maker's purposes. Our approach to the study of public speaking as a liberal art will lead us to explore the demands made upon the speaker by audience, self, material, and occasion. We first turn briefly to certain broad principles that have been observed through the centuries by eminent theorists, among them historic figures of western civilization.

Exercises

WRITTEN

1. Write your own definition of speech.
2. Write your own definition of public speaking.
3. Write a paragraph in answer to each of the following questions:
   A. What is speech made of?
   B. What do we do when we speak?
   C. What is speech good for?

4. Keep a diary of a single day of your activities in which you note all the occasions upon which you found speech to be necessary. In noting these occasions try to describe briefly the distinctive nature of each.

5. After viewing a movie, television, or live theater performance, list those things you observed in the performances of the actors which were similar to or different from those things you have observed in the performances of public speakers.

ORAL

1. Make a short speech in which you describe a specific situation and point out aspects of the situation of which you would have been unaware had you not attended this class and read this chapter.

2. Make a brief public speech on a subject of your own choosing during which you read from the printed page or impersonate some real or fictional character.

Heritage:

The Evolution of

Rhetorical Theory

A clear understanding of any subject is strengthened by a knowledge of its history. The origins of the study, the concepts and ideas handed down for contemporary judgment, the accepted and suspect traditions of theory and practice establish the essential character of the subject. You may not be able to survey all that has been written about public speaking or any other subject, but you will be better equipped to think and apply your thinking if you know the high points of its development and are aware of how present knowledge evolved. With these considerations in mind we shall trace in broad strokes the evolution of that part of rhetorical theory devoted to public speaking.

We shall not be concerned here with the orators whose practices shaped theories and who used them once they were formulated. Neither shall we consider all those whose writings would have to be included in a comprehensive history of rhetorical hypotheses. We shall concentrate instead on the evolution of leading ideas about the art of speech making—on the points of change, the additions and omissions that have appeared in our culture's suppositions about the rhetoric of speaking since ancient times. We invite you to examine this brief and sometimes oversimplified record to acquire background against which to judge the theories and suggestions of this book and your own experience with the complicated art of public speaking.

The Greek Period

The study of public speaking as a liberal art began at Syracuse in Sicily in the fifth century B.C. Descriptions of speech-making and scattered bits of advice on oral communication are found in the Prisse papyrus from ancient Egypt and Homer's works, but it is from the Golden Age of Greece that we have the first record of an organized theory of the art of oratory.[1] Corax and Tisias are usually credited with authorship of a now lost manual of public speaking. We are not sure of its contents but scholars believe that Corax and Tisias developed a theory of how arguments ought to be developed from probabilities and that they laid foundations for a theory of rhetorical organization. These ancient rhetoricians apparently taught that a speech ought to have at least three parts including a proem or introduction to win the favor of the listening judges, a narration or demonstration, and an epilogue. Their primitive work contained only the germ of a rhetorical system, but one to which the citizens turned in their argumentative efforts to reclaim lands and other rights.

It was no accident that rhetoric made its first appearance in Sicily under a succession of tyrants. In the wake of the revolts which deposed them came the inevitable disputes over land and citizenship. These pressing matters and the warm nature of the Sicilian nourished the first systematization of the art of speaking, or more specifically, the art of courtroom speaking.

Some Greek teachers about the middle of the fifth century B.C. were called "Sophists." Most were itinerants who founded no schools. They have left us little by which to judge them. Isocrates, himself a Sophist, refers to them in his speeches "Against the Sophists" and "Antidosis." His allusions and some others in Plato's

---

[1] For further information on the Egyptians see Giles W. Gray, "The 'Precepts of Kagemni and Ptah–Hotep,'" *The Quarterly Journal of Speech*, XXXII (Dec., 1946), 446–454. A discussion of oratory in Homeric works may be found in George Kennedy, *The Art of Persuasion in Greece* (Princeton: Princeton University Press, 1963), pp. 35–39.

works are about all we know of other prominent Sophists. Many of these teachers were allegedly insincere, apathetic toward former students, and motivated by money. They were accused of corrupting youth and regarding success as more important than learning. In truth, they had no uniform standards. They operated quite independently, and their methods and ideas differed greatly. Most, it appears, gave much attention to speech making. Some were well educated and encouraged pupils to think speculatively, an activity their society unfortunately eyed with suspicion.

Protagoras of Abdera (c. 480–410 B.C.) was one of the earliest and most important Sophists. He maintained that the existence of the Gods was uncertain, that truth was relative, and that "man is the measure of all things." In teaching speech he held that there were two sides to every proposition and that speakers should be able to argue either. He practiced his pupils in what were called "commonplaces," speeches in praise or dispraise of such human qualities as friendship, patriotism, and cupidity. These exercises had no reference to any particular occasion but provided students with a stock of set passages they could use when called upon to speak in public. Protagoras founded our system of grammar by classifying and distinguishing parts of speech, tenses, and moods.

Another Sophist, known as the founder of the art of prose, was Gorgias of Leontini (c. 485–380 B.C.). His chief interest was in occasional oratory. His teaching and practice emphasized beauty in diction and style. He held that prose rhythm and word choice were more important than grammar. His own style was florid and exaggerated. Aristotle condemned him for his emphasis upon memorization and delivery of speeches written by others. His portrait in Plato's dialogue, the *Gorgias,* is of one prone to disregard ethics in his attempts to excite emotions. If we may rely on Plato and Aristotle, Gorgias did not care what means he used as long as he realized his rhetorical ends. His lost book, *On the Nature of the Non-Existent,* postulated: nothing exists, if anything exists it cannot be known, even if it could be known it could not be communicated. Gorgias refined the rhetorical theories of Corax and Tisias and was their most artful practitioner.

Prodicus of Ceos (c. 465 B.C.), whose teaching was recommended by Socrates, taught that to face death courageously was a virtue. He propounded the ideals of labor, hardihood, and simplicity in a famous lecture, "The Choice of Hercules." A kind of early semanticist, he loved to study language, and collected and compared words of similar meaning to insist upon accurate usage.

A Sophist we have already mentioned, Isocrates (436–338 B.C.), established a school for speakers and wrote speeches for others to deliver. His rhetorical teachings are occasionally ranked above Aristotle's because he equated the study of speaking with preparation for citizenship. A weak voice and innate shyness kept him from speaking in public, but the excellence of his written speeches earns him a place among the foremost Attic orators. His views in "Against the Sophists" and "Antidosis" reveal that he considered the goal of speech training as the fullest development of the highest human faculties, and that his ultimate aim was to prepare his students for public life. He condemned those who taught rhetoric solely for money and those who claimed that all is possible to him who learns the art of discourse. Isocrates' real love was teaching, and his lasting contributions rest upon the breadth of learning he associated with the art of speaking. He is distinguished from other Sophists by this broader view of the functions of training in public speaking, his ethical bent, and his efforts to improve the prose of his day. His work influenced such Roman writers as Cicero and Quintilian.

Few Sophists were perfectionists. More were practical in their teaching of rhetoric and other subjects. Some used rhetoric for exhibition while others aimed for pragmatic results in speech making. A few ennobled the communicative arts. We can see that despite their reputation for being unscrupulous exhibitionists, the Sophists stimulated new thought, discerned the practical applications of speech, created our grammatical system, and made other contributions to linguistic arts. They did increase the knowledge of their own society and, indirectly, ours.

Plato's main contributions (c. 427–347 B.C.) to the theory of rhetoric appear in two of his dialogues: *Gorgias* (c. 387 B.C.) and *Phaedrus* (c. 380 B.C.). These works view speech-making from opposed positions. The *Gorgias* criticizes rhetoric and inspires others to come to its defense. The *Phaedrus* advances theories which contribute to rhetorical excellence.

The theoretical considerations in the *Gorgias* revolve about the nature of rhetoric. Plato tries to answer two questions: "What is rhetoric?" and "Is it an art?" Rhetoric, he concedes, depends upon speech, but to define it as speech alone is invalid. At one point in the dialogue, he defines rhetoric as producing persuasion for belief rather than for instruction about right and wrong. He declares it to be neither a true art nor a true source of power. Following this line of thought, Plato classes rhetoric with cookery and cosmetic as one of the arts of flattery. The only good use of rhetoric, he contends, is in self-accusation, though it may be nobly used to prevent the punishment of one's enemies. Good rhetoric is based upon knowledge and revelation of truth; bad rhetoric, upon exhibitionism which is not beneficial to the audience and induces belief without knowledge. Those reading the *Gorgias* today will find nothing new in its criticism of training in public speaking.

The *Phaedrus* considers the composition of three speeches on love. Here Plato reversed his position and took the affirmative in the debate on rhetoric. In this dialogue he made several valuable points which all speakers should bear in mind. In essence Plato said:

1. Writing speeches is not in itself deplorable; writing them poorly is a disgrace.

2. A speaker must know the truth about his subject matter.

3. Those wishing to develop an art of rhetoric must be able to define and systematically partition their subjects.

4. Correct diction is necessary in good oratory.

5. To become a notable orator, one must add knowledge and practice to natural endowments.

6. Anyone who teaches rhetoric must have a full knowledge of men's souls.

7. Writing produces forgetfulness, and words once set down cannot defend themselves or know when or to whom to speak.

The impression left by this dialogue is that all speech making is not good, but that well conceived, well intended, truthful public speaking is a powerful instrument which may be employed for social and spiritual good.

Aristotle (384–322 B.C.) was Plato's pupil and rival. He was probably the greatest Greek philosopher and certainly the greatest theorist ever to write on public speaking. His *Rhetoric* is the most influential work ever written on the subject. His theories, written about 330 B.C., emerge in all respectable speech textbooks, and the following pages are no exception.

Aristotle left us a rich heritage. In the three books of his *Rhetoric*, the books of the speaker, the audience, and the speech, —as translators and commentators have labelled them—he treats speech making in ways that are still usable. Aristotle saw popular speaking as a problem in audience adaptation, a position we have adopted. He believed that a speaker must know himself and his intellectual capacities, that he must understand his audience and its emotions, dispositions, wants and fears, and that he must know his material and the ways of presenting it logically, systematically, and strikingly.

In Book I of his *Rhetoric* Aristotle discusses popular speaking as it contrasts to dialectic (analytical discourse among experts). He condemns the speech handbooks of his day for dwelling on irrelevant matters and neglecting the treatment of proofs while concentrating exclusively on pleading in the law courts. He defines rhetoric as ". . . the faculty of discovering in a particular case what are the available means of persuasion."[2] This function, he says, belongs to no other art. He sees the character of the speaker (*ethos*), emotion (*pathos*), and speech content (*logos*) as the forces that bring about persuasion. He discusses at length the nature of rhetorical reasoning and the use of topics or "lines of argument" as guides to invention. Three kinds of speaking, deliberative (of the legislature), forensic (of the law court), and epideictic (of the ceremonial situation), are discussed with reference to their subject

---

[2] From *The Rhetoric of Aristotle* translated and edited by Lane Cooper. Copyright, 1932, Lane Cooper, p. 7, Bk I, Ch. 2. Reprinted by permission of the publisher, Appleton–Century–Crofts.

matter, elements, and ends. This tripartite analysis which Aristotle popularized continues to be influential and useful after twenty-four centuries.

Book II of Aristotle's *Rhetoric* concentrates mainly on the audience. It discusses how emotions affect the judgments of listeners and how such feelings as anger, love, fear, shame, benevolence, and pity are evoked. Age, too, is considered as a factor in the probable responses of listeners. (See pp. 90–93.) After exploring the influence of fortune, wealth, and power upon human character, Aristotle further considers reasoning and the topics of argument. (See pp. 107–120).

Book III, the "book of the speech," says we must pay attention to delivery because of the "sorry nature" of the audience. On the problems of effective delivery, however, Aristotle wrote little. When he turns to style, he discards most of his predecessors' strictures, preferring to emphasize clarity. The additional characteristics needed for effective style are propriety and liveliness, the latter to be gained chiefly through metaphors, similes, antitheses, realism, and rhythm. The final section deals with disposition (speech organization). It offers suggestions for developing the proem (introduction), the narration and ordered arguments (the body), and the epilogue (the conclusion).

After Aristotle little of note was done to advance rhetorical theory until Roman times. As far as we know, it was about 250 years before the next work of major influence on present practice appeared.

The Roman Period

The rhetorical contributions of the Romans were largely those of systematizing and refining the theories of the Greeks. Roman theorists formulated the speaker's problems into five "canons of rhetoric": invention, disposition, elocution (style), pronunciation (delivery), and *memoria* (command of the speech). Classifications of style, methods of amplification, the functions of each division of a speech, and the several kinds of speaking held special interest for them.

The first extant Latin treatise on public speaking, *Rhetorica ad Herennium*, was written about 82 B.C. It is sometimes attributed to Cicero.[3] This concise, plain, technical manual, which resembles a student's notebook, contains the oldest surviving discussion of the canon of *memoria* and the second oldest treatment of style. Style, which includes figures of speech, is given most space. Delivery, treated prescriptively, is also stressed. Little attention is accorded disposition. The book is filled with classifications, some of which are rather complicated. Where definitions appear, they seem oversimplified.

Rhetorica ad Herennium gives extensive but unoriginal treatment to the three kinds of oratory (legislative, ceremonial, and legal) and the five canons of rhetoric. It contends that art in speech making must be attained through study of theory and models, and by practice. A discourse is divided into six parts: introduction, statement of facts or narration, division, proof, refutation, and conclusion. The handbook is noteworthy for providing advice on keeping the details of a speech in the memory, for adding to theories of style, and for its general review of Greek rhetorical teachings.

Cicero (106–43 B.C.) wrote several works dealing chiefly with rhetoric and left many other scattered references on the subject. His most influential books were *De Inventione* (86 B.C.), *De Oratore* (55 B.C.), *Orator* (46 B.C.), and *Topica* (44 B.C.). Less important were his *Partitiones Oratoriae* (54 B.C.), *Brutus* (46 B.C.), and *De Optimo Genere Oratorum* (c. 46 B.C.).

Cicero refined and clarified, but added little to Greek rhetorical theories. He was Rome's foremost orator, more famed for his speeches than for his writings. Well over fifty of his speeches survive. He wrote as an orator for other orators, brilliantly and well. His works reflected the practical cast of mind characteristic of the

---

[3] Professor Harry Caplan, who has made the most authoritative English translation of this work, is of the opinion that Cicero was not the author. See *Rhetorica ad Herennium* (Cambridge, Mass.: Harvard University Press, 1954), pp. vii ff.

Roman of his day. His treatment of rhetoric was not novel, but it was thorough. He related wide general knowledge and excellence in speaking. He also discussed at length the constituents and uses of the plain, middle, and grand levels of style. The language of public speaking interested Cicero greatly; he most admired correctness, clearness, appropriateness, and ornateness.

Cicero was a great artist turned great theorist. That his own speaking met the standards of his theories is a distinctive aspect of his contribution. His mature judgment and long experience as a public speaker, his ability to synthesize and illuminate older theories, and his polished writing made his works classics. Not even Aristotle had a greater influence upon the rhetoric of subsequent generations. Some of Cicero's versions of theory became the bases for rhetorical treatises of the Middle Ages and Renaissance.

Quintilian (c. A.D. 35–95) was the first teacher to be paid by the Roman Empire. The *Institutio Oratoria*, comprising twelve short volumes, is his only surviving contribution to the literature of speech making. It prescribes the education of the orator from the cradle to the grave. Its often-quoted definition of the orator as "the good man speaking well," reveals Quintilian's emphasis upon *ethos*. He looks first to the character of the orator, his competence, integrity, and good motives. Quintilian insists that the student acquire the skills necessary to reveal these qualities and to perfect subject matter for communication.

Books I, II, and XII explain his philosophy of education and consider such topics as the curriculum for the early training of the orator, the individuals who should be allowed to influence him, the importance of adapting training to the individual, and the role of punishment. Because of their subject matter these three books are still discussed in courses in the philosophy of education. Quintilian's remaining nine books contain the curriculum for the orator's liberal education. He covers the five canons in detail, prescribes what the student should read, and suggests the study of such subjects as geometry, music, and gymnastics for the development of the fully educated man.

Quintilian's central thesis—that the orator has to be a good person and conduct himself honorably and responsibly if he is to be more than adequate in speech-making—appears as valid today as it was in his time. Many speech teachers have adopted it as doctrine. But Quintilian did not make his major contribution to present speech education as a theorist or practitioner. He wrote primarily as a teacher of public speaking. Because he was a teacher his main concern was, appropriately, the student. Above all, he warned his successors that the education of a speaker must be individualized, broad, painstaking, and an integral part of general education.

On the Sublime, attributed to an unknown usually called "Longinus" who wrote sometime between the first and third centuries A.D., discusses elevation and inspiration, nobility of soul, and diction. The author sees as the requisites for eloquence: bold sentiments, vehement and enthusiastic feeling, facility with the figures of speech, and majesty of expression derived from judicious word selection and dignified and elevated views. Conciseness, amplification, and imagery are recommended as especially valuable resources in management of language. The attention "Longinus" pays to inspiration and largeness of conception in producing superior rhetoric gives his work its most distinctive cast. *On the Sublime* stands also as the first great work on rhetorical and literary criticism.

The Medieval Period

St. Augustine (A.D. 354–430), who taught rhetoric before his conversion, was the most important theorist of this period. His *Confessions* reveals his turning away from the artificial and exhibitionistic rhetoric taught him in his youth. But many still regard Book IV of his *De Doctrina Christiana* (c. 426) as the best treatise on preaching ever written. To St. Augustine, the purpose of speaking was to teach, to remind the listener of the truth that was within. He discouraged the irresponsibility and insincerity in the rhetorical training of his time. He urged preachers to study the speeches of others as models and to realize full meaning as a foundation for good oral reading. In a time when the popular rhetoric resembled that of the ancient Sophists, St. Augustine focused attention upon speaking as a functional art rather than as exhibitionism.

Such names as Venerable Bede (673–735), Alcuin (c. 735–804), and John of Salisbury (c. 1115–1180) are linked with rhetoric in the period after St. Augustine. Scholarship has only begun to discover what happened to rhetorical theory during the twelfth through fifteenth centuries. Notable contributions to modern theories of the art, especially the Anglo-American tradition, date chiefly from the early years of the sixteenth century.

The Renaissance Period

During the Renaissance rhetoric absorbed poetic and became completely confused with it. The prevalent theory of public speaking was one of ornamentation, as shown in Lydgate's *Court of Sapyence* (c. 1510). The chief purpose of rhetoric was to give pleasure to the ear. In fifteenth- and sixteenth-century England the word *rhetoric* came to mean skill in diction. The view of the period was exemplified by Stephen Hawes (c. 1475–1530), who wrote *The Pastime of Pleasure* (1506). This allegorical treatment of the liberal arts characterized rhetoric as the honied speech of poets. In this era invention (discovering what to say in speaking) was lifted from rhetoric and was often thought of as a poetic experience—the exercise of wit, fantasy, discernment, memory, and judgment. Disposition and delivery were also treated as special poetic problems. Delivery was conceived of as the oral reading of poetry. Only *memoria*, command of what is to be said, retained anything like its classical meaning. Rhetorics of the period gave greatest stress and most space to style; "Rhetoric" and "style" were synonymous to most of the theorists of the time.

At the start of the sixteenth century, what classical writers had treated as rhetorical invention was sometimes seen as matter to be studied in logic. Even Thomas Wilson was less perceptive about the relationship of logic and rhetoric in his earlier work than in his later writings. In *The Rule of Reason, conteinyng the Arte of Logike* (1551) he gave these definitions:

> Bothe these Artes are moche alike, sauying that Logike is occupied about all matters, and doeth plainlie and nakedly set forth with apt wordes, the sum of things by way of argumentacion. Again of the other side, Rhetorike useth gaie painted sentences and setteth forthe those matters with freshe colours, and goodly ornamentes, and that at large.[4]

Petrus Ramus (1515–1572) saw logic as consisting of *judicium* and invention, the apt framing of things and knitting of words together and the finding of matter and searching out of "stuffe" agreeable to the cause. As Professor Donald Lemen Clark says:

> . . . while the survival of the mediaeval notion that rhetoric was concerned mainly with style thus gave over in the English Renaissance *inventio* and *dispositio* to logic, there naturally remained nothing of classical rhetoric but *elocutio* [style] and *pronuntiatio* [delivery].[5]

Books supporting this view were Richard Sherry's *A Treatise of Schemes and Tropes gathered out of the best grammarians and orators* (c. 1550), Henry Peacham's *Garden of Eloquence* (1577), and the *Artes of Logike and Rhetorike* (1584), attributed to Dudley Fenner. Many other books of this era, including John Smith's *The mysterie of Rhetorique unvailed* (1657), continued the faulty tradition of viewing rhetoric as the study of only style and delivery.

Only two important rhetorics preserved classical precepts. They were Leonard Cox's *The Arte or Crafte of Rhetoryke* (1530) and Thomas Wilson's *Arte of Rhetorique* (1553). Cox's primer of ninety-one small pages did not pretend to be complete, but had the distinction of being the first known book on rhetoric in English. It told the schoolboy how to put a speech together and

---

[4] Thomas Wilson, *The Rule of Reason, conteinyng the Arte of Logike*, 1563, fol. 3a, pp. 7–13.

[5] Donald Lemen Clark, *Rhetoric and Poetic in the Renaissance* (New York: Columbia University Press, 1922), p. 58.

stressed invention, the canon of ancient rhetoric which was then least emphasized. Wilson's volume, which came after the *Arte of Logike* already mentioned, passed through eight editions and contributed importantly to the evolution of rhetorical theory by preserving classical tradition at a time when the vision of rhetoric had been badly distorted.

D. L. Clark attributes the perversion of rhetorical theory in the Middle Ages and early Renaissance to the bad judgment of rhetoricians and their ignorance of the classical tradition. In England particularly, the most important classical treatises on rhetoric and poetry, those by Aristotle and "Longinus," were unknown and only fragments from Cicero and Quintilian were used. The most popular work was the *Rhetorica ad Herennium. De Oratore* and *De Inventione* ranked second. The medieval tradition based indirectly upon the *Rhetorica ad Herennium* and on *De Inventione* persisted in England for over a hundred years after it had been displaced in Italy. Quintilian's *Institutio Oratoria* was published in Europe early in the seventeenth century but proved too long to be used extensively; and even when Aristotle's works became available, his *Rhetoric* had almost no immediate influence upon English rhetorical theory. Because of the persistence of medieval tradition, rhetoric in England did not regain its classical meaning until the seventeenth century.

At a time when rhetorical theorists had divided into two camps, one very small and with a marked classical influence, the other large and with a conspicuous emphasis on style, it is impressive that a comprehensive rhetorical theory emerged in the works of the period's most noted philosopher, Francis Bacon (1561–1626). His theory was not presented as a compact set of rules, but Professor Karl R. Wallace has done a masterful job of organizing and assembling the scattered pieces on the subject found chiefly in *The Advancement of Learning* (1605) and *De augmentis scientarium* (1623).[6] On the whole, Bacon condemned excessive stress

---

[6] See Karl R. Wallace, *Francis Bacon on Communication and Rhetoric* (Chapel Hill: The University of North Carolina Press, 1943).

upon style while emphasizing invention and the adaptation of speeches to specific audiences, an almost totally neglected aspect of rhetoric's classical foundation.

Bacon assigns to rhetoric the function of applying reason to imagination for the better moving of the will. His theory of rhetoric is that of persuasion based upon psychological precepts. Bacon declares that we know very little of the actual substance of the mind but are conversant with its faculties—understanding, reason, imagination, memory, appetite, and will—which are the concerns of the logical and ethical sciences. A knowledge of these faculties will aid us in securing action, the goal of all rhetoric. Bacon's theory also has an ethical base, for it insists upon a portrayal of the good as an additional function of true rhetoric. Imagination is to be controlled and subordinated to reason, which must govern all of man's activities.

Bacon does not limit rhetoric to oral discourse. True, he refers to the orator and the speech, but he applies what he has to say to both speaking and writing.

Bacon's major contributions were his observations on invention. His treatment of commonplaces and topics as aids to invention influenced subsequent writers more than any other part of his work. Also influential was his discussion of the philosophical errors deriving from mistakes of inference. In this connection he considered sophistical fallacies, fallacies of interpretation, and his famous Idols of the Tribe, Cave, Marketplace, and Theatre. He viewed rhetoric in broader perspective than others of his time. He saw utilitarian communication as a social art in which reason is applied to imagination to persuade, subjugating passion and establishing good and just causes.

The Modern Period

At this point we must look briefly to France to see a rhetorician of the pulpit who was doing for preaching what classically oriented rhetoricians were doing elsewhere for speaking in general. François de Salignac de la Mothe Fénelon (1651–1715) wrote three dialogues on rhetoric which were first published in 1717, after his death.[7] In them he considered preaching in relation to other arts of expression but without limiting his discussions to sermonizing. Rhetoric was a social instrument in which matter is more important than manner. He preserved the principles of the ancients but did not treat them systematically nor apply them as rigidly as did other rhetoricians of the day. In Fénelon we find a liberal, modern application of a rhetorical theory based upon insistence that man imitate nature in his speaking, that naturalness is a prime requisite for effective communication.

Fénelon disagreed with those who advocated the separation of logic and rhetoric. Nor did he confine his dialogues to style and delivery as was the custom in most rhetorics. Fénelon stressed the close connection between rhetoric and logic, the necessity for proof, vivid portraiture and movement, and the logical and aesthetic dimensions of all acts of literary evaluation.

Unlike others of his day, he did not find things beautiful unless they were true and useful to listeners. In this his teaching resembled St. Augustine's. He believed that real eloquence is an inspired and inspiring art resting upon an ethical base. Once he has given his listeners the "bread" of meaning, the preacher may properly add the "spice" needed to arouse the feelings, stir up emotion, and strike the heart. The philosopher, said Fénelon, acts only to convince, but the orator must go beyond, adding everything capable of arousing sentiments and demonstrating the truth.

Fénelon did not approve the rigid, artificial rules of disposition of his time; he felt that organic unity of discourse is destroyed by complicated, unnatural divisions of subject matter. Style, too, was a matter of aptness, simplicity, and clarity. Delivery was to be unaffected and artless rather than artificial or mechanical.

Fénelon's creed was that man must follow nature in her changes. Oratory and poetic art are rooted in the imitation of

---

[7] Wilbur Samuel Howell, *Fénelon's Dialogues on Eloquence* (Princeton: Princeton University Press, 1951), pp. 36–37.

nature. Their methods are, thus, imitative. Their aims are also similar—to instruct pleasingly. Fénelon's, says Wilbur Samuel Howell, was "the earliest statement we have of what may be said to have become the dominant modern attitude toward rhetoric."[8]

In contrast to Fénelon's viewpoint and separated from it by less than a hundred years was a body of theory called "elocution," the results of which were the antithesis of naturalness. Of this mutation in rhetoric Frederick W. Haberman writes:

> Elocution was an offshoot of rhetorical study. It was an exhaustive and systematic analysis of delivery. The elocutionary movement, which began about 1750, was a response to the demands of the age. This widespread and intense study of delivery was an answer to the eighteenth-century denunciations of oratorical frigidity, to the pressure for professional and educational training in speech, to the new consciousness of the need for standardization of spoken language, to the desire of the people to obtain facility in speaking a language of which they were becoming proud and to demands of those who dealt with democratic movements. The elocutionary movement, however, was more than a simple renaissance of a particular canon of rhetoric. It was rather, a new ordering of an old subject.
> This new ordering resulted from the application of the tenets of science and of rationalism to the physiological phenomena of spoken discourse. The new study of delivery was affected by the impact of science or of rationalism in precisely the same way that the study of history, of economics, of poetry, and of prose style was affected. . . .[9]

Three kinds of textbooks for speakers came out of the elocutionary movement: thorough works treating voice, rhythm, and gesture; elementary rule books; and collections of useful and elegant extracts for practice preceded by prefatory essays. In an attempt to approach speech theory scientifically, the elocutionists developed methods to observe voice, gesture, and language and to record these observations. Elaborate systems of notation and representation resulted from exhaustive analyses. The movement

---

[8] *Ibid.*, p. 46.

[9] Frederick W. Haberman, "John Thelwall: His Life, His School, and His Theory of Elocution," *The Quarterly Journal of Speech*, XXXIII (Oct., 1947), p. 294.

rested upon the philosophy that man is controlled by natural laws. Nature is a compelling force. It has immutable laws in the physical universe and immutable codes in the social universe. These laws and codes are systematic and can be disregarded only at one's peril. These theorists thought speech and all worldly matters to be capable of scientific systematization. So they embarked upon their mission to reduce speaking to system.

In his authoritative work on the movement Professor Haberman identified its four founders.[10] Thomas Sheridan (1719–1788), who published *Lectures on Elocution* (1756), examined the individual sounds of speech as he sought a scientific phonetic basis for pronunciation. Joshua Steele (1700–1791), in his *Prosodia Rationalis* (1775), devised a system of musical notations for the management of the voice. His enterprise stemmed from his interest in melody, rhythm, and pitch in speech and music. John Walker (1732–1807), an actor turned elocutionist, investigated the interplay between inflection and grammatical form. He invented a complete system by analyzing the four inflections (rising, falling, and two circumflex kinds) found in nature and generalizing concerning their applications in the utterance of various grammatical forms. His chief work was *Elements of Elocution* (1781). In *The Art of Speaking* (1761), James Burgh (1714–1775) contended, "nature had given every emotion of mind its proper expression." This belief was not original with him, but the system in which he explained ninety-eight emotions surpassed others in thoroughness and influenced the conception of bodily action during the entire elocutionary movement.

Others, such as Gilbert Austin, John Thelwall (1764–1834), and David Charles Bell (1817–1902) and Alexander Melville Bell (1819–1905), played leading roles in the elocutionary movement. Austin's *Chironomia* (1806) exerted the greatest influence on the theory of gesture by analyzing bodily action in four systems of notation and producing descriptions or chartings for over fifty foot movements, over 100 arm positions and thousands of hand

---

[10] Frederick W. Haberman, "The Elocutionary Movement in England, 1750–1850" (Unpublished Ph.D. thesis, Cornell University, 1947).

positions. Thelwall's distinctive contribution was formulation of a principle of "rhythmus" derived from his explorations in physiology, music, and speech. He applied this principle and elocutionary vocal exercises in his work with the speech handicapped. The Bells devised a physiological or visible alphabet that contained symbols to represent every speech sound. Through the use of physiological pictographs they formulated the first modern system of phonetic symbols to gain prominence and serve useful purposes.

The elocutionists, in their desire to apply the laws of nature to man's behavior, often produced artificial systems. The inflexibility of their notations and rules made their theories applicable only to those public speeches which had been entirely written out. Their systems were designed for and mostly applied to acting and the oral reading of literary works. Their methods would not work for extemporaneous delivery and so were of little influence after 1915. Yet the elocutionists performed valuable service by their thorough investigations, descriptions, and analyses of delivery. Some of these can still help us understand the operation and management of the voice and body during speaking.

Reacting against the elocutionary movement, other British rhetoricians strove to revive, clarify, and strengthen ancient classical theories. Chief among them were George Campbell (1719–1796), Hugh Blair (1718–1800), and Richard Whately (1787–1863). All three were Christian ministers.

Campbell's *Philosophy of Rhetoric* (1776) is a markedly theoretical but useful work which explores the philosophical, literary, psychological, and epistemological foundations of rhetoric. Campbell's topics are the sources of knowledge, evidence, influences upon man's passions, the speaker, analysis of audiences, wit, humor, and ridicule, and linguistic purity, clarity, and vividness. He conceives rhetoric's ends to be enlightening the understanding, pleasing the imagination, moving the passions, and influencing the will. Though his psychology is outdated, he stands as the first rhetorician after Bacon to perceive the inseparability of rhetorical and psychological theories. He treats evidence differently from his predecessors in that he sees analysis of evidence as a solution to

the persistent problems of finding truth and estimating probability. He does not treat the ancient canons of rhetoric systematically, but he tries to explain audience adaptation. His attempt
leads him to discuss invention, arrangement, style, and delivery
in deliberate if unorthodox fashion.

Blair's *Lectures on Rhetoric and Belles Lettres* (1783), as the
last half of its name implies, emphasizes taste, style, and critical
appraisal. Ten of his lectures are devoted to public speaking. Two
trace the history of eloquence from the ancient Greeks to the
time of writing. The next three examine oratory in its settings
—the popular assembly, the law court, and the pulpit. Another
is a critical examination of a sermon. These six lectures are followed by two on the parts of the speech. Two more discuss delivery
and the "Means of Improving in Eloquence." The popularity of
Blair's work has been attributed to its form rather than to its
content. It was widely read in both Great Britain and America.
The reader examines public address from a vantage point unlike
that of other classical theorists because of the emphasis on taste
and beauty. Style, occasion, structure, and delivery are elements
of Blair's view of rhetoric. He had nothing constructive to say of
inventive processes but revitalized other classical precepts.

In his *Elements of Rhetoric* (1828), Richard Whately defined
rhetoric as "argumentative composition, generally and exclusively." He considered it an offshoot of logic. His book on rhetoric
was written after his *Elements of Logic* (1826) and was divided
into four parts: "An Address to the Understanding," an extensive
analysis of invention and arrangement; "An Address to the Will
or Persuasion," primarily an examination of emotional appeals;
Style; and Delivery.

Whately is considered the first to treat argumentation for
popular audiences as a formal branch of speech making. He
stressed argument from probability, and reason occupied the central position in his rhetorical theory.

Other valuable refinements are his distinction between argument from example and argument from analogy and the original
idea that he who argues for a change in the *status quo* must assume
the burden of proof. His treatment of *ethos* was new in that he

discussed the speaker's character in terms of the diverging tastes and intelligence of his hearers. Whately's remarks on the disadvantages of being thought eloquent were also original. Rebelling against the mechanical delivery of the elocutionists, he insisted that a speaker must focus upon what he is saying to speak naturally. To some extent, his theory of delivery resembled Blair's. Whately's treatise was based more directly upon Aristotle's *Rhetoric* than upon any other source, though he also relied on Campbell, Cicero, and Bacon.

The two streams of rhetoric we have been discussing, the elocutionary movement and the classical revival, have both influenced the understandings of our day. The transmission of rhetorical theory from England to America was inevitable. The theories we have described as flourishing in Great Britain reappeared in many versions in the textbooks imported from England and in those written here. They thus became familiar to American students in both the secondary schools and colleges.

A further influence upon American rhetoric came from abroad in 1871 when James Steele MacKaye (1842–1894), actor, director, and playwright, introduced the Delsarte system of oratory and acting to this country. The system had originated about 1839 in France with François Alexandre Nicholas Cheri Delsarte (1811–1871), and was less a system than a pseudo-philosophy which organized all arts and sciences according to a plan rooted in observations on human behavior and orthodox Roman Catholic doctrine. This "science" described and explained phenomena in groupings of threes and nines and was applied chiefly to music and acting, the two arts Delsarte knew best. Professor Shaver explains:

> This trinitary division arises from the Holy Trinity, and each member of the Holy Trinity governs one of the elements of the trinity of any object or idea. Thus man is divided into life, mind, and soul. These are governed respectively by the Father, the Son and the Holy Spirit. Life, mind, and soul are expressed by certain agents: vocal sound (apart from words) expresses life, words express mind, movement expresses soul. This concept of movement as the expression of soul possibly accounts for the emphasis put upon gesture and pantomime

by American Delsartians. It seems unlikely that Delsarte placed any more emphasis on the physical aspects of his system than on the vocal, but in America, the physical aspects became the basis of the system and the Delsarte system became, essentially, a system of physical culture.[11]

By 1900, what had become a routine, mechanical system for teaching expression primarily through gesture, body position, and such exercises as tableaux and statuesque posing was outmoded. Nonetheless, Delsartians had influenced rhetoric by stimulating discussion of the visual and vocal aspects of speech.

Classical and elocutionary ideas have survived, but since the 1920's the elocutionary methods have almost disappeared. In reorganizing and reshaping rhetorical theory for formal study in the classroom, American speech teachers have refined the inherited theories of disposition, strengthened the psychological interpretations upon which theories of audience adaptation depend, enlarged the theory and perfected the practice of extemporaneous delivery, and otherwise added detail and example to the tradition of Aristotle.

An American speech teacher who added significantly to the heritage of rhetorical theory was James A. Winans (1872–1956). Professor Winans made perhaps the most notable contribution to rhetorical theory in this century when he introduced the psychology of attention as the basis for a system of public address. This psychology, which he borrowed chiefly from William James and Edward Titchener, is threaded through his book, *Public Speaking* (1915). Walter Dill Scott (1869–1955) published *The Psychology of Public Speaking* in 1907, but he did not make attention the basis for a comprehensive theory of public speaking. Winans defined persuasion as gaining and maintaining fair, favorable, and undivided attention; he also insisted that logical argument, as well as appeals to emotion, is usually necessary to attain belief. His contribution came in the fullness of time, for without

---

[11] Claude L. Shaver, "Steele MacKaye and the Delsartian Tradition," in *History of Speech Education in America*, ed. by Karl R. Wallace (New York: Appleton–Century–Crofts, Inc., 1954), p. 205.

the psychologists' investigations of attention, his rationale would not have been possible.

Winans' passages on delivery are also notable. He advocated conversational quality rather than conversational style because he thought the latter concept suggested that everybody should speak in the same manner rather than develop individuality. He urged, instead, that public speech be conversational in its elements: lively, direct, and spontaneous. He insisted, however, that good public speaking was neither reproduced conversation nor imitation of informal utterance. Many still consider his discussion of theories of delivery the soundest available.

The evolution of rhetorical theory, the heritage as traced in the preceding pages, is marked chiefly by changes in emphasis. Of the five ancient canons of rhetoric, invention, disposition, style, delivery, and *memoria* or command of the speech, only disposition and *memoria* have missed their hour in the limelight. Neither has ever dominated rhetoric.

The ancient Greeks laid a foundation for the art of speech making which, in many respects, still serves today. The Romans refined and amplified the Greek teachings. Following a medieval period of little growth, a distorted rhetoric was revived in the Renaissance, confused with poetic and absorbed into logic and dialectic. But in this period when rhetoric became style, there were those who clung to classical tradition and regarded invention as the key process in speech composition and delivery. With the modern period came an emphasis upon naturalness. The elocutionists' attempt to convert delivery into a science resulted in mechanical performances which were at least partially responsible for the attempts of British writers to revitalize the more comprehensive classical theory. Most recently the application of modern psychology to rhetorical theory has provided insight into the speech maker's art. Interest in psychology and the use of scientific method in the study of the humanities may yet produce new emphases in the study of the liberal art of public speaking. In the United States public address is today studied with increasing intensity by more diverse methods of research and experimentation than ever before. The yield of such study may well direct us to new understandings of rhetorical theory in the years to come.

Exercises

WRITTEN

1. Write a book review of 1500–2000 words treating one of the works on rhetorical theory discussed in this chapter.
2. Write an essay comparing the treatment of a canon of rhetoric (invention, disposition, style, delivery, or *memoria*) in two of the books cited in this chapter. For example, compare Aristotle's theories of style with Blair's or Quintilian's theories on delivery with Whately's.

ORAL

1. Prepare and deliver a two- to three-minute speech introducing a person whose name is mentioned in this chapter. Assume he is about to deliver a speech on rhetorical theory to your class.
2. After reading in one of the works mentioned in this chapter, deliver a short report on an element of theory which you feel is applicable to speech-making today.

--·*{ 3 }*·--   *First*

Considerations

A public speech has been assigned. A time for speaking has been allotted you. You are expected to appear and perform. A dozen questions crowd your brain. "What must I do to carry off this assignment successfully?" "How can I make sure that what I have to say won't sound as though it had been said dozens of times before?" "What must I do to prepare a speech?" "How can I organize what I have to say?" "How can I be sure I won't faint?" "What speech principles must I expose myself to before I make my first try?"

Ideally, you should know all the theoretical and practical knowledge in this book before making a speech, but a crucial portion of the art of public speaking can only be acquired from experience. Therefore, your personal experiments in formal, spoken communication must begin early. Each opportunity for performance will allow you to explore your own nature as a communicator and to study the behavior of other persons when they listen and react to what you say. Only through steady accumulations of related knowledge drawn from experience and reflection can you arrive at a full understanding of your own potentialities in oral composition.

Your development as an aware speaker will be gradual. As your understanding and control grow, you will become equal to meeting higher standards of performance and more difficult problems in communication. But one must begin with practical experiments immediately if there is to be time for personal growth. In order that your beginning may be a constructive experience, we ask you to study the elemental observations in this chapter before you make your first major attempt at learning about yourself and others through public speaking. These "first considerations" are relevant to all your speaking, but it is important for you to know about them now—before you take the platform.

In the following pages we shall deal with seven topics of which you must be aware if you are to address an audience for the first time with a realistic understanding of yourself and what you are about to do. These topics are: originality in speech making, the basic procedures in speech preparation, readying a first assignment, the modes of delivery, stage fright, rehearsal attitudes, and listening.

Originality[1]

Good speech-making by beginner or veteran requires originality. So the question of what constitutes originality is basic.

You may draw information and ideas from printed or oral sources. You may acquire materials from personal knowledge, magazine articles, essays, editorials, or books. You may glean ideas from lectures, plays, movies, television and radio programs, or conversations with fellow students and professors. But once your information is gathered, you must reflect upon it and stamp it with your own personality. Then you must present it in your own words. *To be original you must be able to discover and convey fresh meaning in known matters.* Rarely does even the greatest speaker discuss what was before the speech totally unknown. To realize a truth clearly because you have experienced it in your own mind produces a degree of originality gained in no other way, even though the base for such originality is to be found in readily accepted axioms.

---

[1] The original version of this section was written by Herbert A. Wichelns and subsequently modified by the authors of this book and others.

If you are to preserve your self respect and gain the respect of your audience you must be prepared to convey newly discovered meanings or new interpretations. Any listener demands as the price of attention that you shall have actively thought for yourself, shall have reached your own point of view, and shall have reacted as an individual to the information you have digested. To be heard with attention and confidence you must exercise judgment in sifting the materials to which you have exposed yourself, and you must test your own reasoning. You must say what you have to say in your own way, choosing your own words. Since individualized choices in both matter and structure are involved, you should be extremely wary of constructing speeches based on a single source. If you rely too heavily on outlines to be found in debate manuals or study files or upon ideas expressed in a *single* book or magazine account, you cannot hope for originality even though you actually speak the words conveying the final message. Ready-made facts, style, and tone promote parrot-like discourse.

Thorough, systematic preparation is the key to originality in public speaking. You must become intimately acquainted with the facts on your subject. You must judge your material. Sifting the important from the unimportant takes time and reflection. For this reason the likelihood of discovering fresh significance in a subject will increase if you begin work early. Ideally, a period of several days should elapse between the period of research and final organization and rehearsal of your speech. During this "gestation" or "cooling-off" period you should mull over the meanings and possibilities of what you know. Ideas should be allowed to grow, to flower into final form, before the finished utterance evolves.

It takes imagination to bring freshness to a subject. You must realize the distinct shapes and the distinct functions of the materials you use to support and amplify points. You must try to see what is unique in these materials, in your relationship to them, and in their meaning and interest for your audience. The function of imagination in this case is not to create the unreal or imaginary but to bring about a true understanding of reality. Imagination ought to reinforce and animate fact and probability.

Clear speech plans reflecting your views, views framed in your own best language and related to your listeners' experiences, result from acquiring knowledge, reflecting upon that knowledge, and applying imagination to it.

What are some tests of originality? You should be able to defend your speech in subsequent discussion. You should be able to add to the information you have presented if called upon to do so. You should know more than you have had time to tell. You should be able and eager to trace ideas to their sources and to credit these sources by citing them in your speech or in discussing their reliability afterward. If you use illustrations or exact quotations borrowed from others, you should acknowledge them. You should be sincere in stating your own ideas and beliefs, and you should be able to publicly evaluate the ideas and beliefs of those you have consulted.

If you wish to be original you will not rely upon others to the extent of repressing your own individuality. You will be sensitive to the dangers of plagiarism and steer clear of passing off the work of others as your own. You will avoid the hackneyed and be free from clichés. You will rely upon your own initiative to produce the fresh synthesis of ideas and wordings which constitutes original public address. Like any other work of artistic merit, your work—your speech—will be the product of your personal experience and insights.

Basic Procedures in Speech Preparation

The processes of preparing any speech are those of guiding your own intellectual behavior by the demands of the nature and frailties of human thought, the conventions of communication, and the nature of listening. We shall consider these processes in detail in later chapters but certain necessities must be understood before you undertake your first experiment in public speaking.

Before you can give a speech you must consider what is to be said. If you do not know what to say, you must decide on some subject worth talking about or someone must assign you a subject.

Given a subject, you must decide what sort of response you may legitimately seek from your particular audience. For example, you must determine whether to inform, inquire, reinforce, persuade, or entertain. This decision made, you must next determine what central idea is to dominate your information, inquiry, reinforcement, persuasion, or entertainment. Let us briefly examine how and why each of these decisions must be made.

DETERMINING THE RESPONSE

You should try to think of a classroom speech as a real speaking event rather than as an unrealistic exercise. Suppose you were asked to speak to a dramatic club "about drama." After agreeing to give the speech, you would have to decide what sort of response you wished to elicit. Should you inform the group of something they do not know about drama and seek the response, "Yes, I understand"? Or should you review and amplify familiar knowledge, thus adding to their information about some phase of drama, seeking the response, "Yes, I understand better (or more fully)"? Or should you persuade the group to change some aspect of its philosophy or some phase of its activity, thus engendering the response: "Yes, we ought to think or do that" or "I agree"? Should you inquire with this group, raising some question with them to excite the response: "We ought to look into that further" or "That bears further thinking"? Or should you reinforce what your audience already believes and inspire them to strengthen their prior affirmations so they respond with, "We ought to reflect more strongly what we stand for" or "Yes, drama *is* a cultural force"? Should you simply amuse the audience with satire or irony or other diverting discussion, seeking smiles, laughter, and "That's amusing" as your responses? These are your normal options in preparing any speech. A subject may be treated in many ways; how *you* should treat it depends first on how you want your listeners to react.

The five purposes which we have just reviewed need not be mutually exclusive in your speech. You may inform in order to persuade or reinforce. You may persuade in order to get a group to inquire. But despite such intermixing and overlapping of purposes, one purpose must dominate and the others must be subordinate, providing a substructure upon which the dominant purpose rests. The reason is as simple as it is inexorable: neither you nor your listeners can think clearly about any subject unless you plainly understand the chief reason for thinking about it at all.

CHOOSING YOUR SUBJECT

As we said earlier, the group that asks you to speak may specify neither subject nor purpose for your speech. A program chairman may simply say, "Come and talk to us about anything you want to." When you must decide upon a subject, there are several guidelines you should follow.

1. First is your own experience. It is unwise to choose a subject about which you know absolutely nothing. Experience, however, is not the whole answer. We think of the student who had much experience with turtles. He was a turtle expert. He spoke first on diamond-back turtles. The class was fascinated with his breadth of knowledge, enthusiasm, and thoroughness. Experience served him well. The second time, he chose to talk about snapping turtles. He was still interested in turtles and he was still experienced, but the audience had heard enough of turtles and turned its attention elsewhere. In this case experience and personal interest did not serve.

We also think of the students who, told to consider their personal experiences in arriving at subject choices, gave speeches on "my summer job as a milkman" and "my days as a lifeguard." Their subjects were not well received, though they had experience and enthusiasm. What they had to say was trite and familiar, incapable of stimulating their audiences to think.

2. Prior knowledge is a second factor to be considered. If you do not know your subject, you must learn before you have earned the right to take your listeners' time. Remember, the five minutes you spend on the platform before an audience of twenty

people consumes 100 minutes of the world's time. Therefore, you will need to decide upon a subject you already know a great deal about or about which you can know a great deal before your speaking engagement.

3. The availability of material becomes a third determinant of the subject choice. Don't choose speech subjects without making a preliminary survey of the resources for obtaining the information you will need. We have mentioned possible sources of speech materials on page 45 and will discuss them further in Chapter 5. Unless you make a preliminary inventory you may find that there is just not enough material to warrant a speech.

4. The audience will also have a bearing upon your subject choice. Age, sex, expectations, knowledge, and socioeconomic level may rule out some subjects which otherwise may seem excellent. We treat these matters more fully in Chapter 4.

5. A fifth determinant of your subject may well be the occasion with its inherent limitations: the reason your listeners will convene, the situation, and the time of day. Some subjects will be inappropriate because of the occasion or assignment.

6. The time allotted for your speech will place further limitations. In your preliminary survey of materials you may realize that your subject is too complex to be handled in the time you have, or too narrow. You may find some subjects too simple to occupy the minutes profitably.

7. Lastly, subjects ought to challenge the audience and the speaker. Something ought to be gained by both. There ought to be "news." Brain stretching and creative cogitation ought to be products of good subject choices. Puerile and parochial subjects do not encourage the kinds of thinking which ought to characterize public speaking as a liberal art.

Sometimes it is not the subject area which is responsible for poor subject choice but your selection of the aspect to be treated. The decisions that determine the merit of a speech often have to do with how to approach and treat a subject rather than with the subject itself.

Given the general topic, drama, for your first speech, your real business in finding a subject begins with deciding what kind of response you want from your audience and with determining how you can narrow this topic to suit your purpose and your time limit. If your assignment or your preference particularizes your subject to something like, "Off-Broadway theatre during the 1950's," you may turn at once to deciding whether to inform, inquire, persuade, or amuse your listeners. On the other hand, a request to "tell about your experience with drama" leaves you with some decisions to make concerning *which* experiences to talk about. These decisions, again, will be chiefly determined by what kind of response you want from listeners. This topic seems to suggest a speech to inform, but you could select experiences to persuade or amuse. Here as elsewhere, your choice of materials and breadth of subject depend upon one crucial decision: What response are you trying to get from your listeners?

LOCATING YOUR CENTRAL IDEA

If you are assigned a "report," you are expected to inform. If the assignment goes one step further and says you must report on a specific subject such as the outcome of a project or an interpretation of a concept, your purpose and your subject are already decided. Having been brought to this stage, your next task is to locate a central idea, a proposition or thesis or subject sentence around which to structure what you will say. In framing this core idea it is helpful to think of it as the hub of a wheel from which supporting spokes extend, as the roof of a pavilion which is supported by pillars, or as the apex of a pyramid supported by blocks of specific information which substantiate the epitomizing statement.

Any praiseworthy speech has a central idea or proposition to which the audience's attention is directed and for which a specific response is sought. Detailed ideas, reasons, or assertions may form primary points in the general framework of your speech; but you must subordinate details to the central subject sentence. Once your subject and purpose are known, your task invariably becomes to decide upon some statement that will express pointedly the encompassing thought to which all that you will say ultimately refers. Once this is determined, you are ready to search for lesser ideas and special material with which to substantiate, amplify, and vivify the central thought in such a way as to evoke from listeners the response you earlier identified as your goal.

To sum up: sometimes you must choose your own subject; sometimes it is assigned; sometimes you must locate a narrower, more specific subject within a suggested topic or subject area. Always you must define the responses you seek from listeners; always you must formulate a central idea that epitomizes the speech's content; always you must locate the subordinate ideas that give meaning to your central thought. We emphasize conscious identification of desired responses, and conscious and precise formulation of central ideas, because of the nature of man. All listeners look for "the point of it all" in what they hear. Their demand must be met.

PHRASING YOUR SUBJECT SENTENCE

Listeners will welcome some ingenuity in the framing of your central idea and statement of purpose. "I shall inform you this morning. . . ." or "Let me instruct you. . . ." or "It is my purpose this evening to persuade you that. . . ." are often unsatisfactory phrases with which to begin. Such wordings suggest lack of regard for the mentality of your audience. Your intentions are stated so bluntly that the audience may back away because they feel you are manipulating them. To say, "This morning I will inform you of the four ways in which pulp is processed," may fulfill the formal requirements for a good subject sentence, but it is rather bald. The purpose stands out obtrusively and is tritely phrased. Though when embedded in content this subject sentence may be acceptable to some, it may offend others by its kindergarten tone. A better subject sentence might be: "I hope you will be willing to work to eliminate Inner Cities like East Harlem, which can be found in every urban area." This invites attention and intrigues the listener.

Given the subject, a listener ought to be able to detect a speaker's rhetorical purpose and his theme from the way in which he words his subject sentence. Assertions are usually used for speeches of information and entertainment. Questions usually indicate that the purpose is inquiry. Propositions are reserved for persuasive speeches of various kinds. Suppose a speaker's subject is community theatre in the United States. For each of the usual rhetorical purposes his subject sentence might be worded in the following ways:

> Informing: The history of the community theatre movement in the United States clearly reveals its purpose and nature.
>
> Persuasion: The federal government ought to subsidize the community theatre movement.
>
> Inquiry: Ought the federal government to subsidize the community theatre movement?
>
> Reinforcement: The community theatre movement in the United States is a worthwhile institution which enriches the lives of many people.
>
> Entertaining: The community theatre movement is too bizarre for words.

Note that each of these sentences does three things: (1) reveals the subject of the speech, (2) states the central idea clearly, and (3) plainly implies the kind of response sought.

Good subject sentences are phrased so that a single idea emerges clearly and unambiguously. They are framed in uncomplicated and uncluttered fashion. They do not funnel thought from a general concept to a specific main heading in the speech nor do they contain two main ideas. Beware of compound subject sentences containing "and" or "but." Conjunctions are often signals that two main ideas are present. Avoid such sentences as "The Bessemer steel process is important, because planes are made of steel" and "The Scottish poets ought to be studied, and the poems of Sir Walter Scott ought to be analyzed by all who study British literature." The first narrows to a specific heading. The second contains more than a single idea.

SUPPORTING THE CENTRAL IDEA

Let us suppose you have completed the initial steps of finding a subject, determining your purpose, narrowing your subject,

53

and framing your subject sentence. You must now discover varied and interesting materials to clarify, to add detail to, or to prove and reinforce your theme. You must, in short, discover (1) facts; (2) testimony; (3) examples, whether long or short, real or hypothetical; (4) stories; (5) statistics; (6) comparisons, contrasts, and analogies; and (7) definitions for the purpose of proving or amplifying your subject sentence. At a later point in this book we shall explain these forms of support and amplification fully. (See pp. 170–182.) For now, it is enough to point out that you must find such pertinent materials and that you must structure them as simply as possible into a coordinated, organically unified whole that becomes a speech. In your first attempts to discover and arrange materials, it will be well to concentrate upon a clear, simple main theme rather than upon an elaborate and complicated structure of points and supporting material. It will also be wise to locate a number of pieces of support and from these to select a half dozen of the best for arrangement in clear, connected order. Once you have delivered one or two simple speeches consisting of one or two main points adequately supported or clarified, you will see that a longer speech is but a series of simple units, each developed individually and originally, and juxtaposed so as to form a larger, more elaborate, more complicated structure.

THE SEQUENCE OF PREPARATION

We have been dealing with the stages of speech preparation prior to arrangement and wording. The full pattern of basic steps in preparing a speech can be completed by adding to the steps already discussed the remaining tasks to be performed in sequence. While some of the following steps may be rearranged in order, you must ordinarily perform all of them to assure proper preparation and final success:

1. Discover the response you seek, often referred to as the rhetorical purpose.
2. Analyze your audience.

3. Analyze the occasion.

4. Discover a subject area.

5. Narrow or expand the subject area to locate your specific subject.

6. Wed the rhetorical purpose and your central idea in a clear-cut statement which stands as the theme of your speech and which may be expressed in a single, unambiguous sentence revealing both the content coverage and the rhetorical purpose of your speech.

7. Gather materials for your speech through such activities as viewing, interviewing, reading, and discussing.

8. Organize your materials into a comprehensive pattern which may be written in outline form.

9. Try out wordings and experiment with language in your mind, or orally, in order to find the sharpest, clearest, and most vivid expression for your thoughts.

10. Rehearse your speech orally in order to gain control of the pattern of ideas, of tentative wordings, of your body and your voice so that you gain a sense of emphasis, of timing, and time consumption.

Though this list may seem rigid, careful consideration will soon reveal that the basic steps are more flexible than they may seem. For example, a speaker asked to talk on his recent experiences as a member of a rehabilitation project in Peru may skip step 4 but must at some time complete all other processes of preparation. Even though he may feel that he can dodge step 7 (after all, he knows all about the subject in question), he will find that to look outside himself and seek subject matter from others will provide reinforcement for his own knowledge. If he pursues step 7 as he ought to, he will find fresh illustrative materials so that his generalizations need not be based solely on personal experience. He may also find the observations of others suggest usable patterns of organization which he might not have thought of otherwise. A speaker who is simply asked to "come and speak for our group" will find that he had better complete all the steps we have outlined. A speaker who is asked to "come and give us the history of the National Association for the Advancement of Colored People" may omit steps 4 and 1 and he may find that his invitation has virtually completed step 6 for him.

Here, we have set down the procedures essential in preparing any speech, long or short, composed of one or many points, for any rhetorical purpose. We do not say these procedures must be carried out in the exact order in which we have presented them; but we do reiterate that all decisions about a speech, for which subject, audience, and occasion are known, are contingent upon a clear and unequivocal identification of the response to be elicited from the audience. Step 1 in the list of procedures offered above must, therefore, be taken as early as possible in the preparatory process. Beyond this we have no wish to prescribe. On the other hand, it should never be forgotten that a listener's confusion about any speech is usually the consequence of some moment of illogical, unsystematic preparation on the part of the speaker.

Preparing a First Assignment

Now that you have seen the procedures involved in preparing a speech, you may ask what should be done to construct a first speech consisting of a single point, one which might well be a segment of a longer speech. Your specific procedure may be as follows:

1. First, select from a subject area of interest to you and your audience a relatively simple, single idea which you wish to clarify for your audience or which you wish them to accept. Sometimes you can arrive at such an idea by making a rough plan for a longer speech and then selecting from it one main point for development.

2. Once this idea has been selected, phrase it accurately in a single subject sentence.

3. Concentrate on a single, simple method of development—a structural pattern. Explain or persuade, for example, by arranging your materials in chronological, spatial, effect-to-cause, or problem-solution order.

4. Draw upon several sources other than personal experience for material to amplify or support your idea.

5. Carefully plan even this short speech; prepare a full-sentence outline though it may consist of only six or eight items.

6. Make each of these items bear upon your subject sentence.

Show the audience that each item does clarify or support your subject sentence.

7. In delivering this single point and its amplifying or supporting material, make each item stand out clearly.

8. A final test of the speech will be an affirmative answer to one of two questions: "Does my audience understand the subject better now that I have spoken?" or "Does the audience more nearly accept the idea I have been proposing?"

A simple outline will serve in planning this first speech. To illustrate how you might locate and outline a single point appropriate for a brief talk, let us imagine that you think a major speech might be given on the subject sentence: "We need to support mental health organizations better than we do." If you ask yourself what might be the main headings of such a speech the following could occur to you:

I. Anxiety is a disturbing phenomenon.
II. Anxiety is widespread in our society.
III. Mental health organizations help people to reduce their anxieties.
IV. Mental health organizations deserve more help than we give them.

Any of these four points could be used as a central idea for a shorter speech although the fourth is least promising because it depends for support on the other three. If you chose the first of these points for a one-point speech, you would need to prepare a simple outline or plan of its development. It might look like this:

Subject Sentence: Anxiety is a disturbing phenomenon.[2]
Supporting Material:

(Example, brief)	1.	A recent article in the *Saturday Evening Post* tells the story of a woman's unwarranted anxiety over the fate of her handicapped son.
(Fact)	2.	The anxiety response is often characterized as objectless, therefore frustrating.

---

[2] This sample outline was prepared by John K. Thorne. Used by permission.

(Definition, Testimony)	3. A group of prominent psychologists, including Harold Basowitz and Roy Grinker, define anxiety as ". . . the conscious and reportable experience of intense dread and foreboding, conceptualized as internally derived and unrelated to any external threat."
(Comparison)	4. Anxiety produces a result like that experienced in marching in place when we only raise the dust around us.
(Quotation)	5. An old saying is that "Anxiety and worry, not work, tire one out."

A comparable plan for a one-point speech amplifying a proverb might well look like this:

Subject Sentence: "A bird in hand is worth two in the bush" is widely applicable in our day.[3]

Supporting Material:

(Restatement of Central Idea)	1. Aesop related this concept in stronger language in *The Fisher and the Little Fish:* "A little thing in hand is worth more than a great thing in prospect."
(Fact)	2. Great expectations may easily become only false hopes, since the future is unpredictable.
(Fact)	3. Psychologically, when one continually gambles on the prospect of a "great thing" and loses, he may develop complexes and may become mentally unbalanced.
(Example, brief)	4. A young girl may physically decay as a result of waiting for "a great thing in prospect."
(Example, brief)	5. The value of a "bird in hand" is exemplified by local policy in football: going for the sure extra point rather than gambling on the two-point conversion.
(Example, extended)	6. It is better to have a date with a local coed for a big week end than to have no date at all. (Tell story.)

---

[3] This sample outline was prepared by James Hamasaki. Used by permission.

You will notice that these sample outlines omit title, opening, and closing. Although you will need to introduce and conclude your speech, we have shown only the amplification or proof for the main point. The pieces of support are labelled to show the types the speakers used and to suggest to you that variety in supporting materials enlivens communication.

Modes of Delivery

There are four general methods of delivering a speech: *impromptu, extemporaneous, read,* and *memorized.* Your first speeches are likely to be impromptu or extemporaneous because these methods best promote development of conversational quality. We shall discuss here the two modes most often used by students and return to the general subject of delivery in Chapter 10.

You may be among those who have always confused the extemporaneous method with the impromptu. The two are not the same. The extemporaneous mode of delivery is one in which your speech is thought out in advance, and planned with care, usually outlined on paper, rehearsed orally, and sometimes delivered with notes. This mode allows you freedom and spontaneity in your final wording. It also permits you the flexibility needed to adapt easily to unforeseen circumstances.

The impromptu mode is one in which you make no formal preparation of any kind until a few minutes before you begin to speak. Usually, the most preparation you will be able to do will be to gather your thoughts together by jotting down a few words on a paper napkin or note card. Impromptu speaking is largely spur-of-the-moment activity which will rarely profit you except as an exercise in self-command and in emergencies.

You may or may not be allowed to use notes for classroom extemporaneous speeches. If you use notes, they should be unobtrusive and kept to a minimum. Do not call attention to them. On the other hand, it is best not to try to hide them in the palm of your hand or under your sleeve. Few in the audience will expect you to memorize a troublesome set of statistics or a long literary quotation. Fewer, however, will feel that you are direct and in control of your ideas if your eyes are constantly on your notes or if you are reading from them most of the time. In some cases you will be allowed to take your outline to the platform and in other cases not. When you use an outline or notes, try to refer to them as little as possible.

In your classroom performances aim to free yourself from preset wordings and from mechanical delivery. Should you freeze fast all your ideas, you will deliver them with exactness and rigidity in wording and gesture; they will have little chance to come alive. You will not achieve what Professor J. A. Winans called a "vivid realization of the idea at the moment of utterance." Should you persist in draining your performance of spontaneity by verbatim memorization, by lackluster reading of what you have written, or by clinging to specific wordings at the expense of the re-creation of ideas, your audience will probably receive your efforts with little enthusiasm. They may react as they would to left-overs of any kind. Cold mashed potatoes served without re-heating are hardly as appetizing to most people as those freshly prepared. While you cannot serve up a "just-prepared" speech, you ought to try to create that illusion. Prepare, rehearse, let the speech lie. Let it go through a gestation period as seeds do. Then re-create your speech with enthusiasm, poise, and verve.

It is easy to mistake extemporaneous speaking for impromptu speaking when you are unsure of the preparation, planning, and rehearsal involved. Many lecturers and some legislators and lawyers appear to their audiences to speak impromptu when in reality they have made extensive preparation during years of authoritative investigation, experience, and practice. Those who seem to speak impromptu when they are really speaking extemporaneously are commonly people who engage in public speaking almost daily, so that formal practice sessions are not an absolute necessity for them. Most of you, lacking such experience and practice, must conduct a specific investigation to enrich each utterance and must gain command over each particular set of ideas by rehearsing them in special, oral practice sessions.

The extemporaneous method of delivery is best for the beginner. By using this mode you avoid the pitfalls inherent in other methods. You will avoid the disorganized, unsupported train of ideas usually apparent in the beginner's impromptu efforts. You will avoid the rigid, mechanical transmission of ideas evident in the efforts of the unpracticed oral reader and inexperienced memorizer. We are not at this point disparaging the reading or memorizing of speeches. Some people read aloud very well, and some can memorize material and recite it so their listeners never know that it is memorized. In Chapter 11 we shall discuss reading in some detail. (See pp. 343–351.) We are saying that the beginner is more likely to achieve conversationality in his speaking if he uses the extemporaneous mode. This mode allows not only for careful, thorough preparation, but also for audience adaptation and for spontaneous regeneration of ideas when the speech is given. We discuss oral rehearsal for extemporaneous speaking in a later section of this chapter. (See pp. 65–67.)

Stage Fright

Stage fright or "speech fright" is a universal experience. You no doubt know its physical symptoms. When some situation demanded that you interview another individual or to stand up alone before an audience, you may have discovered suddenly that your knees were shaking, that your mouth felt as if it were stuffed with cotton, that your voice quavered, or that your heart beat too swiftly. You may have felt faint or perspired in the palms of your hands. You may have felt as if twenty-two butterflies were using your stomach as a football field. Some of these physical manifestations of stage fright were real. Others were imaginary. You actually did perspire, but your saliva flow did not really dry up. All these signs, whether actual and overt or imaginary and covert, were manifestations of a state of anxiety which stemmed from fear. You know that what you experienced was stage fright, but you may have overlooked the fact which the name implies, that fear was at the heart of the matter. Fear provoked the anxieties manifested in your emotional disorganization. These anxieties may have become so severe that you were actually physically ill. Instead of realizing that you were afraid, you may have become preoccupied with the imaginary or real manifestations of your condition and sought to remedy the situation by concentrating on getting rid of the "shakes" or by wetting your lips over and over again. You may have tried to get rid of the physical symptoms without trying to do anything about the real cause of your condition: fear itself.

The fear which caused your anxiety resulted in physiological changes. Many who undergo these changes think they are organically ill, that they have some sort of secretion imbalance. What actually happened was that the flow of adrenalin set off other changes. Blood pressure, the rate of respiration, and nerve conductivity increased. More blood sugar furnishing energy entered the system. More thyroxin may have been secreted, speeding the burning of the blood sugar. More oxygen was taken into the blood. More poisons were removed from your system. As a result of these changes fatigue probably lessened, and you may have experienced the kind of increase in strength that frequently accompanies the release of tensions during anger. These bodily changes may interest you, but they are not the causes of your fear.

The real causes of your fear were psychological. A lack of self-confidence resulted in fear when insecurity threatened. The insecurity stemmed from the uncertainties of the situation in which you found yourself. You may have been apprehensive about how your audience would react. Literally, you were afraid that you would lose control of the audience. Or, you may have been apprehensive about your mastery and control of what you were going to say. You were afraid you wouldn't be perfect or that you would fail. You may have been anxious about how well your voice and body would function, or whether you would choose the right words. In public speaking situations the mere fact that you were physically separated from a group of peers may have been responsible for feelings of insecurity and aloneness. You may have been afraid of listeners' potential criticisms. Or you may have felt that you were compelled to speak against your better judgment. You may have fought with yourself. Your wishes to avoid the situation, to flee from it, may have caused you to make such serious excuses that you finally did not have to speak at all. (After all, you *were* ill.) You may have invented alibis or have inwardly prayed, "If ever I am going to break my leg, let it be now."

If, however, you were unable to avoid speaking or if you faced up to reality and decided that now was the time to speak, you still may have been unable to channel your excess energy so that it worked for you. You squirmed, fidgeted, grimaced, croaked out the words, and visibly shook. Each of these actions called the attention of the audience away from what you were saying. Because of your manifestations of discomfort, those to whom you spoke couldn't hear what you were saying.

How can you reduce fear and, subsequently, the tensions which afflict you? The solutions to this problem can be discovered only by going back to the causes to see what can be done to remove them.

First, realize that everyone else at some time or other experiences the same apprehensions you do. The most any speaker can do is to guess how an audience will react, then calmly calculate how best to promote the responses he seeks and to meet the demands the audience makes. Insights into human behavior come with experience, but they are always less than perfect. Realize this fact, but make educated guesses on how you can best adapt to your particular audience in order to get them to react as you wish them to. They are human beings like you. They may vary in age, interest, and creed, but they are similar to you in more ways than you probably realize. We know it is easy to say, "Feel at one with the audience," "Know that they will be more uncomfortable than you are if you don't succeed," "Remember that they are faced with the same problems, the same fears, and the same reactions to fear as you are." All of this is to say, "Get yourself in the right frame of mind." It is quite another matter to *feel*, once you have adopted attitudes conducive to the feeling. Yet you must make first tries, you must gain composure by repeatedly making speeches in the face of varying conditions. A striving for realistic attitudes, coupled with practice, will help assuage your fear.

Thorough preparation, once the calculated guesses are made, is a further step in combating fear. If your apprehensions result from distrust of your material and your memory, pay close, careful attention to your pattern of organization, to your supporting and amplifying materials, to your wordings and to particularly trouble-some spots in your train of thought. The best antidote to fear is thoroughgoing preparation, but this does not mean memorization.

Proper attitudes, practice, and preparation, then, may all play a part in dispelling fear and decreasing anxiety. Most important, however, is your desire to speak. If you want to speak, you have won half the battle in many instances. If you have more than enough to say and are determined to make the audience under-stand or accept your point of view, you will have come a long way toward releasing your tensions into meaningful, constructive actions which will contribute to the accomplishment of your goals. If your desire to communicate is strong enough, you will forget to worry about your hands or feet or what they are doing. This is not to say that you will forget you have a voice and body which you must control. It is to say that if you bend all efforts toward gaining specific audience responses, you will have your best oppor-tunity to accomplish what you set out to do. You will be like a swimmer in a race who, once he has hit the water, lets nothing divert his attention until he reaches the finish line. All distractions will be swept aside or ignored. With proper practice, you can substitute controlled gestures for wasted motion. Wordings will become economical, because with your mind filled with the busi-ness of communicating that which you know securely, you will say just enough and no more to elicit the reactions you seek. Losing yourself in your speech without losing your self-control will cause you to forget your fears.

Of course, you cannot desire to speak unless you are sure that the subject you have chosen is a worthy one. It must be worthy of you and of the time spent in preparation, and it must be worthy of your audience. If you have misgivings about the ideas and materials you are presenting, you are a prime target for fear. Only by choosing wisely and carefully what you will say can you hope to approach a speech situation with confidence. If you feel that what you are going to say isn't worth much to you or your audience; if you feel that your ideas are shabby, that you have settled for words that are dull or imprecise, or that your speech is just something to get over, of course you will be afraid, and you deserve to be!

Rehearsal and Attitudes
Toward Speaking

Oral rehearsal for extemporaneous delivery assures mastery of your speech plan, control of the succession of points embodied in it, and confidence in your ability to present the speech. The problem in extemporaneous speaking is to transfer your plan to your mind and become thoroughly familiar with its sequence of ideas. As you gain control of ideas and their order, specific word choices will vary with each rehearsal, thus building for you a large stock of verbal resources by which to express yourself during the final presentation of your speech. Sound practice in rehearsing extemporaneous speeches is the first avenue to confidence in public speech; sensible, realistic attitudes toward the act of speaking constitute the second. The suggestions outlined below will repay you in clarity of mind and serenity of spirit if you follow them closely whenever you prepare to speak extemporaneously.[4]

1. Read through your written plan, fixing your mind on the succession of main points. Re-read it, this time concentrating not only on the main points but on the details supporting each.

2. Still referring to your outline, speak through the speech in whatever words happen to come. Talk out loud, not under your breath. You will find it helps to stand up and face an imaginary

[4] The material that follows is adapted from *Manual for Public Speaking, I*, p. 22, by H. A. Wichelns and others (1932) and *Manual for an Elementary Course* by H. A. Wichelns, G. B. Muchmore, and others, p. 19. Used by permission.

audience. Try out gestures as you verbalize. Get through the whole speech. If you bungle a part, go right on to the end without stopping to straighten out the troublesome section. Come back to that when you have finished running through the entire speech.

3. Without using your outline or any memoranda except those notes you will use on the platform, stand up and speak through the speech as before. If you can find a patient listener or group of listeners, so much the better.

4. When you can get through your total speech fairly well, time yourself and adjust the speech to the time allotted for your actual presentation. Such an adjustment may call for omissions or condensations, or it may call for additions or expansions of points. It is important to acquire a sense of time on the platform and develop the habit of keeping within time limits.

5. If, in anticipating the moments of speaking, you tend to panic, fix your mind on the realities of the situation. Focus on facts; do not imagine difficulties you don't yet face.

6. In the moments before taking the platform keep the plan of your speech uppermost in your mind; review it. This is the most constructive outlet for tensions.

7. During preparation and just before speaking renew your desire to share a worthwhile message with others. Remind yourself that the experience before you is not a "performance" but an opportunity. You have earned that opportunity through the knowledge you have acquired and your position as a respected human being in a communicating society.

8. Recall that your auditors are persons not very different from yourself, that they want you to succeed.

9. Don't expect to avoid all tension. Some tension is good for you. Properly channeled, tension can serve you positively by increasing your alertness and your available supply of energy.

10. When you are nervous, exercise autosuggestion. Act alert, at ease, and in control of your subject, and you will actually tend to be alive, relaxed, and in command. You will also find that deep breathing and an erect rather than a slumped posture will contribute to your comfort. You *do* need extra oxygen.

11. As a general rule, avoid last-minute changes in your speech, especially during your maiden efforts. Don't add to uneasiness by entertaining misgivings about choices already made. Adapt to the moment and to other speakers but do not make changes that undermine the over-all plan you established in your mind by systematic rehearsal.

Oral rehearsal is insurance. Fluent discourse demands it. Beginning speakers are often tempted to omit this important stage of speech composition because of self-consciousness or because they have not allocated sufficient time for it in scheduling their preparation. This is a grave mistake. Control over content contributes most to control over self; both kinds of control are established and enhanced in oral rehearsal.

Listening

We have thus far examined basic considerations important to you as a speaker. But where there are public speakers there are listeners. Listening is an integral part of the public speaking experience. There are some elemental facts about listening in general and about listening as a student of speech making which also are "first considerations."

We listen more than we speak. Because our role is so frequently that of listener, we ought to ask: How should we listen?

Before you can profitably listen to any speech, discover your purposes in listening. Are you listening to the speech to gain information? To absorb information you will later be tested on? Are you listening to be entertained? Are you listening to assess critically the speaker's arguments or interpretations? Are you listening to hear the other side of a case? Are you listening to gain information on only one aspect of the subject a speaker is considering? Are you listening in order to appraise the speech as an artistic endeavor?

To answer "yes" to any of these questions would be to give a legitimate reason for listening. But to give a "yes" to more than one question (a definite possibility) would make it necessary to qualify some one answer with the adverb *primarily* in order to determine the posture you ought to adopt as listener. Only by knowing your primary reason for listening can you discover how to listen. Secondary reasons for listening do not help much in determining your focus of attention. Efficient listening for any primary purpose requires that attention be focused in a particular way upon what is heard.

When your primary purpose in listening is discovered, the items in a speech which demand closest attention become apparent. What you will note depends on what you are listening for. Your purpose determines how critically you will examine ideas and their detail, how carefully you will observe the manner in which ideas are phrased or spoken. Conversely, you will relax your attention when you decide what you are hearing is irrelevant to your needs and interests. You have learned to select what you want to hear, note, and absorb. As a speaker you must seek to get your listeners to select for attention what *you* think is of most importance in your speech. As a listener you invariably weigh whether the speaker's view of importance coincides with your own.

Self-discipline is necessary in all comprehensive listening. Careless listening is randomly or erroneously directed. Efficient, comprehensive listening is hard work. It entails clarity about purpose and it requires bringing the sense organs sharply to bear on what you hear or see. Comprehensive listening can be hard work. Louis Nizer says "So complete is this concentration that at the end of a court day in which I have only listened, I find myself wringing wet despite a calm and casual manner."[5] To listen critically, taking in the sum of information conveyed through speech, requires that you curb your tendency to let attention wander. A barking dog, a flickering light, a noisy radiator are stimuli competing with what is being said. These are distractions external to speech, but other distractions emanate from the speaker. He may fidget, speak monotonously, or become confused and disorganized in his train of thought. Still other distractions arise within you as listener. You may be strongly drawn to your own immediate problems; you think of a coming examination, of a letter just received, or a remark recently overheard. Biases and prejudices, too, may provoke strong reactions if a speaker touches a sensitive topic. There is, indeed, clear evidence that one of the most common interferences with effective listening is

---

[5] *My Life in Court* (New York: Doubleday, 1961), pp. 297–98.

the tendency to construct counter arguments in imagination whenever an old belief is challenged by those to whom we listen. To pay attention to what is said in the face of such distractions demands considerable self-control. Purposive, efficient listening does not just happen. It requires a measure of discipline appropriate to the demands of your primary purpose in attending.

Questions concerning speakers' and listeners' obligations often arise in speech classes. It is proper, for both speaking and listening must be examined and understood if communication itself is to be understood. It is useful to ask, Must the whole burden for holding attention rest on the speaker? Do I, as listener, have a duty to perform? Am I, as listener, obligated to attend to what every classroom speaker says whether I want to or not? How far do listening to learn content and listening to observe examples of speech making demand that I pay close attention to all that is said? As a student of public speaking your best answer to such questions is probably the Golden Rule. When your role is that of speaker, you will want others to listen to you so they may make constructive suggestions for your improvement. You will hope they will listen carefully to what you have to say and to how you say it. And if this sort of listening is what you hope for from others, you must be willing to listen to them in the same way, for the primary purpose of evaluating speaking as artistic endeavor. Outside the classroom you are the only listener to whom you can prescribe "duties." But the liberally educated citizen ought to recognize that if he does not listen cooperatively and objectively to both the content and method of what he hears, he will seldom be qualified to judge "what is going on here" in the speaking offered him.

Often what you hear as a listener may puzzle you. You cannot see the sense of it. Depending on your purpose, your job may dictate that you reorganize material which the speaker has neglected to organize or has organized badly. In order to understand, you may have to go over the notes you have taken during listening and put them in a new order that makes sense to you. Some college lectures demand this kind of attention. Conversely, in speaking you will want to avoid placing this kind of burden on your audience, so you will make it easier for them by clearly organizing what you have to say.

The public speaking classroom is a listening laboratory in another sense. As a speaker you will have opportunity to detect whether others are listening to you and you can adjust to what you discover. If a member of your audience stares listlessly into space, fidgets uncomfortably, frowns or shakes his head, lolls sleepily in his chair, or chats with his neighbor, you will know you are not holding his full, favorable attention. You will know you must do something to recapture wavering attention, to start listeners nodding in recognition of what you say, to get them to lean forward in spirit. How you can accomplish this is a major consideration in the chapters that follow. But from the beginning of your study of public speaking you will need to recognize that efficient, purposeful listening is not an invariable condition of communicative settings. You will misunderstand your own responses to the speeches of others if you fail to perceive: (1) that any but haphazard listening is the product of deliberate and organized effort; (2) that what you will gain from hearing other speakers will depend on what purpose governs your listening responses; (3) the responses any speaker wins from listeners depend upon how well he accommodates his speaking to the natural difficulties of listening; and (4) that the public speaking classroom is a laboratory in which you may study the nature of man in the acts of listening and speaking.

The primary goal of listening by the student of public speaking is to discover how method or design in oral communication affects the intelligibility and impact of content. You will find yourself listening to absorb the ideas that other speakers present, to improve your own communication by observing what methods enhance or debilitate other speakers' meanings, and to discover what you can offer your colleagues as constructive criticism calculated to enlarge their potentialities as speakers. You must discipline your perceptions by asking why what was said affected you and other listeners, as it did. Every answer you can defensibly make to that question will add to your understanding of speaking and listening, and in the process of answering you will also acquire much new general information.

In this chapter we have dealt with matters you need to consider before engaging in formal speech making. Originality, we have said, is basic to all effective public speaking. Careful and systematic preparation gives discourse the focus and clarifying structure necessary to both speaker and listener. Since the beginning speaker's need is to acquire conversational directness and flexibility in speaking, the extemporaneous mode of presentation will benefit him most, at least in the early stages of his experience as a speaker. Stage fright, we have seen, is not to be exorcized by any tactics except those that eradicate fear. Extemporaneous speaking, properly prepared, is the mode of delivery that will best permit you to develop constructive attitudes easing tension. It is not enough, however, to view the study of public speaking as a study in how speeches are composed and given utterance; speeches are made for listeners, who have difficulties accommodating to the practices of speakers. The public speaking classroom must therefore become a laboratory of both speaking and listening. To this end, you will probably need to develop in yourself a new kind of listening, which concentrates on the ways by which methods of oral communication affect the impact of content.

Exercises

WRITTEN

1. Read a speech of your own choosing. Note as you read those aspects of the speech which seem to you to be original and those which do not. Hand in a paper containing two lists of items: Original, Unoriginal. Add two paragraphs in which you justify your choices in each of the two lists.

2. Write down five simple, single ideas which you think would be good ones for development in a speech of 2–3 minutes.

3. Select a subject area. Frame a subject sentence for each of the rhetorical purposes: informing, persuading, inquiring, reinforcing, and entertaining.

4. Listen carefully to a speech by one of your classmates. Take

71

notes in outline form on what he is saying. Following the speech, compare your outline with the one the speaker used. Check to see (a) how accurately you noted what was said, and (b) how much you missed noting.

ORAL

1. Deliver a three-minute speech in which you develop a single point which could be one of several main points in a longer speech. In developing your point use at least three different kinds of supporting material. In preparation, prepare a simple outline like that found on pages 57–58.

2. Prepare and deliver a brief speech on a proverb of your own choosing. Select at least five items to support its truth or falsity. In preparation devise a simple outline like that on page 57.

Understanding

Audiences

Until a man knows the truth of the several particulars of which he is writing or speaking, and is able to define them as they are, and having defined them again to divide them until they can be no longer divided, and until in like manner he is able to discern the nature of the soul and discover the different modes of discourse which are adapted to different natures, and to arrange and dispose them in such a way that the simple form of speech may be addressed to the simpler nature, and the complex and composite to the complex nature—until he has accomplished all this, he will be unable to handle arguments according to rules of art, as far as their nature allows them to be subjected to art, either for the purpose of teaching or persuading. . . .

PLATO, *Phaedrus*[1]

Whenever you talk to another person you expect him to respond in some way. You speak to be heard, and you want a reaction. The poet, the novelist, and even some essayists may concentrate on the eternal excellence and beauty of what they write, but you are usually interested in the reception accorded your message now —at the moments of speaking. Even if you want your message to reach beyond the immediate audience, you still aim for a particular set of effects. In either case you loose speech to do specific kinds of practical work under conditions you can describe

---

[1] Plato, *Phaedrus*, trans. B. Jowett in *The Works of Plato* (New York: Tudor Publishing Company, n.d.), III, p. 446.

rather precisely. This is why successful speakers do not dwell on the beauty of their speeches; they concentrate, rather, on the practical effects of what they plan to say. For the same reasons a speaker's success is measured not so much by the timelessness of his remarks as by the responses they evoke at the time of the speech. Speakers, unlike other literary artists, seldom address all men in all ages; speeches are, before all else, composed and delivered to and for particular audiences in particular times and particular places. If a speech becomes part of the cultural heritage it is because the subject matter happened to have importance for many audiences and the speaker was skilled enough to meet the demands of a special situation in ways that were not inevitably local or bound in time to the moments of his address.

Since practical effect is the chief measure of success in speaking, your degree of achievement will depend heavily on your understanding of how men and women listen and respond. And in that fact lies a problem. It is not easy to regulate one's speech making according to the dictates of what is known about listeners. Like the serpent tempting Eve, self-love whispers to each of us that the world ought to be as we wish. We tell ourselves listeners ought to wait attentively to hear what we have to say. "I know what they need to hear," we tell ourselves; if we then discover "they" didn't listen, we complete the self-delusion by saying, "Well, that's their loss, for I am right and I spoke for their good. They could have caught my meaning had they tried." But the mistake was our own. We spoke to please ourselves, not to influence people as they are. This easy self-deceit should be a reminder that all men and women prefer their own discourse over the talk of others. Just as you prefer your own ways of thinking about any question, every other person—every listener—prefers his way. Therefore, if the speaker is to reach the minds of listeners, he must forget himself enough to fit his thought to their preferences, understandings, and interests.

You have certainly felt, when talking to a friend, that although he seemed to hear you, he was not thinking about what you were saying. Each of us has played this role of polite but evasive listener, actually engrossed in private thought. Most of us have witnessed the same phenomenon in public situations. In the novel, *Phineas*

Finn, Anthony Trollope described Mr. Daubeny announcing to the House of Commons the resignation of the British Ministry. Now, the political plums would have to be redistributed. A new and special kind of self-interest stirred the politicians in the audience. How this would affect their listening is plain. That part of Daubeny's speech which dealt with what his party might have done had it been left in power, Trollope says, "was generally felt by gentlemen on both sides of the House to be 'leather and prunella,' . . . very little attention was paid to it. The great point was that Lord de Terrier had resigned, and that Mr. Mildmay had been summoned to Windsor."

Like all listeners everywhere, the politicians' thoughts and concerns were with how the new situation would affect them and those in whom they were personally interested. Mr. Daubeny thought his speculations important; but since he spoke of his concerns instead of his listeners' concerns, he spoke almost unheard. This scene reflects not only what happens to speaking and listening politicians but also accurately portrays the basic nature of audiences and the basic problem of speakers.

A speaker cannot presume audiences will give him attention just because they and he are in the same physical place. What counts is meeting psychologically. Speakers must learn how listeners behave, what controls their willingness to listen favorably, and what resources exist by which listeners can be made willing participants in spoken messages. Whether acquired from instruction or from experience, this knowledge distinguishes the effective from the ineffective speaker.

The remainder of this chapter deals with how listeners behave and what controls their willingness and ability to listen favorably. All the rest of this book deals directly or indirectly with the resources by which speakers can engage willing attention.

What Is an Audience?

In thinking about listeners the speaker has a choice. He may begin by trying to understand a single person in the act of listening and generalize his understandings to encompass the audiences that public speaking always involves. Or he may try to think out how people behave when brought together as audiences and give minimal attention to the behaviors and experiences of individual listeners. Both alternatives have limitations from a speaker's point of view, so we shall raise what may seem a simple question: What is an audience?

Audience is a common word, yet we do not always think clearly about the common characteristics of the groups of people whom public speakers ordinarily address. Some conceive of an audience as a mass of faceless beings who present a gelatinous surface on which the speaker may make whatever imprint he chooses. Some imagine that groups of listeners respond automatically to appeals or to techniques alleged surely to influence behavior. Neither of these views can be adopted safely by speakers.

An audience listening to a speech is not faceless or will-less. Neither is it a group of people whose responses will be mindlessly automatic. Whether it consists of one person or many, an audience is made up of individuals, each intent on his own and his group's life and happiness, each preferring the pursuit of these private interests to any form of activity. Though each tends to conform in some degree to the standards and expectations of those about him, he seldom surrenders his individuality to the group. Whether any member will choose to attend to what you say normally will depend much more on him and on you than on the behavior of the other people in the audience. Thus the two most important things a public speaker must remember about listeners are: *they are individuals*, and *they do not have to listen unless they want to*. If you consider your own behavior you will see the truth of these propositions.

You undoubtedly have sat in a class in American history. Sometimes you gave active attention to almost everything your instructor and classmates said. At other times you found nothing of special interest was being discussed, so you allowed your thoughts to wander. If you liked the subject or the teacher, you probably attended more carefully than if you disliked either or both. And no doubt, every now and then some historical fact or an especially clear, interesting, or impressive statement seemed literally to seize your attention and your thoughts. But in all of these experiences of listening *you* retained control over what you would admit into your consciousness and over the ways you would respond to what you admitted. Doubtless there were many times when you restrained your enthusiasms or fought your boredom out of regard for others, but generally you remained yourself. Though you were among many, you were not the speaker's puppet. As part of an audience, you were somewhat affected by those about you; but you and each of your classmates remained individuals, granting or withholding attention according to your own interests, ideas, attitudes, and desires.

But, you may say, "A classroom listener does not play a typical role. How is it that large numbers of people are deeply moved as in religious revivals or great political rallies?" In such mass meetings, people take encouragement from discovering that others feel as they do. They *seem* to be swept along by the power of a speaker when they are only allowing themselves the luxury of acting in an unusually uninhibited fashion on the basis of prior attitudes, enthusiasms, or dislikes. Dramatic outbursts illustrate that listeners will express strong beliefs and feelings with greater freedom once these have been intensified by the words of a powerful speaker and encouraged by the visible support of fellow listeners. But the facts seem to be that people do not lose their own identities when they join together as an audience, although most do not like to appear very far ahead or very far behind their fellows. Evidence further indicates that all of us are anxious to have our predispositions confirmed by others; though few follow the herd blindly, most want to be within the bounds of what is approved by our associates. When we become members of audiences, we all trim the sails of our behavior to the winds of group opinion and practice; yet each sails his own vessel, however much he likes to keep the fleet in sight.

Any speaker who thinks of his audience as a "crowd" or "mob" or "mass" possessing attributes that the listeners do not also possess as individuals endangers his own goals. A far more reliable view of audiences is that expressed by the British social psychiatrist, J. A. C. Brown:

> . . . the main lesson to be drawn from our present study
> of propaganda is how very resistant people are to messages
> that fail to fit into their own picture of the world and their
> own objective circumstances, how they deliberately (if uncon-
> sciously) seek out only those views which agree with their own.[2]

Speakers need to recognize that audiences are aggregations
of individuals with some tendencies to behave alike. Here, you
may find advantage. Favorable responses from some listeners may
encourage like responses from others. But this is only one aspect
of an audience. Each audience is also an aggregation in which each
member acts on the basis of his private needs and knowledge.
Here is challenge. The public speech must contain meaning for
all the kinds of individuals the speaker wants to influence. But
you cannot, practically, motivate each audience member independently of the others. Hence, the direction of your thought
about listeners needs to be like that which has served effective
speakers for centuries: you must make your plans and conduct
yourself on the basis of what your listeners have in common, both
as individuals and as an aggregation.

One thing all your listeners have in common is their humanity. They are people; hence, you can predict some of their
characteristics whether you think of them as individuals or as the
kind of group we call an audience.

PAYING ATTENTION

A distinguished German zoologist has written, "The outside
world—the world perceived by the senses—is the source of all
that a form of life is and does, thinks and feels."[3] If you accept
this view, it makes an enormous difference what a human being
pays attention to—how he uses his senses. He does not, of course,

---

[2] *Techniques of Persuasion* (Baltimore: Penguin Books, 1963), p. 309.

[3] Wolfgang von Buddenbrock, *The Senses*, trans. Frank Gaynor (Ann
Arbor: The University of Michigan Press, 1958), p. 12.

take into himself and therefore form himself by everything that he can sense:

> Which stimuli get selected depends upon three major factors: the nature of the stimuli involved; previous experience or learning as it affects the observer's expectations . . . ; and . . . his needs, desires, wishes, interests . . . in short, what the observer wants or needs to see and not to see. Each of these factors can act to heighten or to decrease the probability of perceiving, and each can act on both exposure and awareness.[4]

The propensity for paying attention to what goes on outside one's self is basic; we attend instinctively and as a matter of conscious choice. Therein lie tremendous opportunities and important resources by which speakers may influence the behavior and experience of audiences.

Whatever yields strong sense experience, especially that which appeals changefully to the senses, has primary power to draw the attention of any of us. Imagery, too, has special power to draw and hold attention, for images enable us to "see," "hear," "feel" vicariously. And we naturally attend to relations among the stimuli presented directly or vicariously to our senses; we notice especially the similarities and differences of things and their nearness to each other or to ourselves. These and other tendencies can be of great value to speakers who supply through talk those behaviors, images, comparisons, and contrasts that gratify the human urge to inspect what impinges on the senses.

Something of these possibilities can be seen from a simple example of how attention typically operates in communicative settings.

Imagine yourself entering a room and sitting down beside a friend. What happens inside your friend? First, he becomes conscious that you have come into the room. Probably he looks at you. He may smile or speak a greeting which says he is aware of you—even that he is glad to see you. In the same moment he may casually notice what you are wearing or whether you look

---

[4] Bernard Berelson and Gary A. Steiner, *Human Behavior, An Inventory of Scientific Findings* (New York and Burlingame: Harcourt, Brace & World, Inc., 1964), p. 100.

tired or refreshed. So far, he has been carrying on a swift, internal conversation; his greeting was an automatic reaction of which he was hardly conscious. What occupied him was his feeling toward you and toward your sudden appearance. In these earliest seconds, his thoughts were focused on you as a person and not at all on communication with you. But if you speak, he will begin to listen, for he was already focusing his attention on you. He only needs to shift attention from your person and his feelings about your presence to what you are saying. This he will usually be willing to do as long as your remarks strike him as interesting. If your talk begins to bore him, he may turn his thoughts back to your person, or to the way you sound when you talk, or to another part of the room, or to other thoughts of his own. Your meanings no longer affect him.

The above is neither a complete nor an entirely scientific description of how one individual grants and takes away his attention. But you should note it mentally as an approximate description of every listener. Each member of an audience first grants attention to your presence; then he responds to whatever internal feelings your presence arouses; next he transfers his attention, tentatively, to whatever communication you initiate. Thus far he will go voluntarily; what happens afterward depends on whether the communication keeps him interested and favorably disposed toward you, the source of the communication. These are the typical first stages of each of your relationships with audiences.

To secure attention from listeners is relatively easy. Introductory "gimmicks" are seldom necessary. But to hold attention is another matter. Here, you need inventive effort and design.

The attention of listeners is fickle and must be enticed, guided, managed, commanded by the speaker. Samuel Taylor Coleridge's "The Rime of the Ancient Mariner" envisaged the control over attention of which speakers dream:

> He holds him with his glittering eye—
> The Wedding-Guest stood still,
> And listens as a three years' child:
> The Mariner hath his will.

> The Wedding-Guest sat on a stone:
> He cannot choose but hear;
> And thus spake on that ancient man,
> The bright-eyed Mariner.

But a wordy observation, dullness of expression, or an ill-adapted theme may tell your listener there is nothing for him, and set his mind to search for more pleasant exercise. Such an irrelevance as a flashy tie, graceless speech, or awkwardness of manner may overpower your words and throw attention back to your person or demeanor. It is, in short, unobtrusiveness of manner and identification of your concerns with those of your listeners that hold their attention.

PURPOSES AND INTERESTS

Lacking the Ancient Mariner's wonderful power to hold attention by a look, speakers must seek other means of controlling listeners' perceptions. The speaker is committed to try for such control through the stimuli of his own speech behavior. It is up to him to devise ideas, language, and behavior that at once support his own purpose and touch the experience and expectations of his hearers and their needs, desires, wishes, and interests. Every speaker can safely assume that all his *listeners are anxious to hear about what affects their own purposes, wishes, and interests.* Conversely, those listeners will usually deny attention to what has no apparent bearing on their affairs as they understand them. These are reasonably sure generalizations you can make about your listeners. They will behave in these ways simply by virtue of being human beings. "Man is aware," says an eminent social psychologist, "of only those aspects of his environment that have some bearing on his purposes in the 'now' that he must judge and act on."[5]

You read this book because you suppose your personal affairs

---

[5] Hadley Cantril, *The "Why" of Man's Experience* (New York: Macmillan, 1950), p. 175.

may be affected by something said here. If you decide that you cannot use what we are saying, you will soon set the book aside or turn the pages to hunt for something that promises to be useful. In this you are like every listener who has heard or will hear you. "Of what use is it to me?" your listeners are always asking. Therefore, your earliest and continual need as a speaker is to satisfy those listeners that what you are talking about can help to meet some need or relate to some previous experience of theirs.

Some of these listeners' needs are predictable, at least in a general way.

BIOLOGICAL NEEDS

Certain dreams, jobs, and ideas affect our interests and purposes simply because we are mammals of the species called man and have the bodily and organic needs of our kind. We are always in some degree interested in satisfying these needs. We want gratifications for hunger, for thirst, for our need of oxygen, for our sexual drives, and for other natural demands made by our peculiar biological system. We want to preserve ourselves from injury, punishment, or other physical discomfort. Thus, we get another useful generalization: *every human being is anxious to learn how his biological wants and needs can be satisfied with the least sacrifice of his other goals and purposes.*

In this group of wants common to all men and women lies a whole series of possible answers to the listener's question, "Of what use is it to me?" Show him that what you have to tell him will help him find such satisfactions as we have just discussed, and he will listen to you—at least until he begins to doubt your promise or to suspect that your goals conflict with his stronger wants and needs. Whenever you can link your thought to the physical needs of listeners—even indirectly—you increase the probability that you can hold their attention.

Even more promising possibilities are open to you, for man is a social as well as a biological creature.

SOCIAL NEEDS

Because they are human beings, listeners are more than creatures driven by physiological needs. When people live together they also develop social desires. Since we discuss the social more often than the physiological, people's social desires offer numerous avenues for approaching their minds, holding their attention, and influencing their behavior.

Almost all people want to be rich (or to be thought rich) in whatever values their societies hold in esteem. A Spartan or an American Indian warrior was especially interested in what would increase his strength or prove his bravery. Athenian listeners of ancient times were greatly concerned that their decisions should prove their judgment in practical affairs. North Americans readily attend to those who tell them how to win out in the various competitions for success and esteem. Each society and each group within a society has special ways of thinking about life, the rest of the world, and the sources of happiness. Consequently, each member of the society or group carries within him some of these special goals, judgments, and points of view derived from his milieu.

These themes might be developed at length were our study sociology or anthropology, but our concern is with how you as a speaker can use sociological and anthropological knowledge. That can be quickly said though not quickly acted upon.

Every time you speak, it is important to locate some of the social needs and goals which your listeners, or most of them, value highly. Then, your job is to associate the thoughts you wish to communicate with the social needs you have identified. The process need not be complicated or pretentious to be effective. Presumably, one of the social aspirations of most American citizens is to have law and order triumph against crime. President Dwight D. Eisenhower laid the ground work on which to rest a plea for public support on behalf of labor legislation that had bogged down in Congress, and to do so he made use of his hearers' regard for public order.

This nation needs a law to meet the kind of racketeering, corruption, and abuses of power disclosed in many instances by the Senate investigating committee headed by Senator Mc-Clellan. For two years, I have advocated such a law. For many months, newspapers have carried extensive accounts of racketeering and corruption in labor-management matters. Many of you have actually witnessed disclosures of this corruption on television in your own homes. It is a national disgrace.

The legislation we need has nothing to do with wages, or strikes, or problems we normally face when employers and employees disagree. Nor am I talking of any new approach to collective bargaining. Nor about any new labor-management philosophy.

I am talking solely about a reform law—a law to protect the American people from the gangsters, racketeers, and other corrupt elements who have invaded the labor-management field.[6]

STEREOTYPES

There are those who prefer not to admit, or who admit but deplore, that all of us simplify the world in order to get on in it. Fortunately or not, everyone thinks by means of stereotypes much of the time, and one cannot understand the humanity of audiences if he disregards this truth. Audiences are constantly perceiving and responding to what they hear by referring new ideas to the stereotypes or special simplifications they have elsewhere acquired.

To change preconceptions is difficult at best, and it can only be done through using other beliefs and knowledge previously acquired by the people addressed. The character of much of that belief and knowledge was described by Walter Lippmann in his noted chapter, "Stereotypes":

For the most part, we do not first see, and then define; we define first and then see. In the great blooming, buzzing con-

---

[6] Text as it appears in Donald C. Bryant and Karl R. Wallace, *Fundamentals of Public Speaking*, (New York: Appleton–Century–Crofts, Inc., 1960), p. 544 (3rd ed.).

fusion of the outer world we pick out what our culture has already defined for us, and we tend to perceive that which we have picked out in the form stereotyped for us by our culture.[7]

Each speaker must recognize that when he speaks to anyone, he must talk to him of values, facts, and patterns of experience that his listener already understands.

To tear a listener away from the comforting assurances that his cultural simplifications and stereotypes give him is probably to lose him, perhaps to irritate and frighten him. It will certainly impair his ability to understand. Carried too swiftly out of his world of familiar ideas, customs, goals, each of us becomes uncomfortable, uncertain, insecure. Each listener wants assurance that his old direction signs are still accurate. Hence we can formulate another generalization about how audiences must be treated just because they are human: *if we speak of what listeners already know and want to reinforce, we shall probably win and hold attention; if we show disrespect for their beliefs, simplifications, and expectations, our listeners are likely to ignore or suspect what we say.*

Thus it behooves the public speaker to ask himself how the members of his audience have defined and come to think about the subject he wants to discuss, and all subjects closely related to it. President Eisenhower's remarks, quoted previously, illustrate the outgrowth of this kind of inquiry. Here, it furnished the basis for a plea in support of a legislative act. What are the stereotypes of lawlessness and disorder which American culture has conditioned us to use when we consider law and order? Gangsters, racketeers, and corruption. When Eisenhower spoke, it had been demonstrated that criminals had associated themselves with some labor unions. The president had the choice of speaking of these "corrupt elements" in general terms only or of defining the problem in simplified, popular terms. By resorting to the concepts of racketeering, gangsterism, and corruption, he quickly and vividly set forth general conditions justifying the law for which he sought support.

---

[7] Walter Lippmann, *Public Opinion* (New York: Harcourt, Brace, 1922), p. 81.

AUTHORITY

One pair of psychologists has put the matter this way:

> Size and magnitude yield only to the prestige of authority as inhibitors of reflective thought. . . . *Prestige of authority* is a general term which refers to many forms of influence. The source of authority may be expert opinion, official pronouncements, religious symbols, the pomp and ceremony of institutional practice, the sayings or doings of the socially elect, or even the printed word or the tone of voice.[8]

Let us illustrate the practical applications of this universal tendency to accept without much question the assurance and advice of a favored authority. Are you speaking to engineers or other students of science? Show them the system you are explaining rests on physical laws they know and trust, and you will probably renew their attention and secure their belief. Would you address a group of businessmen? Make it clear that your proposals have support in the business world. If you know that your listeners will have a wide variety of intellectual and personal interests, search for the community and cultural experiences they have in common, then consider what opinion leaders, symbols, and institutions those experiences will have raised to the level of authority. Identify your thought, as a speaker, with the voices of the leaders and institutions of your listeners' social and private creeds. All men do not have the same values or the same hierarchies of authority, but they all have some values and some sources of authority. We may therefore generalize: *to reach listeners' minds and influence their behavior, you must discover their favorite sanctions and authorities and use these to illumine or justify the new thoughts you offer.*

FAMILIARITY AND NOVELTY

For reasons that probably lie very deep within us, we all tend to reject, even fear, what is alien to our experience, yet

---

[8] Daniel Katz and Richard L. Schanck, *Social Psychology* (New York: Wiley, 1938), p. 313.

certain levels of novelty simultaneously attract and fascinate us. In greater or lesser degrees we are all timidly bound to the familiar and adventurously drawn toward the unknown. Thus, while it is true to say that speakers must discover and use their listeners' stereotypes, sanctions, and authorities, it is equally true to say speakers must offer their hearers "news." We all demand that the new and the old be blended in the ideas and language of effective speech.

Whatever is familiar (especially if it appears in a strange setting) or whatever seems strange (especially if it appears in a familiar setting) can crowd almost everything else out of our perceptions. You do not notice the flawless playing of sixty musicians when the sixty-first player blows a discordant note. You do not pay much attention to twenty cars in a parking lot or to twenty different hats worn at a meeting; but your eye unerringly picks out your car or the hat similar to yours. These dual tendencies of the mind, to embrace the familiar and inspect the new, afford the speaker many opportunities to command attention by mingling elements of the new and old.

Parables are, of course, the classic examples of how one can secure acceptance for a new thought by imbedding it in stories about well-known activities or familiar kinds of persons. Likewise, one can see in the King James version of "The Sermon on the Mount" the attention-compelling power of the new when linked to the familiar—especially when what is familiar has the prestige of authority. In this sermon Jesus introduced six successive sections of new instruction with the words: "Ye have heard that it was said by them of old time. . . ." In these two clauses Jesus was able to reassure His audience that the new thoughts only extended and amplified what was already accepted on the authority of the lawgivers. When Abraham Lincoln wanted to convey his fears about the spread of slavery, he expressed his disturbing view in a familiar figure: "A house divided against itself cannot stand." Parables, references to old and familiar law, and Lincoln's metaphor illustrate some of the means by which speakers may supply the needed reassurance of the familiar while introducing ideas that are essentially new or strange.

Though too much that is unusual disturbs listeners, they still expect any worthwhile experience to contain some novel elements. Aristotle expressed it in his *Rhetoric*:

> Words are like men; as we feel a difference between people from afar and our fellow townsmen, so it is with our feeling for language. And hence it is well to give the ordinary idiom an air of remoteness; the hearers are struck by what is out of the way, and like what strikes them.[9]

He was speaking of style, but the unexpected idea, like the unexpected or out-of-the-way word, has power to catch and hold attention.

The speaker who uses—as he must—man's curiosity about the new and his affection for the old should also remember that attention is transient. Men do not usually look deeply into what is new nor contemplate the familiar. They tire easily, especially when listening. The key to holding their attention through the means we have just been discussing is that *it is the shift from the familiar to the unfamiliar and back again that pleases and holds the mind.* It is change that controls attention. The speaker who remembers this important generalization will see to it that his listener has, at every possible point, something familiar to which he can cling for assurance and something new which will give him a sense of learning and, possibly, adventure. Too much of the old bores; too much of the new baffles.

We have been considering what forces grip attention. We have seen that people tend to grant attention first to your presence; second, to the feelings your presence arouses; and finally, to what you communicate. We have observed that a speaker must work wisely and carefully in order to hold and control this attention, which was casually granted and may as casually be withdrawn. To this end, speakers must be guided in speech preparation and in all utterance by the general truth that listeners usually are eager to hear that which seems to affect their immediate purposes and interests, but will deny attention to what seems irrelevant to their affairs. You will better understand this

---

[9] From *The Rhetoric of Aristotle* trans. and ed. by Lane Cooper. Copyright, 1932, Lane Cooper, p. 185, Bk. III, Ch. 2. Reprinted by permission of the publisher, Appleton–Century–Crofts.

important generalization about audiences if you mind the following subsidiary propositions whenever you prepare a speech:

1. Whatever can be closely linked with the immediate physical needs of those who are listening will probably receive their sustained attention.

2. Whatever can be shown to be consistent with and favorable to the social standards and purposes of listeners probably will receive attention, provided it does not conflict with some stronger physical desire or drive.

3. Whatever can be shown to have the sanction of known and respected sources of authority has a better chance of being received attentively than that which must be presented without evidence of such approval.

4. To sustain attention, any subject matter must be presented to listeners in such a way that the new and the familiar will engage their minds alternately or in combination.

These basic generalizations must govern selection of materials and planning for any public speech.

Against these standards you, as a public speaker, must test your choice of a speech subject, your mode of developing each point, your choice of each piece of supporting material, and your language. Your first business is to enter the minds of those who hear you and to deposit there the propositions which you have brought to the rostrum. You can gain admittance to the mind of another by any number of means, but you cannot remain there long enough to transact your business unless you demonstrate that your errand meets one or more (preferably all) of these charges which every listener levies as the price of his continued attention.

Attributes of Listeners

Affecting Attention

We have just seen that there are characteristic ways in which nearly all human beings respond to events. There are also special conditions of life that further modify how your audience will listen. Where these conditions work against your cause, you must neutralize them by offering compensatory justifications for your listeners' full attention. Where these conditions make interest in your cause, take advantage of them.

What are these special conditions that consistently affect listeners' behavior? Five are invariably at work within every listener. These are *age, sex, expectation, knowledge,* and what social scientists have come to call *socioeconomic level.* These five conditions of life almost always affect your listeners' perceptions and preferences. Speech cannot change the conditions themselves or the ways in which they affect people's outlooks, but speech can be adapted to those outlooks. How this can be done is our next consideration.

AGE

The age of your listener affects your options in dealing with a given topic. The young, the middle-aged, and the old give their closest attention to different aspects of ideas, to different examples, arguments, behavior, and language, and they often judge these features of speaking by different standards. Shakespeare's famous description of the ages of man in *As You Like It* and Aristotle's detailed analysis of how age influences the interests of auditors form, together, an unsurpassed survey of this condition of life as a force affecting the receptiveness of humans. Shakespeare's Jacques said it this way:

> At first the infant,
> Mewling and puking in the nurse's arms.
> And then the whining school-boy, with his satchel
> And shining morning face, creeping like snail
> Unwillingly to school. And then the lover,
> Sighing like furnace, with a woeful ballad
> Made to his mistress' eyebrow. Then a soldier,
> Full of strange oaths, and bearded like the pard,
> Jealous in honour, sudden and quick in quarrel,
> Seeking the bubble reputation
> Even in the cannon's mouth. And then the justice,

In fair round belly with good capon lin'd,
With eyes severe, and beard of formal cut,
Full of wise saws and modern instances;
And so he plays his part. The sixth age shifts
Into the lean and slipper'd pantaloon,
With spectacles on nose and pouch on side,
His youthful hose, well saved, a world too wide
For his shrunk shank; and his big manly voice,
Turning again toward childish treble, pipes
And whistles in his sound. Last scene of all,
That ends this strange eventful history,
Is second childishness and mere oblivion,
Sans teeth, sans eyes, sans taste, sans everything.[10]

Aristotle addressed himself specifically to "the proper means of adapting both speech and speaker to a given audience." His characterizations of the young, "men in their prime," and the elderly can only be summarized here, but they are well worth a full reading in the original source. Most of what Aristotle had to say of the men of his day applies as well to modern men and women.

In youth "men have strong desires, and whatever they desire they are prone to do. Of the bodily desires the one they let govern them most is the sexual; here they lack self-control. They are shifting and unsteady in their desires. . . ." They are "quick to anger, and apt to give way to it," and they are "fond of honor" but even "fonder of victory." Money means relatively little to them "for they have not yet learned what the want of it means." They are not cynical; rather, they are trustful "for as yet they have not been often deceived." Being quick to hope, and living much in anticipation, "they are easily deceived." Though brave and spirited, they are also shy. Being idealistic, "in their actions they prefer honor to expediency" and are dogmatic. "All their mistakes are on the side of intensity and excess. . . ."

In middle life, Aristotle thought, people "will be neither excessively confident . . . nor yet too timid; they will be both confident and cautious. They will neither trust everyone nor distrust everyone; rather they will judge the case by the facts.

---

[10] *As You Like It*, Act II, Scene 7.

Their rule of life will be neither honor alone, nor expediency alone. . . ." They will temper valor with self-control, and they will be neither parsimonious nor prodigal with their possessions. Generally, "all the valuable qualities which youth and age divide between them are joined in the prime of life."

The aged have characteristics opposed to those of the young. Thus, "they err by an extreme moderation" and are "positive about nothing" for they have lived long and been disappointed much. They tend to be cynical and "put the worst construction on everything"; they are suspicious, and sometimes small-minded. They "aspire to nothing great or exalted, but crave the mere necessities and comforts of existence." They are constantly apprehensive and "live their lives with too much regard for the expedient and too little for honor." What other people think means little to them, for they "live in memory rather than in anticipation."

Aristotle concludes: "Now the hearer is always receptive when a speech is adapted to his own character and reflects it. Thus we can readily see the proper means of adapting both speech and speaker to a given audience."[11] It is true. In Shakespeare's and Aristotle's descriptions you may find almost the sum of things on which men and women in each age of life bestow eager attention. Here are useful generalizations about the changing interests of man, generalizations that tell the wise speaker how he must approach his themes to come within the interests of each age group represented among his listeners. He cannot, of course, always gratify the idealism of youth and the caution of age with the same argument. But more often than most speakers realize, ideas are at once expedient and honorable. For example Medicare has humanitarian, economic, and security-assuring aspects. Which one or ones you should stress will depend in part on the distribution of age groups within your audience. Recognizing that age affects your listeners' perceptions, you find materials that will invite the attention and favorable judgment of the age groupings

---

[11] From *The Rhetoric of Aristotle* trans. and ed. by Lane Cooper. Bk. II, Ch. 12–14, pp. 132–137. Reprinted by permission of the publisher, Appleton–Century–Crofts.

likely to comprise your audience. The elemental fact that all people have lived for "X" years directs the effective speaker's rhetorical invention.

SEX

Whether the listeners are mostly male or female or evenly divided must also be considered in selecting and using materials for speeches. In an era when women receive essentially the same education and share many of the same responsibilities as men, it is certainly possible to overemphasize alleged differences in the interests and motivations of the sexes. Nevertheless, anyone who wishes to influence the behavior of both sexes or of audiences in which one sex predominates must remember that men and women do not share all kinds of experience. They will accordingly attend to some topics with differing degrees of willingness.

Matters of business policy, mechanical construction, and team sports touch the experience of most men while being foreign to the experience of many women. Women apparently are more interested in government than in problems of corporate or international finance. Similar examples are plentiful. These differences probably result from special values inculcated by experiences peculiar to each group, and the values which influence the kinds of knowledge and interest each group prizes. Whatever the reasons, the practical fact for speakers is that men and women are not equally persuasible on all subjects. Given any specific topic, it is important for a public speaker to ask himself whether the normal differences between masculine and feminine experience should influence his treatment of the subject.

Chivalric and romantic attitudes still live in our society. They, too, affect the tone of discourse. Many of us feel that while argumentative pressures, cumulation of overwhelming amounts of evidence, and bluntness of statement may sometimes be appropriate in dealing with masculine listeners, these methods are inappropriate in addressing women. Female listeners ought to be persuaded by gentle suggestion. When speakers attempt "the hard sell" in dealing with female listeners, some men and some women withhold serious attention. It is a moot point whether in public speaking, as in love, women listeners must always be treated as beings

> nobly planned,
> To warm, to comfort, and command;
> And yet a Spirit still, and bright
> With something of angelic light[12]

At any rate, speakers certainly have little to lose and often much to gain by respecting some of the conventions of chivalry when dealing with women as listeners.

EXPECTATION

Your listeners' expectations will also affect their willingness and ability to attend to what you say. What we expect to perceive has much to do with what actually invades our consciousness. The intention, inclination or expectation of a listener makes him peculiarly alert to whatever is consistent with his preconception of the speaker, the speech, and the occasion. A psychologist has put it: "The organism goes out and determines what it is going to respond to, and organizes that world. One organism picks out one thing and another picks out a different one, since it is going to act in a different way."[13] Practical examples are easy to find.

If you go to church to worship and hear a preacher deliver a political harangue, you are likely to become uneasy and consequently inattentive. If you expect radio and television broadcasters to report the news without editorializing, you will be irritated by a reporter who injects opinion into his newscast. You may even agree with these speakers, but you become disturbed over whether their comments are appropriate for the time, the speaker's position, and the occasion. When this happens you cannot keep

---

[12] Excerpt from "She Was a Phantom of Delight" by William Wordsworth.
[13] George H. Mead, *Mind, Self and Society* (Chicago: University of Chicago Press, 1934), p. 25.

your mind on the whole of what he says. You focus on the fact that he is violating your expectations; afterward, you may not be able to remember what he actually said. Conversely, when your expectations are realized, you are able to attend fully and can usually recall the gist of the communication. Your preconception "is in a way a rehearsal of an expected experience. When the experience comes it is like meeting an old friend."[14]

A listener may base his preconception of your remarks on what he knows about you, on what he thinks would be appropriate for the occasion, or on his understanding of your announced subject. If the occasion is formal and dignified, he prepares himself to hear a formal address touching themes that grow out of the situation. If the occasion is informal, he prepares himself to hear pithy, relevant remarks delivered without much fanfare. A juryman expects the attorney to give reasons for making a decision, and the alumnus at a homecoming banquet expects to hear reminiscences and news of his alma mater. People prepare themselves, often unconsciously, for most experiences in listening. They set up standards which they expect speakers will live up to, and they are disturbed if those standards are not observed. Speakers can conform to their listeners' expectations, or they must justify their deviations from expected practice. The speaker is fortunate whose purpose and foresight enable him to fit his whole speech to his hearers' expectations; the speaker who must violate preconceptions may safely do so only by drawing the listeners' thoughts from the "old friend" they expected to meet to the new and better "friend" whom the speaker feels bound to introduce. Listeners do not respond predictably if taken unaware.

We discover, then, another set of tasks always involved in preparing a speech: trying to calculate in advance what the majority of any audience will expect. If you can make reasonably informed calculations, you will know when your speech material will conform to expectations and when you must tread cautiously,

---

[14] Edwin G. Boring, Herbert S. Langfeld, and Harry P. Weld, *Foundations of Psychology* (New York: Wiley, 1948), p. 220.

justifying your need to introduce unanticipated sets of ideas, methods of development, and language.

KNOWLEDGE

Your listeners' education and general knowledge will affect the ways they can respond to your speech. We have already seen that what human beings know governs what they are ready to hear and what they can understand. It is difficult to generalize about the specific effects that education has on attention and understanding, but it is known that the more catholic the listeners' knowledge and experience, the more topics can grip their attention and interest. The more listeners already know, the fewer subjects there will be to baffle or frighten them. If you try to evaluate what your audience is likely to know and what it will not know, you will surely come closer to meeting them on their own grounds.

A veteran of World War II who was assigned to transport Chinese troops from one battle area to another reports that in this task communication was sometimes all but impossible because some Chinese troops could not understand the hazards of flying. There were occasions when soldiers, not realizing they would be killed by the fall, tried to step out of planes in flight. Since they had no experience to which they could relate their danger, they could not understand it despite explanations. Such extreme difficulties should remind us that all listeners have their blind spots. Where knowledge is lacking, listeners must be taught what they did not previously know before they can think and feel about such information in relevant ways.

It is entirely conventional to advise speakers to find out all they can about each audience to be addressed. The advice is sound. We would add that a major reason for preliminary "audience analysis" is to discover how you may take advantage of what your listeners will probably know and how you must compensate for the blind spots they are likely to possess—in short, how to adjust your speaking to a given listener's level of knowledge.

SOCIOECONOMIC LEVEL

Among the conditioning factors that deeply affect the knowledge and expectations of listeners are their cultural, social, and economic experiences. How these forces condition the lives and perceptions of everyone is one of the most fascinating topics of inquiry in anthropology, sociology, and social psychology. It is a subject we can touch but lightly in a work on public speaking, but it is one of enormous importance to an understanding of audiences.

One limitation of studying public speaking in college is that you will have too few opportunities to explore directly the influences of cultural, social, and economic forces upon audiences. You may not come into contact with them fully until you enter the nonacademic world. Just now most of your listeners are essentially like yourself in age, educational attainment, expectations; even sex differences are probably as limited in influence over opinions as at any time in life. More important, college or university life makes more alike those whom it touches, even where cultural, social, and economic differences are concerned. The authors of one study of attitudes held by college students have said:

> . . . you can infer a college student's economic philosophy if you know only what political party has his sympathies and what college he is attending, and further information about the economic level of his family will not substantially improve the prediction. The same clues will lead to a rather accurate inference regarding his stand on an economic issue with humanitarian overtones. If, however, you wish to infer a college student's attitude towards a current economic issue which reflects conflicting class interests, then additional information about his family's economic level will increase the accuracy of your guess.[15]

Because you are a college student speaking to college students, you will probably find more common ground and more identity

---

[15] Rose K. Goldsen, Morris Rosenberg, Robin M. Williams, Jr., and Edward A. Suchman, *What College Students Think* (Princeton: Van Nostrand, 1960), p. 116.

of interests than you would find if you addressed a nonacademic audience. You must, then, guard against assigning to nonacademic audiences the uniformity of opinion and the relative indifference to cultural, social, and economic conditioning that you find among fellow students. Outside the college or university these conditioning forces produce marked differences in viewpoints such as you only occasionally see in student life.

To illustrate the disparity of attitudes and opinions held by people from different walks of life, we have no need to use the varied outgrowths of primitive and sophisticated cultures. There are numerous sharp differences of outlook within our own society. For example, according to one study, white American males of "lower occupational strata" are more likely than males of "higher occupational strata" to insist that woman's place is in the home. Higher occupational groups of males have more faith in the value of machines than do manual workers. The higher groups tend to think success and wealth are achieved through ability, but significant numbers of males from lower occupations attribute success to "luck, pull, and superior opportunities."[16] A summary of findings, published more than two decades after the study just quoted, clearly indicates that two wars and unprecedented prosperity have not changed the differences of knowledge and values that are associated with socioeconomic differences in our society:

> Lower-class people . . . participate in fewer voluntary associations and other organized activities. They have less facility in reading and writing. They read fewer magazines and listen to the "less serious" radio and television programs. They know less about political issues and have less expressed interest in them. . . . They are more timid about expressing their opinions to poll interviewers and more often give more "don't know" answers. They know less about such matters that concern their economic and social interests as income taxes, price controls, birth control, and consumer's cooperation.[17]

---

[16] Richard Centers, "Attitude and Belief in Relation to Occupational Stratification," *Journal of Social Psychology*, XXVII (1938), 158–185.

[17] Bernard Barber, "Social-Class Differences in Educational Life-Chances," *Teachers College Record*, LXIII (1961), 108.

These comparative differences in views and knowledge only suggest the vast array of dissimilarities among listeners whose cultural, social, and economic experiences are dissimilar. Plainly, any speaker will err if he fails to investigate the socioeconomic experience and resulting viewpoints and values of his prospective listeners. To carry a message from one culture to another—even from one subculture of our own society to another subculture—is a most difficult assignment. Only careful analysis of what knowledge and attitudes the alien culture tends to implant can tell a prospective speaker what expectations and knowledge he dares take as bases on which to build his message.

It deserves repetition that your college experience as a speaker is unlike the experience you will have outside the college in respect to the impact of cultural, social, and economic forces upon your listeners. The moment you turn from your college-oriented audience to a general, unsifted audience, sociological differences among auditors become critical factors to which you must adjust. It is not too much to say that when any speaker asks, "Who will be there?" he ought to insist upon as precise a sociological answer as can possibly be secured.

FACTORS OF ATTENTION

Because listeners and listening are as we have described them, one can specify certain qualities which engaging talk needs to exhibit. These factors of attention, as they are often called, are meaningful attributes which an idea may have by virtue of its own nature or by the way it is expressed. Below is a brief statement of these factors or qualities of speech with a reminder of the general reason each quality is likely to control the attention of an audience.

Factors of Attention	Basis of Influence
1. *Activity:* actual movement in speaking or suggestion of movement through verbal imagery.	Noticeable *change* always tends to attract attention; real or imagistic movement introduces change.

Factors of Attention	Basis of Influence
2. *Proximity:* showing things as near in time or space to the listener or as near to one another (actually or figuratively).	Adjacency is among the simplest relationships to perceive, and adjacency to a listener implies his self-interest is involved.
3. *Realism or vividness:* pictorial or other sensory qualities introduced by imagistic language or action or physical illustration.	Learning through the senses, directly or vicariously, is the basic experience by which knowledge is gained and survival defended.
4. *Familiarity and novelty:* association of ideas with what listeners know or presentation of what was either unknown or never before seen in the way proposed.	All human beings prize and attend to what they have experienced before; they also enjoy or are curious about experience that is new.
5. *Conflict and suspense:* showing either animate or inanimate things in opposition to one another or in competition with one another, the details or the outcome being in either case uncertain in some degree.	Opposition is the most obvious of differences, hence easily perceived. When active clash or competition is present *change* and the *unknown* are both present to draw man's attention.
6. *Vitality:* associating ideas or objects with matters of direct concern to the lives of people —especially the lives of the listeners.	Personal interests and purposes are prime reasons for granting attention; what seems to touch life itself has special significance for all.
7. *Specificity:* presentation of precise detail.	The more concrete or specific any concept, the more easily it is acquired by human beings.
8. *Intensity:* the force of any aspect of communication—of voice, movement, or energy of language. Wide variations in intensity levels are possible in speech: of sound, of physical energy, of vividness or color in language.	Within certain limits too complicated to explain here, the strength of impact of any stimulus tends to vary with the intensity of the stimulus; also, noticeable changes in stimuli and *contrasts* between intensities of stimuli draw attention to the *dissimilarities* and *change*.
9. *Humor:* introduction of exaggeration, incongruity, irony, word play, unexpected turns of thought or phrase.	The nature of response to humor is not fully understood, but the attractions of the *novel* or unexpected and satisfaction derived from safely regaining reality—the *familiar*—after having expectations built up, then reversed, appear to be involved.

We hope you will see from studying the tabulation above that the general qualities for which you must strive in speech are not qualities invented by pedagogues nor outgrowths of arbitrary doctrines of taste or correctness. It is because men and women are as they are psychologically that speech must symbolically represent activity, proximity, realism, familiarity and novelty, conflict and suspense, vitality, specificity, intensity, and humor. Only so can it seize and hold the attention of listening human beings.

It is all too easy to interpret superficially what we have just said. Just any adaptation to the interests of listeners will not serve your speech, nor will just any active image or bit of suspensive development. The speaker's problems are to understand his listeners as human beings and to understand the resources of speaking. It is his further task to fit together the particular complex of materials and methods that can win and hold human attention in a particular time and place. His question becomes: Given the range of what he might say and how he might say it, what content and what methods fit this particular audience's humanity, special purposes and interests, biological and social needs, stereotypes, regards for authority, age levels, sex, special expectations, knowledge, and cultural experience?

A careless or cynical response to the speaker's great and perplexing question might yield the view that listeners can never be confronted with messages to which they are not already prepared to give assent. This view would be a grave mistake. Audiences are no more changeless than faceless or purposeless. True, a speaker who would change the viewpoint of a listener must begin by accepting him as he is and adapt a message to the hearer's human and particular condition. But the very object of adapting —of working within the listener's frame of reference by methods that will grip his attention—is to enable that hearer to see what he did not see before. Rhetorical adaptation of ideas to the natures of audiences is a means of achieving change in listeners—the only means open to man, short of force.

In this chapter we have been trying to discover some useful generalizations about audiences. We have said that audiences are composed of listeners who must be thought of as individuals, though each will behave as it is the nature of human beings to behave. Listeners can be depended upon to give attention to what seems to affect their immediate physical needs or social purposes; to what presents an interplay of the familiar with the new; and to ideas that seem associated with whatever sources, institutions, and patterns of experience already hold their confidence. These concerns have inevitable claims on the attention of all men and women in all circumstances. The speaker who always designs his message and his speaking to touch these concerns will have a much better chance of being heard and believed than one who neglects them or touches them randomly.

Listening is also a special kind of activity, as we pointed out in Chapter 3. We have therefore tried to discover what conditions of life peculiarly affect men's ability or willingness to understand. Five such conditions have special importance for public speakers: age, sex, expectation, knowledge and experience, and cultural-social-economic background. Whether listeners will it or not, these conditions of life invariably regulate their ability and readiness to respond.

If we knew precisely what commands the attention of, let us say, a man of thirty who holds a law degree and is attending a Chamber of Commerce luncheon, public speaking would be more nearly a science than an art. But we do not know all the ways that the above conditions can singly or in combination influence a given man's responses to a particular message. We have, instead, a few crude generalizations. Even with these rough tools, the diligent speaker can refine his command over the minds of his listeners; if he remembers to use the tools he has and to make the inquiries he ought to make, he will recognize at least some of the existing opportunities and limitations. As Plato implied in the passage quoted at the head of this chapter, it is by discovering the natures of hearers, by experience in bringing different messages before differing audiences, and by imaginatively adapting content to them that speakers can ultimately achieve artistic, insightful social control.

We have tried to show that, despite all the differences that affect particular auditors, there are qualities that are universally useful in commanding the attention of audiences. These factors of attention exist, apart from the special interests and the special conditions of listeners, as ever-present resources available to speakers. They are the basic ways of adjusting communication to mankind. They do not solve the problems of speakers, but through them solution of those problems is begun.

More specific solutions to more specific problems begin to emerge as we turn from the nature of audiences to the ideas and feelings that must be adapted to audiences. Ideas and feelings are pliable, but only to a degree. Force is not weakness; nor love, hate. Speakers therefore must understand not only their audiences and the basic ways of commanding their attention but the role of content in speaking as well. In the next three chapters we shall concentrate on the problems of discovering and sifting speech material.

Exercises

WRITTEN

1. Write a careful description of some specific audience with which you are familiar (fraternal group, political or other club, religious congregation, or other) giving special consideration to the following:
   a. Chief biological wants and needs, if any, that affect this audience;
   b. Chief social wants and needs, if any, that affect this audience;
   c. Favorite sanctions and authorities of this audience;
   d. Any special characteristics of age, sex, expectation, knowledge, and socioeconomic level that all speakers addressing this audience should take into account.
2. You are to prepare a short speech using the central idea: "Reading is superior to listening to radio or watching television as a means of acquiring education." Outline the major points you might make in such a speech if it were to be given to

audience *a* below; then outline the major points you might try to make if the speech were for audience *b* below. Justify any differences there may be in the two outlines.

a. An audience of 20 college students aged 17–22, made up of 10 men and 10 women, assembled for an informal class on study habits organized for students whose academic records do not "meet the potentialities indicated by standardized aptitude-test results."

b. An audience of 20 college students aged 19–22, all cadet teachers in an elementary school attending one of a series of weekly seminars. The seminar topic for this meeting is "Motivation." There are 18 women and two men in the group.

3. Using the text or a recording of any speech, identify the points at which the speaker seems to have adapted content for the specific purpose of suiting it to one or another of the audience characteristics discussed in this chapter. Identify and evaluate the effectiveness with which he took advantage of factors of attention.

ORAL

1. Give an expository speech on one of the following subjects: stereotypes, the psychological process called suggestion, the psychological process called conditioned response, social (or ethical or other) values of the American college student, the expectations of audiences assembled on ceremonial occasions, unique expectations of audiences assembled to legislate or determine policy, theories of crowd behavior, authority as a source of persuasion.

2. Prepare and deliver an oral report on the methods of audience analysis and adaptation used by an outstanding trial lawyer, preacher, or political speaker.

3. Prepare and deliver a talk on some aspect of audience research and advertising or market research and industrial design.

---{ 5 }---   *Invention:*

                      Basic Processes

I would not be hurried by any love of system, by any exaggeration
of instincts, to underrate the Book. We all know, that as the human
body can be nourished on any food, though it were boiled grass and
the broth of shoes, so the human mind can be fed by any knowledge.
And great and heroic men have existed who had almost no other
information than by the printed page. I only say that it needs a strong
head to bear that diet. One must be an inventor to read well. . . .
When the mind is braced by labor and invention, the page of whatever book we read becomes luminous with manifold allusion. Every
sentence is doubly significant, and the sense of our author is as broad
as the world. We then see, what is always true, that as the seer's hour
of vision is short and rare among heavy days and months, so is its
record, perchance, the least part of his volume.

RALPH WALDO EMERSON, "The American Scholar"

Let us suppose. You are a psychology major standing in the foyer
of the library. A friend hails you: "I just saw Professor Perception.
He says there's a meeting of underclassmen Friday afternoon at
the Student Union. Some of the academic departments have been
asked to pick upperclass majors to talk at the meeting about their
departments. The Psych Department wants you to speak for them.
So get in that library and hit the books; you've got to write a
speech."

This is the way most of us become involved in speech making. Someone sends word, or calls. The request is a little indefinite. A speech subject may be suggested or not, and if suggested the proposal is vague. Whether the subject is given or we find it ourselves, we soon learn that the work of creating a speech has scarcely begun when the speech subject has been located.

Consider what your state of mind would be if, in the foyer of your library, you received the message we just imagined. Would a speech suitable for an audience of underclassmen spring full-blown into your mind? Would you know what to read if you entered the library? Could you even tell a friend precisely what it is like to be a psychology major? If you had never taken a similar assignment before, you would certainly possess no speech fit for public presentation, nor any clear method for getting such a speech. Some random thoughts about psychology and the social sciences might flit through your head. A good phrase or two might come to mind. But like all other speakers in the first moments of realizing that a speech must be made, you would find no ready speech in your thoughts.

This situation demonstrates what introspective speakers have known for centuries: once you know you must speak, and about what, the next task is to form a strategy for finding potentially useful ideas and information. A systematic search for ideas is preferable to an impulsive one, so we shall turn next to the ways one may conduct such a search. Though we shall defer discussion of choosing subjects to the next chapter, much that we shall say in the immediately following pages will be as applicable to searching out subjects for speeches as to searching for ideas pertinent to subjects already chosen or assigned.

The Discovery of Ideas

Your speeches will be as good as your capacity and willingness to find ideas worth talking about. This is why we contend that method in inventing what is to be said is more important than hours spent in intellectual and emotional agitation.

As you stand in the library foyer, your problem is not really whether to enter the library or rush to the Department of Psychology. Your immediate problem is to direct your thoughts toward where you will ultimately find useful ideas about academic majors in general and psychology in particular.

Not every idea connected with academic majors or psychology will be appropriate in talking to underclassmen. Therefore, it is foolish to collect ideas at random. Some available ideas will be too technical, some too remote from the experience of underclassmen, and some you will be unable to formulate clearly and exactly enough to communicate. Your need is for a way of identifying ideas that will prove negotiable between you and your hearers—ideas that can be exchanged between the parties like coins, with each negotiator understanding the nature and value of the items traded. But how does one do this?

FINDING LINES OF THOUGHT

One of the earliest and most useful systems for guiding intellectual explorations of a creative, rhetorical sort was detailed by Aristotle in his *Topics* and his *Rhetoric*. Simplified, that procedure can draw your thoughts toward the best hunting grounds for ideas suitable to your particular speaking assignment.

The Aristotelian theory of how a speaker should search for negotiable ideas rests on the assumption that the basic kinds of things we say to one another are fewer than thoughtless people suppose.

First, the theory runs, there are times when speakers want to give advice and when audiences have to make up their minds about courses of action. Whenever this is so, the basic question for both speaker and listener is: What shall be done or left undone? Aristotle called this a *deliberative* setting. In the language adopted in this book it would be called a *persuasive* setting in which a proposition of policy is to be discussed—one in which the speaker's central idea will contain the words "should" or "ought to" or their equivalents. Put in contemporary terms, Aristotle's idea was that a speaker frequently knows he must persuade on behalf of a central idea like "The United States government ought to recognize the Communist government of China" or "Regional government should replace municipal and county government in metropolitan areas," or "You ought to vote for John P. Findley." Aristotle contended that if a speaker knows he is going to function as an adviser, this knowledge tells him something about what to say and so narrows his field of research. For purposes of advising, ideas that have to do with the expediency of alternative courses of action are the ones that are most negotiable. These are ideas that have to do with rewards and punishments lying in the future and with the prospects of happiness or unhappiness for those who are going to take an action or refuse to take it.

By this reasoning, whenever a situation demands that your central idea concern the future behavior of your listeners, you will know immediately that you must hunt especially for ideas touching the expediency or inexpediency of the actions you expect to recommend. If your audience needs or wants advice, most of your initial preparation time ought to be spent finding ideas that concern the consequences of whatever actions your listeners are free to choose. By simply recognizing what advising involves, one isolates a particular type of material his speech must include.

A second class of situations in which men speak are those in which the audiences function as "judges" rather than as deciders of future action. In discussing these circumstances Aristotle talked almost entirely of judgments at law, but we require a broader view. Audiences have to or want to render judgments about facts and events in many different situations. Every speech to inform is such a case. Most of what one says in a speech of inquiry deals with what the facts are, though when solutions are being considered the situation becomes concerned with policies and future actions. All persuasion about propositions of fact succeeds or fails according to the judgments finally rendered by the listeners. So, if your central idea must focus on what something is, or whether it exists, you will be asking your listeners to function as judges of accuracy, truth, propriety, or legality. The most significant point about any such situation is that to make judgments your listeners must interpret facts or events in light of some "code." The code may be the law of the land, the theory of probabilities, the standards of historical research, the canons of artistic excellence, or personal standards for distinguishing truth from error. But your judges will need two distinct kinds of knowledge: (1) knowledge about the facts or events they are to judge and (2) knowledge about the standards against which they are to measure the facts or events. Once more, noticing what listeners will be asked to do quickly reveals what kinds of ideas to give them.

To restate this guide: If in informing, inquiring, or persuading you are going to ask for judgments, you will especially need ideas that define and clarify whatever is to be judged and the standards to be used in judging. You may need other information too, but these two kinds of content are certain to be crucial for you and for your listeners.

Rhetoricians who came after Aristotle suggested that three kinds of information had special usefulness in speeches that require judgments of listeners. These kinds are: (1) information about whether there really are any facts or events to talk about; (2) information about what the existing facts are; and (3) information about how any acknowledged facts or events are to be interpreted in light of whatever codes properly apply to them. Put another way, speakers about facts always have to answer one or more of these questions: Is it? What is it? What is its quality? These questions are simply extensions of what we have already said. They further narrow the hunt for ideas and they encourage an early decision on what class of information about facts will be important in speeches about facts.

We emphasize that there are simple questions by means of which any speakers, and especially speakers who inform, persuade about questions of fact, or conduct inquiries, can quickly focus on the kinds of information they will need when they speak. It makes sense for these speakers to collect the most important types of information at the beginning of preparation.

The third class of speaking situations that Aristotle and other writers of classical times perceived was one in which audiences behaved more as spectators or admirers of speech-making than as deciders or judges. For many reasons this conception needs to be modified in order to be useful in our own day.

We can begin by saying that audiences often expect to have

old ideas strengthened, familiar beliefs rendered more firm, convictions deepened, new or old knowledge rendered amusing or diverting. Using the language we have adopted for describing the purposes of speaking, these are situations in which speakers try to persuade by reinforcing belief or feeling, or in which they try to entertain their listeners. In these settings new judgments and new courses of action are neither sought nor wanted very much. Commencement exercises are such occasions. So are many worship services, service club meetings, fellowship meetings, banquets, and political rallies. Those who attend commencements already accept the worth of education; worshippers accept the greatness of their deity; fellowship groups accept the worth of being together and wish their association to be strengthened by being made more enjoyable. Whoever prepares to speak to such audiences must, then, locate the kinds of ideas that deepen, enrich, magnify, or even exaggerate the listeners' current knowledge. The chief end of the worship service may be to strengthen faith that already exists; the chief end of the club dinner may be, not calorie intake, but some magnification of the joys of friendship.

To sum up the implications of this third class of situations in which we speak, when one's purpose is to reinforce beliefs and feelings or to entertain, his need is for ideas peculiarly familiar to his prospective audience. Aristotle's advice on preparing for the more serious of the occasions we are now discussing was: Look for ideas that connect your subject with such well-known virtues as justice, courage, temperance, grandeur, magnanimity, liberality, gentleness, prudence, wisdom, or with the opposites of these. The advice is sensible. Whatever has these virtues becomes impressive and admirable, and whatever lacks them or is incompatible with them becomes the object of ridicule and disdain if not disgust. If lightheartedly done, assigning these virtues and their opposites where they do not belong is a standard way of rendering subjects amusing.

Thus, your preparation begins with a hunt for the virtues possessed by whatever you and your audience are committed to and for the non-virtues possessed by what you and your audience disapprove. Except for incidental uses you do not need ideas that deal with what is an expedient action or with the existence and legitimacy of facts and events.

Such are some ancient suggestions on how to begin a search for useful, negotiable ideas. If we imagine again that you have to "think up" a speech on psychology, we now can apply the advice we have summarized.

Though they didn't say so, the Psychology Department probably hopes you will tell the underclassmen what kinds of psychology courses are open to them and what requirements govern those who major in that department. Since other departments are to be represented at your meeting, the gathering evidently is not organized as a recruiting session for any particular department. Still, you ought to make studying psychology seem inviting.

As soon as you accept presumptions like these about your assignment, you have roughly defined procedures for preparing your speech: (1) you do *not* need to hunt up much material on long-range matters such as whether psychology majors have better professional opportunities than other majors; (2) you *do* need to get the facts about specific courses and the regulations governing the psychology major, because enabling listeners to pass some kind of judgment on the study of psychology in your college is a major part of your assignment; (3) you *do* need to find out by what standards underclassmen and other people measure the worth of a course of study, for these are the codes by which the facts you present will be judged. Your prospective listeners are going to function primarily as "judges." Settling that much puts you in a position to begin gathering information efficiently. Having decided not to try to make these listeners commit themselves to any course of action just now, you can bypass much information having chiefly to do with the rewards of studying psychology. And since your hearers will not already be devoted to the study of psychology, there will be no point in hunting for ways of associating that study with generally accepted virtues.

On the basis of these decisions, you need stand indecisively in the library foyer no longer. Take two immediate actions: (1) obtain information about psychology as it is taught in your college; (2) find out how underclassmen distinguish "good" from "not-so-good" in thinking about academic subjects. If you enter the library, you will want to read the college announcement or catalogue; if you don't go in, you will be wise either to set off for the Psychology Department's offices or to conduct some interviews to see what standards (codes) underclassmen use when they make judgments about the attractiveness of courses and subjects. Any other actions on your part will probably be irrelevant to your speech preparation.

These are the general ways you can point thinking and research in potentially useful directions. Decide what you are going to ask your listeners to do: decide about courses of action, make judgments about facts or events, acquire stronger attitudes toward something of which they are already aware. Notice the particular kind of ideas naturally associated with the behavior you want to achieve. Go after that kind of material first.

The system we have been discussing suggests only broad classes of speech materials that different speakers will need in different proportions—materials relating to expediency, happiness, justice, accuracy, truthfulness, virtuousness, and their opposites. Ancient writers went much further in trying to forecast the specific ideas speakers would need in the usual circumstances for speaking. Aristotle enumerated hundreds of specific "lines of argument" in his *Topics* and *Rhetoric*. It seems hardly possible that even astute speakers actually reminded themselves of such detailed catalogues of what might be said in a given case. To guide the modern speaker, we need some more concise scheme of reminders of what one can say or ought to say.

You need not read many modern speeches to see that the ancients were right when they contended that speakers repeatedly use a small number of themes, varying their treatments widely but not the themes themselves. This is not surprising, nor is it a sign of laziness. People make speeches chiefly about human affairs, and the customary ways of thinking about human affairs are limited within any particular culture.

One of the clearest illustrations of the recurrence and predictability of these basic themes appears in a speech by Professor William G. Carleton. Notice the specific ideas Professor Carleton identified as necessary to establish a comprehensive case for what he believed would be an expedient American foreign policy. Talking about "Effective Speech in a Democracy," Professor Carleton at one point said:

> Will you permit me to illustrate my point by demonstrating for a moment how I would construct a speech on current American foreign policy? It so happens that I favor the following foreign policy: In the countries of Asia and Europe where the non-Communists are in control, I would, where conditions indicated, put the United States squarely behind a policy of social democracy or even democratic socialism as a way of combating Communism; and in the countries where the Communists are in control, I would play upon the nationalistic tendencies everywhere evident in Communist governments and Communist parties, to attempt to divide Communist countries from each other on national grounds and thereby contribute to the restoration of a multiple balancing-of-power system, a system which would prevent the Communists from acting together in a Communist front and threatening to upset the balance of power. For if we can remove the Communist threat to the balance of power we can remove the real cause of another great war.
> In order to present effectively my point of view on the importance of playing wise social politics, it seems to me that I would have to show how and why conditions in Europe and Asia are converging to produce collectivist movements there and why laissez-faire capitalism there is not feasible [1]; also I would have to show the difference between totalitarian socialism and democratic socialism [2] and examine the reasons why I believe America's backing of social-democracy and even democratic socialism in Europe and Asia would check Communism and serve America's national interests [3]. In order for me to present effectively my belief that nationalism within Communist countries and parties could be used to divide Communism and restore a multiple balance-of-power system, I would have to examine in some detail the degree to which Communist revolutions and movements are in fact nationalistic in aim, method, and development [4], and actually point out the specific grounds of possible national conflict between specific Communist countries [5].
> However, even when I had done all this my intellectual task would not be completed. I would have to point out why other

courses in foreign policy would not serve America's national interests as well as the policy I favored [6]. This would involve my examining the reasons why political isolation would not work today; why a policy of mere military containment of Communism through the United Nations would not be enough and would not work permanently [7]; and why if it worked it would be the hard way to do something that could be done with less possibility of war and fewer long-time sacrifices [8]; why a policy of mere military containment of Communism by the United States alone—a policy of American imperialism— would be even less workable and less desirable than a policy of military containment through the United Nations [9]. In short, in order to carry intellectual conviction on so large and controversial a question, it seems to me I would have to construct a speech that analyzed critically all courses—those I oppose as well as those I favor [10].[1]

Here is a realistic representation by a political scientist of how a serious speaker explores what it is necessary to say in a given situation. Most important to you is the fact that the topics Professor Carleton says need to be covered in the speech he is imagining are "lines of thought" that almost *any* speaker talking about *any* matter of policy would have to consider for possible development.

How can we pick out these "lines of thought" so common to all speaking? *Feasibility* is one—how and why a thing can or cannot work: note the remarks just preceding [1]. (Bracketed numbers refer to the quotation from Professor Carleton's speech.) *Similarities and dissimilarities* is another: see the statement that differences would have to be defined, in the clause before [2]. *Causality* would have to be established before anyone would think Carleton's preferred policy would in fact "serve America's national interests" [3]. *Degree* must be discussed if Carleton is to show there is enough nationalism in Communist systems to allow his plan to work [4]. And the *existence* of circumstances that make national conflicts likely must also be treated [5]. Another set of *similarities and differences* ought to be treated [6]; and to explain

---

[1] William G. Carleton, "Effective Speech in a Democracy," *Vital Speeches of the Day*, XVII (June 15, 1951), 540–544. Reprinted by permission of the publisher and author.

these, a new set of *causalities* would have to be discussed [7]. Incidentally, a comparison of the *potency* or power of alternative policies to bring *desirable* results would have to be treated [8]. Then, Carleton finds he would need to consider a further set of *similarities and differences* among the *desirable* and *feasible* features of several policies [9]. All these specific lines of thought would need to be discussed, says Carleton, in order that his speech might have the kind of *substance* or quality ("carry intellectual conviction") he would want it to have [10].

Professor Carleton actually enumerated most of the topics or themes that we normally develop in any speech about popular affairs. A tolerably complete list of such topics for development might be set forth thus:

A. Attributes commonly discussed:
   1. *Existence* or nonexistence of things.
   2. *Degree* or quantity of things, forces, etc.
   3. *Spatial* attributes, including adjacency, distribution, place.
   4. Attributes of *time.*
   5. *Motion* or activity.
   6. *Form,* either physical or abstract.
   7. *Substance:* physical, abstract, or psychophysical.
   8. *Capacity to change,* including predictability.
   9. *Potency:* power or energy, including capacity to further or hinder anything.
   10. *Desirability* in terms of rewards or punishments.
   11. *Feasibility:* workability or practicability.
B. Basic relationships commonly asserted or argued:
   1. *Causality:* the relation of causes to effects, effects to causes, effects to effects, adequacy of causes, etc.
   2. *Correlation:* coexistence or coordination of things, forces, etc.
   3. *Genus-species* relationships.
   4. *Similarity or dissimilarity.*
   5. *Possibility or impossibility.*

Every speaker does not develop all of these topics in any particular speech, nor is every imaginable thought suggested as soon as one asks himself whether he needs to talk about one or another of these eleven attributes and five relationships. Nonetheless, this simple list of topics can be easily mastered and used to generate ideas for possible use in any speech. Let us try it on a subject that might very well be discussed in your speech class.

Let us suppose you are preparing a speech on how space exploration has effected industries. If you discipline your thinking as we have proposed, your first step in planning will be to notice that your audience will be judging or interpreting facts, not choosing a course of action or modifying existing attitudes. From this observation you will quickly know that you need two kinds of materials: the facts about the impact of the space age and the standards your listeners ought to apply in judging the truth, significance, or other meanings of those facts. Now, you could use the checklist of attributes and relationships to suggest or generate likely ideas about facts and standards related to space exploration and industry.

First, try *existence*. Will you need any facts showing the existence of, say, the space age? Not unless yours is a primitive audience. But what about the existence of a "space industry" or of "space markets"? Asking yourself this question could remind you that it may be worth while to show your audience that a space industry does indeed exist now within the general business system we call industry. That kind of information would be appropriate to your speech and useful to your audience. You might have thought of the same item without asking yourself about the topic, *existence*, but to ask the question increases the probabilities that this and other possibly useful ideas will come to your mind.

Continuing your canvass, you might ask, Will I need to talk about the *degree* or quantity of anything? Unquestionably. You will want your listeners to know how much change has taken place. How much of industry is now space industry? How much of our industrial output depends on the government's space program? Similar lines of thought will occur to you if you pause over the topic of *degree*. What about *time*—the order in which the features of space industries emerged? This theme may prove important in developing some details, but it will probably not be a major topic in your speech unless you decide to stress something like the rapidity or slowness with which space enterprises have developed during the last few decades. The theme of *motion* or activity does not suggest much material to be included in your speech. Were you explaining how a space-shot is accomplished, you should include information about preparatory, launching, and orbital movements, but you probably will have little need to discuss such procedures.

Form, as a topic, ought to suggest that you can discuss such matters as whether space industries have grown up independently or inside other types of organizations. *Substance* (the essential natures of things) seems unlikely to suggest many kinds of information you will need, unless you choose to discuss the importance of research in space science, opportunities for industrial growth, or perhaps the youthfulness of those who work in space industries. *Capacity to change* suggests an important question: whether space industries are stable or change rapidly as scientific technology advances. And the topic, *potency*, ought to suggest that you need to know what spurs and slows an industry's capacity to compete in production of space goods.

The *desirability* and *feasibility* of various industrial practices will also need to be touched—not because your audience must approve any courses of action but because they should understand why practices in production, financing, and organization had to change as space industries developed.

When you turn to the common relationships for suggestions of information, your judgment will tell you that information about *genus-species* relationships will be relatively unimportant to you—except when you distinguish space and non-space industries from one another. Otherwise, you will seldom classify or define things in this talk. But *causes* and *effects* will certainly have to be discussed. For example, what are the effects of our space industries' having grown so large (*degree*)? What *causes* space industries to be so volatile and speculative as places to invest money? What are the *effects* of the industries' dependence on governmental expenditures? You should know enough to discuss the *similarities* and *dissimilarities* between space and traditional industries. And to try another likely topic, whether there is any reliable *correlation* between the amount of research done by a space industry and the industry's growth or profit is just one of the correlative matters you will probably need to talk about.

These are examples of the directions in which thought and research can be stimulated and guided by the process of reviewing sixteen familiar themes for discussion. The values of this kind of autosuggestive review will be evident in your speech. Your examination of your own knowledge is likely to be thorough, fruitful, and relevant to the business of discovering what is discussable. Reviewing a checklist of possible topics for development assures that you will not overlook either significant information lodged in your own mind or significant topics for detailed research.

From the time of Aristotle to the days of Francis Bacon it was periodically proposed that the way of searching for ideas which we have just described was the only feasible way a speaker could have any assurance that he had properly reviewed his own knowledge of his subject. Bacon put it best:

> . . . a faculty of wise interrogating is half of knowledge. For Plato says well, "whosoever seeks a thing, knows that which he seeks for in a general notion; else how shall he know it when he has found it?" . . . The same places [topics] therefore which will help us to shake out the folds of the intellect within us, and to draw forth the knowledge stored within, will also help us to gain knowledge from without; so that if a man of learning and experience were before us, we should know how to question him wisely and to the purpose; and in like manner how to peruse with advantage . . . books and parts of books which may best instruct us concerning what we seek.[2]

Whether it is worthwhile to use in the twentieth century the methods of autosuggestion and brainstorming that have been little used for three hundred or more years is a fair question. We put the matter to you: If you can't think of the word you want and need, you go to a dictionary or thesaurus. When you don't know what book you want from the library but do know the subject you

---

[2] *De augmentis scientiarum*, V, p. 3, *Works*, IV, p. 423.

want to learn about, you search the indexes of your library or the Library of Congress. We propose that the intellectual method of searching that works for words and books also works in searching for ideas that would be useful in a speech. The alternative is to trust impulse, accidents of memory, and sheer inspiration. The only other aids to speakers' invention discovered in 2,400 years are those we have just explained: (1) reflecting on the kinds of subject matters your listeners will need in order to make the decisions you ask of them; (2) stimulating your own memory and creative powers by referring to some systematic set of suggestive topics or themes.

There is, indeed, modern psychological justification for the use of topics in investigation. "The solution to a complex problem is generally approached via several increasingly specific considerations," write Berelson and Steiner in summarizing what is known of creative thinking and problem solving. These authors enumerate the stages of such human thought as, "starting with a general scanning of the class of possible approaches [examining the speech situation and estimating the kinds of decisions required of listeners], moving to a selection of one or more 'functional solutions' [determining the broad *kinds* of material needed], and then narrowing to one or more of these in specific, operational solutions [deciding what specific themes or topics need to be developed]."[3]

The procedures for identifying the kinds of useful material which we have proposed can also assist you in planning the development of individual points within a speech. For example, if you see that at some point in a speech you must distinguish between the effects of sales taxes and income taxes, the checklist we have provided might help. It might remind you that one way of making this distinction is to emphasize that the income and sales taxes are different *species* of taxation and, therefore, exert their influence (*causal effects*) in different ways. This observation would direct your search for detailed materials toward such items as examples,

[3] Bernard Berelson and Gary A. Steiner, *Human Behavior, An Inventory of Scientific Findings* (New York and Burlingame: Harcourt, Brace & World, Inc., 1964), p. 202.

comparisons and contrasts, formal definitions, and other data that are useful in describing the natures of things.

RESEARCH

Systems of classifying speech situations and systems for suggesting discussable themes do not of themselves provide information. They only stimulate recall of things previously learned. Inventional schemes such as we have been discussing chiefly show you what to look for. Once you have by these means decided what kinds of information you need, the routine work of research for speaking begins, and a few general suggestions about this stage of preparation may be useful. We shall repeat some advice familiar to you, because all of us need reminding that some ways of digging for information are more practical than others. We shall mention some sources you need to know, but nothing short of personally investigating the research facilities of the library available to you can equip you to prepare speeches adequately.

Though books are among the very best places to go for information, they are not the only wells of knowledge. We have already pointed out that *you* are a valuable source of information. Perhaps instead of talking about research for speeches, we ought to speak of "recall, recovery, and research for speeches." Ask yourself: What have I already read about this subject, or this point? What have I heard in conversation, in lectures, on radio or television? What have I seen firsthand or in photographs? Such questions often stir the memory. Hence, each speaker ought to explore his memory and check his notebooks as an early step in research.

Other people are excellent resources too. What photographer is not happy to answer questions about photography? What traveller is not all too pleased to reminisce about what he has seen? What professional man is unwilling to talk about the problems and accomplishments of his profession? We all know people who would be happy to supply information; yet, just as we often forget to probe our own minds, we neglect convenient, willing resource persons.

Public officials, teachers, and popular personalities are often overlooked as sources of valuable information. One must be cautious about seeking assistance from such persons because of the heavy demands on their time, but even the busiest people are usually willing to grant limited aid to those who know what they want and are able to draw out needed information efficiently. The carefully planned, prearranged interview is the usual way to secure such help, and the speaker who has previously identified the kinds of ideas he needs should be able to conduct himself as a business-like interviewer. Interviewing available authorities ought to be a normal part of an effective speaker's preparation.

Personal investigation is another neglected avenue of research. We would think ill of a speaker who, after urging us to read the works of Joseph Conrad, turned out to have read only one of Conrad's books. What, then, of speakers who deplore the low level of television programming without having checked the full program listings and explored the viewing options open to their particular audiences? To take other examples, you are fortunate if you have never been subjected to speeches on juvenile delinquency by speakers who had never visited a youth court, a settlement house, or even talked with young people of the kinds they discuss. One need not be an ex-convict to speak of prisons or a parent to discuss children, but to neglect obvious and convenient opportunities for firsthand inquiry is to miss some of the most vital and immediately relevant information.

We do not disparage reading as a source of materials for speeches. We wish only to stress the fact that the printed word is never the sole resource available. Printed materials are, of course, your most varied sources; best of all, they are available when you need them. But the printed page, like people and personal experience, needs to be approached thoughtfully, systematically, and imaginatively if it is to render its best service.

Comprehensive books, encyclopedic articles, surveys, and reviews in periodicals are the most promising sources of background material, and usually these are the sources to which one goes first. Before looking for detailed information on the classical Greek theatre, you will be well advised to read some brief, general, but authoritative work on ancient Greek society. G. Lowes Dickinson's *The Greek Way of Life* or Edith Hamilton's *The Greek Way* or the general article on ancient Greece in a good encyclopedia are sources of this kind. The way you read such works makes a difference too. The object of reading general works is to accumulate enough broad understanding so that when you find more detailed materials you can see them in their proper context. To this end one reads general works attentively but swiftly.

General source materials usually do not contain the detailed information a speaker needs if he has to establish, say, the precise *degree* or *desirability* of what he speaks about. If your speech subject concerns the role of advertising in our society, you may need to know how much advertising is handled through advertising agencies and how much is purchased directly by the advertiser. You are unlikely to find these details in general books or articles on advertising. To putter among the encyclopedias at this stage is to waste time and effort. Examine your library's card catalogue and such indexes as *The Readers' Guide to Periodical Literature* or the *International Index to Periodicals* to locate up-to-date reports and studies on the organization and economics of the advertising industry. The procedure is the same no matter what your subject: after obtaining general knowledge, you must locate specialized information, usually in specialists' reports and studies.

Your mode of reading will change also. The point is easily illustrated. Assume you are working on a speech dealing with John C. Calhoun as a public figure. You would certainly find Professor Richard Hofstadter's "John C. Calhoun: the Marx of the Master Class" (in his *The American Political Tradition*) a relevant, general essay. However, you could not talk competently about Calhoun's political influence without acquiring a clear understanding of what Hofstadter calls "the king pin of his political system"—his proposal to amend the Constitution to provide for settling contested national issues by "concurrent majority." Hofstadter's essay, like most general works, gives but a few lines to Calhoun's theory. An obvious place to go for more detail would be Calhoun's own *Disquisition on Government*. There the idea and reasons for it are spelled out in full. Some sections of the

Disquisition would demand your intensive study, but others, such as those dealing with the Polish, Iroquois, Roman, British, and other constitutions, would probably be irrelevant to your needs. From full but relatively light reading of Hofstadter's essay, it would be necessary to shift to highly selective but intensive reading when attacking the more technical and specialized *Disquisition*.

There also comes a time when exact bits of evidence—statistics, authoritative estimates, dates, facts about topography or design or authorship—are needed to fill small gaps in your speech. What were the exact dates of Calhoun's life? What was the population of the North and South at the time he popularized his "concurrent majority" concept? If your speech were on some other subject you might find yourself needing to know the area of a battlefield, the height of a building, the probable authorship of the "Letters of 'Junius,' " or the date the Warren Report on President Kennedy's assassination was issued. When this is the class of information required, it is time to explore some of the many volumes of classified data: biographical dictionaries, *The World Almanac, The Statistical Abstract, Facts on File,* concise histories of this or that literature, *Bartlett's Quotations,* Jane's *Ships of the World* or *Aircraft of the World.* These are the kinds of resources you need when in search of isolated items of fact, and study of such materials is still more selective than one's general reading or intensive reading on special topics.

In all the exploratory activities that most speeches impose upon you, you ought never to forget that the purpose of it all is to extract what is necessary to create *a communication that will serve as your personalized way of getting a particular set of responses* from a specific audience that is going to gather on a specific occasion at a specific time. One does not assemble a speech; he collects specific kinds of raw materials out of which he can mold a personal message—a unique composition. Research for speechmaking properly ends whenever you have collected most of the raw materials for weaving together an original, informed communication that will have a specific purpose with the audience that will hear it.

Before we pass to considerations that should control your efforts while you are composing, something needs to be said about recording research findings to aid composition. Speaker after speaker compounds his difficulties by jotting research information randomly on page after page of notebook paper. If he paused to ask how he was going to use these notes later, he would adopt different methods of note taking.

A speaker must discover which of the facts and ideas he has found deserve inclusion in the speech he will actually give. But how can he decide whether he ought to spend much or little time talking about, say, the types of cancer, if what he has found out about the forms of cancer is scattered through a dozen pages of miscellaneous notes on the control of diseases? He must dig out the bits of information that deal with the types of this particular disease. This would be a far simpler task if all his notes were on individual cards or slips of paper, each labelled according to the special subject covered. Were this so, he could in a few moments shuffle the cards marked "Cancer—Kinds" out of his pack of notes, examine them, and determine whether this sort of information seemed important enough to present to his audience.

There are many satisfactory ways of recording information for convenient use during speech composition. This is one:

Humor—Kinds

Donald J. Gray, "The Uses of Victorian Laughter," *Victorian Studies*, X (Dec. 1966), 175–176.
". . . nonsense does not end in laughter. And its laughter is the product of devices and habits. . . . The laughter of nonsense is not a surprised recognition of the savagery of nature or the brutality of man. It is rather . . . laughter of release, a happy acceptance of the chance to look at something trivial or profound, pointless or terrifying, without thinking about it."
(Donald J. Gray: Assoc. Prof., English, Indiana University. Specialist on Victorian poetry and humor.)

The requisites of a good record of information are simply that it be complete enough to obviate a second trip to the original source, that it provide an accurate representation of what was found, and that it allow individual items of information to be separated, sorted, and compared in any conceivably useful way.

Thus far in this chapter we have been dealing with stages of speech preparation that precede the actual composition of the speech. We have suggested a simple series of topics and questions that can direct thought toward the types of information you need for a given speech. These same topics and questions can efficiently guide explorations of your own mind, the minds of others, and the world of print. We have pointed out that different kinds of source materials are needed at different stages in research and that they must be studied in ways appropriate to their natures and to what you need to draw from them. Finally, we have observed that it is laborious and confusing to record the results of research in any way that does not allow you to sort and study related pieces of information. But a speaker is more than a bibliographer or research clerk. He investigates in order that he may compose and deliver an informed speech that will do what it needs to do with the particular audience he is going to meet.

Humanizing Ideas

Let us go back to the supposition with which this chapter began. You are to speak to underclassmen on the psychology program at your college. Suppose that you have picked the brains of professors and underclassmen and have read generally and specifically on your subject. Your pockets may bulge with notes inscribed on labelled, three-by-five cards. You still have not created a speech. Your raw materials still must be molded into a communication from one human being to a particular group of other human beings.

The gist of your intended talk may be clear in your mind: "The psychology major here makes sense; it offers a course of study that helps a person understand himself and other people. It will never be irrelevant to anything you do afterward." To crystallize in this way what thought and research have taught you is the first and indispensable step toward composing a meaningful communication. But because your communication is to be a speech rather than an essay, the ways you may develop these leading thoughts are peculiarly restricted. The position you have taken about the study of psychology is yours, and you have a right to it. You have no cause to give it up, no matter what audience you address or under what circumstances you meet them. Whether it is sensible to present your ideas in exactly the form that appeals to you is quite a different matter. You are not the one who is going to receive this communication. Nor will the listeners hear you in circumstances like those under which you worked out your own position.

Your listeners will be people who have lived different lives, whose knowledge differs from yours and from each other's, who have all the general and special susceptibilities discussed in Chapter 4. Yet they, not you, are going to be the final judges of whether the study of psychology is justifiable, compelling, inviting. And they are going to make these judgments at a time when other people are "talking up" other studies offered in your college. The whole tenor of the meeting will be one that says to your listeners: "Look over all your opportunities for study. Don't decide quickly or thoughtlessly on any concentration of courses." Your job, then, is to prepare a communication that will clarify the study of psychology and its benefits despite all the human variables represented by the kind of audience you have and the tone of the occasion on which you speak.

No matter what seems compelling to the speaker he dares not apply only his personal judgments of adequacy, clarity, or persuasiveness in the communication he composes. No communicator is completely free, but because they always face particular audiences on specific occasions, speakers are less free than essayists, poets, or writers of imaginative literature. An essay, a poem, or a novel can be composed as an expression of private feelings and can be published to the world on a take-it-or-leave-it basis. A listener gets the speech at whatever time and in whatever place he and the speaker happen to come together. If the listener is unready for the speaker and his message, the speaker must create readiness. He cannot retire to the bookshelf to wait until the listener falls into a mood to seek out what he has to say. The composition of a speech thus becomes an exercise in transforming your understanding of a subject into stimuli that will evoke a like understanding in people who are different from you, at a place and time that may or may not be ideal for either of you.

It is not enough for you to know a truth. You must give that truth vitality within another person's life—whether or not he is entirely ready for the experience. Through the design of your speech, you must make data humanly significant. You must establish mutual acceptance between yourself and other people whose lives are momentarily linked with yours because you happen to have the platform and they the seats. All of this means that you, as speaker, must accommodate yourself and your ideas to whatever demands of audience, time, and place you can foresee.

Some people feel that personal integrity and accommodation to the demands of an audience are scarcely compatible. The issue they raise goes like this: How can you sort, pare, rearrange, and perhaps even suppress things you know or think you know, and still be faithful to yourself and to your audience? Quite rightly, those who ask this kind of question are impatient with answers that say only, "You have to do these things in order to win your audience." The questioners properly ask in their turn, "Are there not men it is demeaning to please?"

The authors of this book think the questioners misconstrue what adaptation requires of a speaker and that they fail to understand the very nature of human communication. In the first place, the questions we have just cited imply that integrity and candor require publication of everything known about a subject—that simplification is misrepresentation. This can be the case, but it is not normally so. Second, the same questions presuppose that there is one faithful version of a discussable subject. The reply that "you must do these things" is vapid because it accepts the same supposition. The facts are that in human affairs almost no version of anything is perfectly true in the sense of being complete and universal. Even physicists and mathematicians would be prepared to say that perfect truth for all conceivable cases is rare in their areas. The supposition that any of us can be so perfectly right about any matter of human affairs that all alternative perceptions must be wrong simply does not hold for any matter that is really discussable.

Discussable subjects are also susceptible to various presentations, all valid from some points of view though not equally comprehensive. Both of the following propositions are in some senses true: By studying psychology one comes to understand himself. By studying psychology one comes to understand his fellows. Believing both, a prospective speaker might reason: "I have only five minutes to talk. That means I can either treat superficially both benefits of studying psychology or one of them fully. To show I really know what I'm talking about, it's better to be thorough than superficial. I'll develop one benefit only. Which? Most people are more interested in themselves than in others. Also, I can be more specific about how we can observe and understand our own behaviors. I shall put my emphasis on the thesis that the study of psychology helps one to understand himself. Maybe some other time I'll have an opportunity to talk about the social insights a knowledge of psychology can give."

This monologue fairly represents one aspect of the accommodation speakers must make to audiences and occasions. Unquestionably some of what this speaker thinks is going to be suppressed in his speech, not for purposes of misrepresenting anything but for the purpose of fully and properly representing a portion of what he thinks. This speaker would serve his audience less well if he attempted more and gave his subject a shoddy treatment.

Adaptation of subject matter is not always a problem in simplification or partition. The subtle decisions speakers are sometimes called upon to make are suggested by this illustrious example of audience adaptation: St. Paul's sermon on Mars Hill in Athens. The Revised Standard Version of the account in The Acts of the Apostles, Chapter 17, runs as follows:

> And they took hold of him and brought him to the Areopagus, saying, "May we know what this new teaching is which you present? For you bring some strange things to our ears; we wish to know therefore what these things mean." Now all the

Athenians and the foreigners who lived there spent their time in nothing except telling or hearing something new.

So Paul, standing in the middle of the Areopagus, said: "Men of Athens, I perceive that in every way you are very religious. For as I passed along, and observed the objects of your worship, I found also an altar with this inscription, 'To an unknown god.' What therefore you worship as unknown, this I proclaim to you. The God who made the world and everything in it, being Lord of heaven and earth, does not live in shrines made by man, nor is he served by human hands, as though he needed anything, since he himself gives to all men life and breath and everything. And he made from one every nation of men to live on all the face of the earth, having determined allotted periods and the boundaries of their habitation, that they should seek God, in the hope that they might feel after him and find him. Yet he is not far from each one of us, for

'In him we live and move and have our being';
as even some of your poets have said, 'For we are indeed his offspring.'

"Being then God's offspring, we ought not to think that the Deity is like gold, or silver, or stone, a representation by the art and imagination of man. The times of ignorance God overlooked, but now he commands all men everywhere to repent, because he has fixed a day on which he will judge the world in righteousness by a man whom he has appointed, and of this he has given assurance to all men by raising him from the dead."[4]

The story of this speech closes with these words:

Now when they heard of the resurrection of the dead, some mocked; but others said, "We will hear you again about this." So Paul went out from among them. But some men joined him and believed. . . .[5]

Looking at this account of a speech carefully designed to win a hearing within Greek culture raises some questions about rhetorical adaptation on which reasonable men may differ. Would Paul's personal religious convictions have been better honored had he not suppressed, for this speech, his strong distaste for

---

[4] (New York: Thomas Nelson, 1959), Acts, XVII, 19–31. Copyright by the Division of Christian Education of the National Council of the Churches of Christ in the United States of America. Reprinted by permission.

[5] *Ibid.*, 32–34.

paganism? This was his first meeting with Athenian philosophers, all of whom were pagans in Paul's eyes; yet he chose not to deplore their views outright but to use one facet of their paganism as a means of getting into his own subject. Certainly what he chose to say did not represent his complete view of Greek religious doctrines. One could argue that Paul or any other speaker who withholds private views in order to adapt to an audience misrepresents himself. But without knowing the motives and judgments behind the adaptation, there can be no final proof of the argument. It is thus with most questions concerning the ethics of rhetorical adaptation to audiences; one must know or guess at the speaker's private thoughts and intentions in order to pass upon his ethics. Our guess—and it is only a guess—is that Paul's adaptation to the Greek philosophers did not violate the core of his religious belief; we surmise that the tolerant spirit expressed in his speech fairly reflected his attitudes toward the Greeks. But this estimate cannot be supported to everyone's satisfaction, nor can its opposite. What can be supported far more successfully is that Paul's mission of converting the Greeks would have been ill-served if he had chosen to be completely outspoken. The choices he made were wise and artful ones, rhetorically; without knowing his motives, we can only guess at the ethical quality of his simplifications and suppressions. So it is in many cases of adaptation to audiences. We can see the artistic quality of the choices made, but only the speaker really knows whether he is choosing ethically.

If he is to be responsible, any speaker ought to distinguish between those accommodations to audience and occasion that leave the communication essentially faithful to what he knows or thinks he knows and those accommodations that convey to the audience a meaning other than what he knows or thinks he knows. The latter choice is either clumsy or unethical. A remark attributed to Confucius constructively suggests another direction in which adaptation ought to tend: "The nobler sort of man emphasizes the good qualities in others and does not accentuate the bad. The inferior sort does the reverse."[6]

---

[6] *The Sayings of Confucius*, trans. by Lionel Giles in *An Anthology of World Prose*, Carl Van Doren, ed. (New York: Literary Guild, 1935), p. 4.

In addition to accommodating his materials to audiences and occasions, a speaker must recognize that not all kinds of content are communicated through the medium of speech with equal efficiency. Thus another kind of adaptation is required. An attorney normally prepares a brief to accompany his oral plea; the judge studies the brief at his leisure. Our courts recognize that some content is better communicated in print than in speech, and vice versa. If an engineer or any other speaker must deal with highly technical details, he is likely to reinforce what he speaks with visual or other more efficient communication. The architect prepares floor plans, sketches, sectional drawings, and models, recognizing that building plans are never adequately communicated by speech or writing. Likewise, each speaker must discriminate between what can be told through speech and what is better conveyed in some other way.

Despite the examples we have just cited, the balance of effectiveness is not always against speech as a communicative medium. A man's attitude toward a proposition or toward another person is exceedingly difficult to picture and more difficult to convey through writing than through speech. A degree of feeling or emphasis is better conveyed in person than in print. Speech best communicates the relationships between ideas and human experience. Aspects of an idea or event that have strong human significance are "naturals" for oral communication, and ideas that lack human significance must either be deliberately associated with other matters of human concern or consigned to another medium.

As a public speaker you have both auditory and visual resources. (Never forget that *you* are your most versatile visual resource.) You will need to choose and emphasize content which lends itself to communication through your media and subordinate or exclude from your speech whatever materials cannot be effectively communicated through speech and action.

Adaptation of content for a speech has still another dimension. What an audience can absorb and what speech can efficiently communicate sometimes vary with the time and place. We would miss much of St. Paul's artistry in adapting his material if we did not know that he had previously been speaking in the market place at the foot of Mars Hill and that it was a group of philosophers who "brought him to the Areopagus" at the top of the hill. We would miss more of Paul's achievement if we did not know that this hilltop had for centuries been the site of Athenian deliberations on matters of law, ethics, and morality. Some scholars have even thought that the philosophers were members of a formal council that met there regularly. Whether this is true or not, we see more clearly the fitness of Paul's choice of ideas when we realize that few places and few audiences in all Greece more naturally invited discourse about comparative religion and ethics. The very details of the setting gave St. Paul cause to reason about whether a true god needed man-made offerings, for the speaker's stone on the hilltop was flanked by altars for sacred offerings. This, then, was a place and an occasion for reasoning and discussion, but not for pronouncing and evangelizing. What better topics than the proper *substance* of worship and the *potency* of the "Unknown God"?

Every speaker sooner or later must adapt to situational problems. The after-dinner situation establishes a tone of conviviality and relaxation. This tone must be respected, at least at the beginning of a speech. A Great Books discussion group will tend to establish reflective and informal communication as its norm, so unusually vigorous expression will be looked upon as inappropriate. Most radio and television situations demand more personalized and informal communication than is customary on public platforms. The reason is that sitting at home before their receivers, listeners tend to identify more easily with direct and conversational speakers than with orators addressing thousands in rally halls. The composer of a speech needs to be initially sensitive to these special demands that settings for speeches impose upon speakers.

To return to the thought with which we ended Chapter 4, it is unfortunate that college students seldom can move from one unique speech situation to another except in imagination. Because there are limited opportunities to test your skill in adapting to a wide variety of settings, it is important for you to recognize that upon entering the nonacademic world, you will almost never find speaking occasions as free from special demands as the academic settings. It is true that Winston Churchill was able to turn a Westminster College convocation platform in Fulton, Missouri, into an international forum that would accommodate his famous address, "Sinews of Peace," in 1946. But most of us will never have Churchill's prestigeful power to rule occasions instead of being ruled by them. We shall have to adapt ourselves and our materials to the requirements of the occasions, places, and special times in which we are privileged to speak.

We have focused on external forces that hem you in as you plan and compose speeches. But there are resources upon which you can draw to compensate for these restrictive pressures. In succeeding chapters we shall discuss these resources in detail. Here, we shall present preliminary observations about these compensatory opportunities.

There is seldom only one way of handling an idea. For example, if you find it impossible to demonstrate the *existence* of life on another planet, you have other options. You can discuss whether conditions on the planet are *potentially* capable of supporting life. Again, many distinctive qualities of a great piece of music are scarcely communicable through words, but this need not prevent you from speaking about the musical work. Though you cannot say all, you can verbally draw attention to some aspects of its structure or *form*. This is precisely the method Leonard Bernstein, musical director of the New York Philharmonic Orchestra, used to make meaningful the verbal portions of his justly famous televised lectures on musical comedy, jazz, rhythm, conducting, etc. If one attribute or relationship of a subject does not lend itself to oral communication in a given setting, there is always the possibility that some other theme or line of thought, almost equal in importance, is orally communicable.

Speakers confronted with ideas that are difficult to communicate or with purposes difficult to accomplish are subject to the same dangers as scientists confronted by the fact that absolute certainty and rigorously demonstrable answers are not always possible:

> There is in the first place the temptation to sloppy thinking
> —if one knows that rigor can never be attained one is tempted

to do less than one's best and let a piece of analysis go that one sees could be improved if one took more time and pains with it. There are situations where a defeatist attitude is too easily adopted instead of pressing the attack to one's utmost.[7]

Very seldom is there no usable analogy, no example, no familiar principle, no easily imagined experience that will create at least an approximate impression of what you want to speak about. We have seen how St. Paul turned to the methods of philosophical deduction when he wanted to show the superiority of his "Unknown God" to the philosophers so used to this kind of discourse. Thomas Huxley once explained the principles of scientific investigation to an audience of English working men by showing how this kind of investigation resembled investigations of crimes. Huxley's speech is still a classic model of exposition, but it would certainly not be had he decided to disregard the limitations of his auditors and proceed by rigorously defining induction, evidence, and generalization.

Edmund Burke had a similar problem: how to explain the proper relation between political representatives and their constituents. Speaking to his constituents, he said:

Parliament is not a *congress* of ambassadors from different and hostile interests, which interests each must maintain, as an agent and advocate, against other agents and advocates; but Parliament is a *deliberative* assembly of *one* nation, with *one* interest, that of the whole—where not local purposes, not local prejudices ought to guide, but the general good, resulting from the general reason of the whole. You choose a member, indeed; but when you have chosen him he is not a member of Bristol, but he is a member of *Parliament*. If the local constituent should have an interest or should form a hasty opinion evidently opposite to the real good of the rest of the community, the member for that place ought to be as far as any other from any endeavor to give it effect. . . . Your faithful friend, your devoted servant, I shall be to the end of my life: a flatterer you do not wish for.[8]

---

[7] P. W. Bridgman, *The Way Things Are* (Cambridge, Mass.: Harvard University Press, 1959), p. 9.

[8] "Speech to the Electors of Bristol," November 3, 1774. *Works* (London: John C. Nimmo, 1887), II, pp. 89–98.

Some six years later the same subject came up in Parliamentary debate. Addressing fellow members of Parliament, Burke spent little time defining; rather, he clarified his point by focusing on how a proper representative acts and feels toward himself and his constituents:

> Faithful watchmen we ought to be over the rights and privileges of the people. But our duty, if we are qualified for it as we ought, is to give them information, and not to receive it from them: we are not to go to school to them, to learn the principles of laws and government. In doing so, we should not dutifully serve, but we should basely and scandalously betray the people, who are not capable of this service by nature, nor in any instance called to it by the constitution. I reverentially look up to the opinion of the people, and with an awe that is almost superstitious. I should be ashamed to show my face before them, if I changed my ground as they cried up or cried down men or things or opinions—if I wavered and shifted about with every change, and joined in it or opposed as best answered any low interest or passion—if I held them up hopes which I knew I never intended, or promised what I well knew I could not perform. Of all these things they are perfect sovereign judges without appeal; but as to the detail of particular measures, or to any general schemes of policy, they have neither enough of speculation in the closet nor of experience in business to decide upon it. They can well see whether we are tools of the court or their honest servants.[9]

A weak speaker might have said the constituent-representative relationship was too abstract a subject to be explained to ordinary voters. But Burke found, in contrasts between agents and representatives, between hostile interests and the interests of people of the same nation, between "member of Bristol" and "member of Parliament," and between flattery and faithful service, the concepts by which to convey his basic meaning—that the responsibilities of representatives extend beyond the boundaries of the constituents' district. For addressing other representatives, however, Burke found he needed a very different set of contrasts: duty vs. subservience, higher vs. lower political capacities, what

---

[9] "Speech on a Bill for Shortening the Duration of Parliaments," May 8, 1780. *Works* (Boston: Little, Brown, 1869), VII, pp. 71–87.

the constituent can accurately judge as opposed to what he cannot, feelings of personal integrity against feelings of deceit. What we see is that Burke located a dozen or more *similarities* and *dissimilarities*, all of which could be used to make somebody understand this one idea.[10] Knowledge of one's subject, persistence in preparation and composition, and a bit of ingenuity can overcome very many of the restrictions imposed upon speakers by subject matter, audiences, and occasions.

Speakers too easily adopt defeatist attitudes also when they realize their audiences have no strong, initial interest in their subjects. One had probably better remain silent than try to discuss the romantic movement in English literature with members of a primitive New Guinea tribe; but there are fewer such impenetrable situations than inexperienced speakers realize. The little narrative that follows is true, and it illustrates how fully respectful, sympathetic adaptations to an audience can overcome ignorance and initial indifference.

Bob Barth was one of a class of fifteen students, all but four of whom were college freshmen. Nine were women and six were men. In conference with his instructor Barth revealed that he would like to explain the operation of jet aircraft engines in his next speech to the class but, he said, this probably would not be wise since it was already clear that only two of the fourteen students who would be his audience had even an elementary knowledge of mechanical and physical principles. Barth's judgment on his audience was exactly right; most knew nothing and seemed to care nothing for the world of physics and mechanics. Nonetheless, Barth's instructor contended that this was a golden opportunity for an experiment with what careful selection of ideas and methods could accomplish with a difficult audience. Barth reluctantly agreed to do what he could and set doggedly to work designing a speech that assumed little interest and no mechanical knowledge on the part of his hearers.

On the day of his speech Barth began by saying:

---

[10] See Chapter 6, pp. 170–183 for discussion of the speaker's options when his need is for means of amplification as distinguished from proof.

I am going to talk to you today about jet engines. I suspect you think you aren't interested. Probably what's in your minds now is something like this.

Here Barth uncovered a rough but clear drawing of a jet engine "pod" covered with such words as "dangerous machine," "complicated," "for mechanics only," "expensive." He continued:

> The fact is that in principle at least jets aren't complicated. They're rather simple. If you've ever blown up a toy balloon and then let it out of your hands to watch it shoot through the air as the wind escaped, you not only know something about jet propulsion, you've used it. Let's begin right there—with the air escaping out of the balloon.

In this vein, Barth covered simply but accurately the elemental facts about the construction and operation of ram-jet and turbo-jet engines. There was nothing unusual about his delivery, except that it was not as direct and forceful as it ought to have been. The language of the speech was simple and the examples were always from everyday life, but there were no other marks of artistry. Even the charts and sketches that communicated things hard to put into words were free-hand crayon drawings on cardboard sheets of different sizes. Yet when Bob Barth ended his talk there was a ripple of applause—the first applause heard in that public speaking classroom. At the end of the hour two young women who had been in the audience exchanged these observations as they walked from the room. "I learned more today than I do in most class periods," said one. Her companion replied, "Yes. And imagine! I even thought I understood that engine."

What happened? A speaker accepted his audience as he found it, adjusted to its limitations and its needs, and gave it as much information as its little knowledge, his inventiveness and art, and the time would allow. Without fanfare Barth offered his listeners two always alluring reasons for attending: I can help you understand what's been a trifle mysterious to you, and you'll find the whole experience much easier than you expect. Scarcely any subject is unusable in speaking if speaker and audience approach it in this spirit. Aristotle said it well:

> . . . for style and reasoning alike, . . . in order to be lively they must give us rapid information. . . . What we like are those [arguments and expressions] that convey information as fast as they are stated—so long as we did not have the knowledge in advance—or that our minds lag only a little behind.[11]

To gain attention and interest one must give information the listeners can rapidly comprehend. Adapting to the interests of audiences does not mean we are to tell them what they already know. This is a splendid way to bore them. A most important task in speaking is to bring "news" at the exact rate at which the hearers can absorb it. If one can achieve that, there are few occasions on which he need feel that what he wants to say will be rejected.

Thoughtfulness of others, a willingness to hunt for and experiment with alternative ways of handling ideas, and a reasonable amount of patience and persistence are attributes the composer of speeches needs in large portions. But no amount of rhetorical skill and ingenuity can ever compensate for the absence of thorough knowledge of one's speech subject and clear vision of what one wishes to accomplish by speaking. We have explored the avenues along which your mind may travel in search of useful ideas, some considerations relevant to your research, and the problems and opportunities you will encounter in humanizing ideas. We shall therefore turn next, in Chapter 6, to the problem of coordinating one's information to form a speech that is both manageable for you and clear to your audience.

Exercises

WRITTEN

1. Assume you are to speak to your classmates in favor of majoring in the academic field that interests you most. Identify

---

[11] From *The Rhetoric of Aristotle* trans. and ed. by Lane Cooper. Copyright, 1932, Lane Cooper, p. 207, Bk III, Ch. 10. Reprinted by permission of the publisher Appleton–Century–Crofts.

three lines of thought (topics) that it would be useful to discuss with this audience. Identify three other lines of thought that are relevant to your assumed speech subject but which you would not choose to discuss in a speech to your classmates. Explain the grounds on which you include or exclude each of these lines of thought.

2. Assume you are to give a classroom speech on "Censorship of Motion Pictures Should (or Should Not) Be Discontinued." Which of the sixteen lines of thought listed in this chapter suggest the most promising lines of research for this speech? Explain why the remaining lines of thought are not potentially useful as guides to promising information for this speech.

3. Identify the lines of thought (topics) used in some brief, familiar speech such as Lincoln's "Gettysburg Address," St. Paul's "Sermon on Mars Hill," Shakespeare's version of Mark Antony's speech over the body of Caesar in *Julius Caesar*. Defend or criticize the speaker's choice of these lines of thought. Were there other lines of thought he might as wisely have chosen? If so, illustrate how one of them might have been incorporated into the speech.

ORAL

1. Give a short speech in which you explain two different ways in which a specific proverb may be interpreted or a process explained.

2. Give a brief report on a speech or editorial you have heard or read in which you believe the speaker either made exceptionally inventive use of the lines of thought available to him or failed to take advantage of promising lines of thought open to him.

—⁓{ 6 }⁓—   *Invention:*

                                        General Tactics

The audience-centered attitudes and judgments of which we have
written in the preceding pages are indispensable, but they do not
directly yield the tactics you will need to use in selecting and
adjusting materials to your listeners and your purpose. This chapter and the next deal with such tactics. Here we shall consider
those specific steps in rhetorical invention that are important in
all public speaking regardless of specific purpose; in the next
chapter we shall discuss ways in which goals of speeches further
modify discovery and selection of ideas.

   There are three broad problems of intellectual discovery that
every speaker confronts, however experienced he may be or whatever his purpose in speaking. First, every speaker must find a suitable subject for his speech. We shall try to show you that some
tactics in choosing subjects work better than others. Second, how
do you build proof? What tactical choices do you have in selecting
and developing ideas that will affect what listeners think? We shall
address ourselves to these questions. Third, how can one clarify
and reinforce ideas, to enhance the likelihood that auditors will
grasp ideas as intended? Our final considerations will deal with
this question.

Choosing Subjects

Choosing subjects on which to speak is more troublesome in the classroom than in professional life. In the business or professional world, most occasions for speaking in public will suggest appropriate subject matter. Your professional and avocational competencies, the settings in which the speeches are to be given, and the terms of the invitations will sharply narrow the range of subjects open to you. Now, as a student of public speaking, you will have much more freedom in choosing your subjects. That freedom gives you both opportunities and difficulties and, since your classroom needs are immediate, we shall concentrate on them in the next few paragraphs.

The specifications for a good speech subject are easy to state in general terms. Any subject on which you talk ought to be timely, significant for you and for your audience, appropriate for you as a speaker and for your particular audience and occasion. You should also be sure you can present a reasonable treatment of your subject orally in the time available to you. To list requirements in this way gives the "tests" of a suitable subject, but it does not provide any procedures by which you can locate a subject that will satisfy you as well as the demands imposed by your own capacities, the capacities and readiness of the audience, and the conventions of the situation in which you will appear.

For some students, finding subjects for speeches seems to present more problems than testing their suitability. So, let us see how inviting as well as suitable subjects can be discovered.

To find a subject which can interest you and also have significance for your listeners, let your mind run freely over all kinds of subject matters. Suspend your doubts and critical inclinations temporarily. Just try to see what is interesting in the world about you and within you. The next paragraph illustrates how the process sometimes called "brainstorming" can work. The subjects and subject areas discovered are printed in brackets following the stimulus that brought them to mind.

This paragraph is being written in a motel apartment. That

fact will affect the thoughts that spring to mind [the power of suggestion; hotel-motel-hostelry operations]. The highway is visible from the window [mass transportation problems, highway construction, auto and truck licensing, highway safety, scenic routes]. Across the highway is a row of shrubs [horticulture, landscaping, plant breeding, land use, plant pathologies]. The storm windows are still on the motel [insulating materials and properties, maintenance industries, glass making, fabricating for the construction industries, custom building vs. prefabrication]. A school bus passes [the topic of education calls up too many possibilities to enumerate]. The typewriter is before me [mechanisms of communication, the publishing industry, business machines, automation]. A bookshelf is at my side. On it stands *The Ugly American* [foreign policy, diplomacy, the responsibility of the press], a murder mystery [escapist reading, paperbacks, censorship], Chaim Perelman's *Traité de L'Argumentation* [foreign language study, foreign travel, methods of persuasion, the study of philosophy, the relative merits of different academic subjects].

Twelve minutes passed while this little "brainstorming" experiment took place and the results were typed out. By the most conservative count thirty-two different, discussable subjects and subject areas emerged. It is difficult to imagine an educated man or woman who could not, by further narrowing one of these thirty-two topics, find a timely, significant, manageable subject on which to give a worthwhile, ten-minute speech.

"I have nothing to talk about" or "I cannot find an interesting subject" is almost never a statement of fact. Either assertion really means "I have not truly opened my mind to the possibilities." Discussable subjects are everywhere about you. Look at the newspaper headlines. Walk along library shelves noting book titles. Scrutinize any group of people, animals, machines, plants. Or take any class of things as your starting point and begin enumerating members of that class. Try *vehicles, buildings, clothing, inventions,* or *authors* as a start. The fund of potential speech subjects is virtually inexhaustible if you let your mind run freely in one direction after another. But keep some record of the often strange, often familiar ideas free-wheeling thought grinds out.

Once you have noted a considerable list of *available* subjects and subject areas, it is time to reactivate your critical powers and judge the results. Cull the list for timely, significant themes that interest you. Do not ask, yet, whether a subject is manageable, and don't worry about whether your audience will be interested. If a subject is timely and interests you, there may be a way to trim or expand it to meet the manageability test. If you are as careful a workman as Bob Barth, whom we described in Chapter Five, you can find ways of fitting it to your hearers and to the occasion. Your immediate problem is to draw from a random list of ideas those that are potentially timely and potentially significant for you.

To be a live option, a subject need not be patently within your present knowledge and preparation. It need only be one you can and want to learn more about than your audience already knows. Given this much, it is probably within your power to command some phase of the subject and to make it vital for your audience. So we see that choosing a subject involves opening one's mind to possibilities and then culling the results to discover the live options. We cannot tell you which option to choose; that must be your decision, made with due regard for your own interests but with equal regard for the circumstances under which you will speak. However, we warn you against two enfeebling practices: dawdling and choosing overworked subjects.

One mistake many speakers make is to dawdle over choosing a specific subject and purpose. A colleague of ours has studied diaries of more than a thousand college students in public speaking classes and has found that a consistent difference between good speakers and poor speakers is that the good speakers choose subjects for speeches carefully but swiftly, and then stick with their choices. Most of their available time goes into preparation. Poor speakers consistently reported in their diaries that they spent days trying to settle on an acceptable subject. We do not know whether indecisiveness is related causally to poor speaking, but the evidence is clear that good speakers choose subjects promptly and stick with them; poor speakers do not. If indecisiveness is your problem, it could be useful to keep a simple chart of the hours you spend on each phase of speech preparation: choosing a subject, locating your specific purpose, doing research and reviewing topics for further ideas, outlining, rehearsing. Perhaps if you see in graphic form where you actually spend your time, you will be able to use time more efficiently by setting deadlines for the various tasks involved.

A second practice that endangers success in speaking is choosing only subjects that are already known to listeners. Listeners want news, and speakers need challenges to do their best. If you choose subjects already familiar to everyone, both you and your listeners will end by being indifferent. Choosing shopworn subjects is also a poor tactic because you can never learn what your own powers really are until you test them against a task that demands skill and creativity.

Building Proof

A speaker has several tactical alternatives as he chooses and develops ideas intended to alter people's perceptions. Broadly expressed, these options concern giving purpose to the speech, injecting satisfying support for what is said, and clarifying and reinforcing ideas in ways that will make listeners grasp them and respond to them with some eagerness.

PURPOSIVENESS

It is important both to you and to your listeners that what you say be clearly and recognizably focused. Whether you formally state your purpose or not, some clear goal must be plain to you if your speech is to be prepared and presented efficiently. And if your speech has been developed under control of a clearly conceived purpose, its overall meaning (even if initially hidden) will gradually become apparent to your listeners. If this is to happen, you should be able to express your purpose in a concise sentence that specifies: (1) the kind of experience you intend your listeners to have; and (2) the essential content you will put into your speech. Some standards for evaluating this kind of statement have been discussed (see pp. 51–53), and others will be considered in the chapter to follow. Whether you tell your listeners what your purpose is or withhold it, you must be clear about it if your preparation is to be efficient and your speech effective.

Consider first your own need for an unmistakable purpose. How will patiently phrasing a statement of purpose pay off for you? First, any subject can be treated in several different ways. You cannot speak cogently until you have decided in which of these possible ways you are going to approach your audience. One dares not be vague. "I want to tell you about psychology" does not say which of the hundreds of possible speeches on psychology you are going to prepare now. "I want to help my listeners to understand what requirements a psychology major must meet" does identify a specific speech about psychology. Focus on such a specific statement, and you will have good prospects of developing an original, coherent talk. "I shall explain three milestones in the development of psychology as a science" identifies another, different speech about psychology. "I shall show you that important psychological research is lagging for want of public support" identifies still another speech. You could make a coherent, influential speech by adopting any of the last three statements of purpose; but a vague conception like "I want to talk about psychology" directs your thought and speaking scarcely at all. To direct your own thinking you need a precise statement covering your (1) aim and (2) the range of subject matter to be covered. Without both you cannot know what speech you are preparing.

A sound conception of purpose will also focus your attention throughout the stages of preparation—from searching for ideas to delivering the speech. By saying this we do not mean a purpose, once chosen, should never be modified. You should always feel free to revise your aim as you learn more about your subject and think more about your audience and occasion. Your vision of what you can or ought to achieve through speaking ought to change as your bases for judgment mature. Be ready, then, to modify your purpose statement and your coverage, but be sure that your most recent version of your specific purpose is clear to you. If it is not, you will ramble in your work and in your speaking, and when you speak your listeners will probably lose their ways.

It is also important to your listeners that your speech exhibit the unified thrust precise purpose can provide. Listening is not an especially efficient way of acquiring ideas, and listeners need all the help they can get to extract the right ideas from public speeches. If they know what your specific purpose is, that knowledge will help them to see how the details of your speech relate to one another and to what you are asking of your audience. Hence, telling your audience your purpose often gives you advantages.

There are times, however, when more will be lost than gained if you tell your hearers exactly what you are trying to do and how. This is usually the case with a doubtful or hostile audience. To tell an audience of scientists, "I want to show you how science is undermining morals," may arouse so much defensiveness that the scientists will close their minds to what you have to say. So experienced speakers often withhold their specific purposes in order to be sure the listeners give the fullest possible attention to the "proofs" of the speech and are not prematurely disturbed by the conclusions.

The expectations of the audience and the demands of the occasion and the subject must govern whether you reveal your purpose early, late, or not at all. Whether he knows your statement of purpose or not, your listener will invariably understand a unified message better than a disorganized one, and it is the statement of intent that lies within *your* mind that will unify your speech.

Do not mistake the central idea of what has just been said: careful attention to formulating statements of purpose for speeches is important, not because a textbook says so, but because speakers and listeners expend their energies inefficiently if they lack the guidance a clear sense of purpose gives. How the forms for expressing your purpose may vary according to the response expected from listeners has been touched on in Chapter 3, and will be further explained in Chapter 7. Here, we wish to establish the broader proposition that the demands of subject matter, speakers' capacities, and listeners' capacities all conspire to make formulation of clear and settled purposes essential to an effective speech.

PROOF

The purpose that governs a well conceived speech does not in itself accomplish the work it forecasts. Ideas, language, and behavior are deployed to do this work. Here we are concerned with deployment of ideas—and the somewhat military connotations of the words *deployment* and *tactics* are worth keeping in mind as we explore the ways in which ideas can be made to serve the aims of public speech.

There is no completely reliable way of predetermining exactly what an idea or way of speaking will accomplish with an audience. There are, however, dependable ways of assuring that a whole speech or any part contains the different kinds of content or "proof" that usually make communications influential. Just what that statement means we must pause to consider.

Any well-stated purpose reveals that the speaker is chiefly interested in securing one of five responses. A statement of purpose may indicate that the speaker wishes, in the main, to *inform* listeners. A specific purpose may show the speaker aims at leading his listeners into an *inquiring* exploration of a subject. It may reveal that he wants to *reinforce* ideas and attitudes that his listeners already possess. Again, the statement may show the speaker hopes to *persuade* listeners to adopt some view or take some action. Finally, the statement of purpose may indicate the speaker aims at *entertaining* his listeners. Whatever aim the speaker adopts, he is always seeking to induce change in his listeners' experience. He must get them to accept information and use it in special ways if he is to inform; they must experience heightened desire to investigate if he is to provoke inquiry; they must revalue their prior knowledge if he is to reinforce their beliefs and attitudes; they must accept his interpretations of things and of their own interests if he is to persuade them; they must suspend some serious concerns if he is to entertain them. Whatever he attempts, every speaker is asking his listeners to shift their outlooks. So, to ask what makes people change viewpoints is to ask what people accept as sufficient "reasons" or "proofs." We have placed *reasons* and *proofs* within quotation marks just above to draw your attention to an important point: What listeners think of as "reasons" may or may not involve extensive reasoning, and what they take as sufficient "proof" may involve much logic or none at all.

Here are the proofs that listeners demand of a communication before allowing it to change their views.

1. They demand that either the communication or their own experience reveal a connection between what the communication asks of them and their own personal interests. (See Chapter 4, pp. 81–103.)

2. They demand that either the communication or their own experience provide rational justifications for believing what is said to them.

3. They demand that the source of the communication (the speaker and his sources and sponsors) seem worthy of confidence—at least on the subject of the communication.

A speech, or any part of it, must in some way satisfy these general demands if there is to be change in the attitudes and beliefs of those who listen. You have often made these demands on speakers, though you expressed them within your mind as questions.

Suppose someone is talking to you about an engineering curriculum. Certain questions constantly pop into your mind: Why should *I* care about the engineering curriculum? Why bring this up *now*? Why should I believe the curriculum *is as you say it is*? Why is what you urge on me *better* or *truer* than an alternative? Why should I listen to *you* on this matter?

Anyone talking about engineering curricula can expect these questions to arise again and again in any listener's mind. And if we substitute another subject for engineering curricula, we shall find listeners raising precisely the same questions. They are commonplace, recurring questions asked by listeners of any speech on any subject.

Notice that some of these questions ask whether the listener's personal interests are going to be satisfied (Why should *I* care? Why bring this up *now?*); some ask for rational justifications (Why should I believe things *are as you say they are?* Why is what you urge on me *better* or *truer* than an alternative?); and another asks about the speaker's qualifications (Why should I listen to *you* on this matter?). If you see to it, when you speak, that these five questions are satisfactorily answered either by what you say and do or by something your listeners are already aware of, your speech will have the personal-interest, rational, and source justifications that audiences demand as the price of shifting their attitudes and beliefs.

To deal with how one builds up personal-interest, rational, and source justifications, we shall have to talk about these kinds of justification separately, but as you read the discussion you should bear in mind that these influences never operate separately from one another. You can demonstrate this by examining your own behavior. When a speaker shows you that something is in your own interest, do you not think better of him for that same reason? Do you not almost always find your friends more reasonable than people you dislike? Have you never said, "I see no flaw in your reasoning, but I don't accept your conclusions anyway"? We are dealing with proofs that are almost always intricately interrelated, but to talk about them clearly we must treat them separately.

Developing Personal-Interest Justifications. "Why should *I* care?" and "Why bring this up *now?*" are primitive questions. They spring from man's basic attributes. We say in Chapter 4 that listeners are anxious about things that seem likely to affect their private purposes and interests, that people tend to shut out what has no apparent bearing on their immediate affairs, and that all of us behave in this way by virtue of being human. You, as a speaker, must give your listeners some satisfying answers to why they should care now.

To see how listeners may be shown that their own interests

justify what you say, we review some elemental psychological concepts. Many modern psychologists posit that we behave as we do in consequence of internal forces commonly called needs and drives. Drives are internal stimuli that induce us to act in certain ways. Needs give rise to these drives and direct them toward simple or complex goals. These goals are conditions likely to satisfy our needs and hence cause our drives to cease.[1] Some of our needs, and therefore our drives, are physiological (the need for food and drink evokes hunger-thirst drives); some are social as well as physiological (the basic need for physical safety and the learned need for social approval may evoke a variety of drives toward the goal of gregarious experience). Experience teaches us that certain behaviors satisfy specific needs, relieving us of the tensions we experience when drives associated with these needs are stimulating us. Thus, we soon acquire predictable patterns of activity to which we regularly resort when we experience the tensions of specific drives. For example, we learn that to drink a cup of coffee at mid-afternoon "picks us up." So, under tension of drives toward relaxation, we go through a thirst-satisfying activity. We do not feel any the less gratified because the drives that induced us to act in this way had less relation to thirst than to a need for relaxation.

Similarly we all develop predispositions toward a host of intellectual activities. These are the behaviors of special importance to speakers. We learn that experienced people are often better advisers than the inexperienced; so, we become predisposed to accept what, say, a world traveller tells us. Or we learn that Midwesterners are more friendly than New Englanders. We are thereby predisposed to react approvingly if we hear that we shall find it more pleasant to live in Winona, Minnesota than in Pittsfield, Massachusetts, although we may know nothing of either

---

[1] This and the immediately following statements are simplifications of highly complex concepts widely and often somewhat differently used in psychological explanations of behavior. They should not be taken as definitive or universally agreed-upon descriptions of reality. We offer them only to furnish a tolerably acceptable framework within which to examine the options a speaker has in trying to reach the interests of those who hear him.

place. Everyone has acquired hundreds of ready propositions—infrequently verbalized, often contradictory to one another—that constitute his fund of attitudes.[2] These predispositions become our guidelines in judging what does or does not conform to our own needs or interests. And what is especially important to speakers is that *these attitudes, though infrequently verbalized, are nonetheless expressible in words, as needs and drives are not. Listeners' attitudes, therefore, can be thought of as yes-no propositions capable of taking their places amidst the propositions which the speaker offers.*

The paragraphs above present a vastly oversimplified view of human behavior. They do, however, present concepts with which we can think meaningfully about the tactics of building personal-interest justifications into speeches. It is crucial to understand that we do not reach human needs directly with words; we can, however, awaken need-produced attitudes which, being susceptible to verbalization, can in effect become an integral part of language-bound experience within a listener. A speaker can weave a tapestry of need-justified experience within listeners if he sets off attitudes that coherently intermingle with the information his language supplies.

See how a masterful political speaker did this for a Detroit audience during the economic depression of the 1930's. The speaker was Franklin D. Roosevelt. We have broken a quotation into separate thought units and have suggested, opposite each, the kind of favorable or unfavorable predisposition which that thought probably energized in most listeners.

Take another form of poverty in the old days.	Unfavorable to "poverty"; perhaps to "old days" also.
Not long ago, you and I know, there were families in attics/—in	Unfavorable to attic living and poverty that causes it.
every part of the Nation—	Increased unfavorableness to widespread poverty, etc.

---

[2] For a brief summary of the general theory of attitude change on which our abbreviated summary is based see Irving L. Janis, Carl I. Hovland, *et al.*, *Personality and Persuasibility* (New Haven and London: Yale University Press, 1959), pp. 1–16.

in country districts and in city districts

—hundreds and thousands of crippled children who could get no adequate care,

crippled children who were lost to the community and who were a burden on the community.

And so we have, in these past twenty or thirty years, gradually provided means for restoring crippled children to useful citizenship;

and it has all been a factor in going after and solving one of the causes of poverty and disease.[3]

Still more unfavorable to universal poverty.

Unfavorable attitudes toward poverty now reinforced by unfavorable attitudes toward neglect of crippled children.

Earlier attitudes further reinforced by unfavorable attitudes toward losses and toward economic and other burdens.

Now favorable attitudes toward "restoring" actions are evoked. They are the stronger for the "restoring" actions suggest ways of relieving the unpleasant drives caused by contemplating widespread poverty, neglect, losses, and burdens. Moreover, the speaker was himself permanently crippled by poliomyelitis.

Favorable attitudes are now transferred to those ways of acting that promise to eliminate what is unpleasant to contemplate. Some hearers may begin to "learn" a new attitude here—one favorable to governmental action to end poverty and its consequences.

Here, no reasoning is offered nor does Roosevelt make any verbal attempt to show himself uniquely qualified to say what he does. The thoughts expressed are nonetheless justified by his own crippled condition and by a series of attitudes that become, inside the listeners, proofs of the goodness or badness of whatever Mr. Roosevelt is mentioning. The speaker evokes these attitudes in series, creating out of them a kind of argument leading to the conclusion: Neglect of the impoverished is thoroughly bad when we know how to get rid of the pitiful and costly effects of poverty from the lesson taught by our good experience with the crippled,

---

[3] Franklin D. Roosevelt, "The Philosophy of Social Justice through Social Action," a campaign address delivered in Detroit, Michigan, October 2, 1932. Text as established by L. LeRoy Cowperthwaite, "A Criticism of the Speaking of Franklin D. Roosevelt in the Presidential Campaign of 1932" (Ph.D. thesis, State University of Iowa, 1950), 2 vols. Used by permission.

including Franklin D. Roosevelt himself. The speaker sets off images, recollections, and ideas in his hearers' minds; associated attitudes do the rest—stamping poverty and neglect as "bad" and "going after and solving . . . the causes of poverty and disease" as "good." By ideas-borne-on-language and ideas-born-of-his-own-handicap Mr. Roosevelt regulates the mixture of need-produced attitudes and his own perceptions of how things have been and could be. This is the complex process that occurs when listeners' perceptions and self-interests are enlisted as proof for what speech says.

You will find many points in your speeches for which your hearers will have the best proofs already within them. How silly it would be to prove by statistics, quotations, and arguments that skillful teachers are more desirable than unskillful ones, if the audience were made up of students! Any student's attitudes will supply proofs far more potent for him than any assembled outside his skin. Every student's needs and experience have taught him such attitudes as: disorganized lectures get in the way of learning; teachers who don't allow discussion are inferior; a showman isn't necessarily a good lecturer; good examinations ought to teach something; good teachers show interest in individual students. Such attitudinal propositions, whether or not they have ever been voiced, have only to be triggered by the mention of disorganized lectures, showmen, and so forth, to become proofs of that which you associate with them.

To identify all the attitudes possessed by even a single audience would require research by a corps of social scientists. Some political candidates and certain other communicators have the benefit of such research data, but most public speakers must work without these advantages. Most of us must discover the attitudes of our hearers—and thereby the personal-interest justifications open to us—from using such generalizations as were discussed in Chapter 4. Even so, we are not wholly disadvantaged.

You will not need the Harris polling organization to tell you that the young people in your audience will be more disposed than their parents to endorse idealistic and unqualified propositions. Nor need you be a social scientist to predict that members of a taxpayers' association will be cost conscious and, therefore, harbor proofs favorable to hints at control of public expenditures. To compose public speeches effectively, you need a readiness to ask yourself what your prospective listeners identify as "good for me and mine" and "not so good for me and mine." If you ask yourself this question, common sense often will tell you which attitudes can be called up to sustain attention and to justify your ideas—and which must be carefully skirted lest they leap into a hearer's consciousness as proofs against you.

We began this section by saying that answers to "Why should *I* care?" and "Why bring this up *now?*" must either be obvious to your listeners or supplied in your speech. The gist of what we subsequently said is that one place where answers for these questions can be found is in the systems of attitudes your listeners bring with them. Your listener may call up an attitude himself, or you may remind him he possesses it. However it arises to his consciousness, the attitude will teach him why he should care *now.* It is your task to direct his caring toward the conclusion you have in view, not let it subside or become associated with something other than the viewpoints you are urging. When Franklin Roosevelt juxtaposed the plight of crippled children and poverty, he exercised three such controls at once. He awakened dormant attitudes favorable to the proper care of children, took advantage of strong, Depression-bred attitudes unfavorable to poverty in any time or place, and aligned these so they would "prove" that government ought to "go after and solve" other causes and results of poverty. When you wish to use listeners' attitudes to support propositions your hearers have not yet "learned," your method must be essentially the same as Roosevelt's.

Developing Rational Justifications. Sometimes "Why should *I* care?" or "Why bring that up *now?*" cannot be sufficiently answered by triggering attitudes. Then you may have special need to answer the questions people ask when they are in doubt: "Why should I believe things *are as you say they are?*" or "Why is what you offer *better* or *truer* than some alternative?" When this is your need, you will not work primarily through existing attitudes but through propositions you supply and which you relate in ways your listeners consider rational.

What constitutes a rational justification in a given circumstance is a human question, not a scientific one. The example below can illustrate how variable judgments of rationality are, and how rational justifications are created in speeches. The example comes from a speech that was predominantly persuasive, but the lessons that can be learned from it apply to speeches with other aims.

On January 25, 1959, Mr. Oliver W. Hill, then chairman of the Legal Committee of the Virginia State Conference of National Association for the Advancement of Colored People Branches, delivered a radio speech from Richmond, Virginia. His specific purpose was to show that segregation of races in public schools was unconstitutional and unwise. At one point in his speech he argued as follows:

> The segregationists complain that in 1896 the United States Supreme Court decided that racial segregation did not violate the provisions of the 14th Amendment in the case of *Plessy vs. Ferguson.* But for some unexplained reason, they ignore the fact that in the Plessy case—which, incidentally, involved segregation on street cars—the United States Supreme Court arbitrarily determined that racial segregation did not violate the rights of the Negro as guaranteed by the 14th Amendment. No evidence was introduced in the case on this question. In the *Gong Lum* case, in 1928, neither the detrimental effects of segregation nor the right of a state to make racial classifications was an issue, because the little Chinese girl conceded the right of the state to make racial classifications.
> But in the School Segregation Cases [1954], for the first time concrete evidence was presented to the Court which overwhelmingly preponderated over any evidence to the contrary that racial segregation was in fact harmful to Negroes.
> Faced with this history and these facts, there was no logical or just conclusion that the United States Supreme Court could reach other than to hold racial segregation in public schools unconstitutional.[4]

---

[4] Oliver W. Hill, "Reply to Broadcast Address to the People of the State," *The Crisis*, March 1959, pp. 184–185. By permission of *The Crisis*.

Here is a relatively uncomplicated unit of speech by means of which a speaker hoped to root out one point of view and replace it with another. It is plain he meant to do this by supplying reasoning and evidence—rational justifications. If we rearrange the leading ideas of the argument we shall be better able to see what this reasoning and evidence provided to the attentive listener.

DATA: that from which argument starts	WARRANT: justification for making the CLAIM about the DATA	CLAIM or conclusion concerning DATA

| Segregationists [rest their arguments on] the 1896 decision in *Plessy vs. Ferguson* |  So, ⟶ (WARRANT) | [Segregationists' grounds for believing racial segregation is legal are unacceptable.] |

Since

[The kind of evidence used in Plessy case was too limited to make it an acceptable precedent for conclusions about the legality of racial segregation in schools.]

↓

(BACKING)

On Account of:

1. Plessy case involved street cars [not schools].

2. The Court was arbitrary [in going beyond its evidence in a case where] no evidence on rights of Negroes under the 14th amendment was introduced.

3. In [the related] *Gong Lum* case neither effects of segregation nor states' rights to make racial classifications was considered.

4. [When in 1954] the Court did consider evidence showing the effects of segregation on Negroes, it concluded segregation in public schools was unconstitutional.

The English logician, Stephen Toulmin, has devised a way of "laying out" arguments[5] which, if used here in simplified form, will help us identify the chief constituents of Mr. Hill's rational justifications.[6] Unspoken but implied material is placed in brackets in our layout.

We could analyze Mr. Hill's argument by other methods or in more detail, but this analysis of it will serve our needs. The points to see are several. First, Hill has (1) drawn his listener's attention to a piece of alleged fact (DATA) and (2) implied a CLAIM or conclusion about it. Second, he has taken pains to justify his CLAIM by giving reasons why the Plessy case is a poor precedent for segregationists to use in forming their own claims. Third, he has not expressed the WARRANT for his implied claim. He has left that to be understood by the listener —presumably to be inferred from the kind of BACKING he gives. His assumption seems to be that if we think his points of BACKING are convincing, we will then think something like: The kind of evidence used in the Plessy case was too limited to make it an acceptable precedent for deciding the present question. We would thus supply a WARRANT. If we do this, Mr. Hill's implied CLAIM—which he also leaves us to discern and formulate for ourselves—will seem justified.

The point of analyzing Mr. Hill's bit of speaking is not to teach you speech criticism nor to teach Professor Toulmin's way of describing arguments, though criticizing speeches is part of your task in the public speaking classroom and understanding Toulmin's theories would benefit you greatly. What we wish to set before you here is that in building a piece of reasoning Mr. Hill adopted some tactics open to him and disregarded others. You will always do the same.

---

[5] Stephen E. Toulmin, *The Uses of Argument* (Cambridge, Eng.: Cambridge University Press, 1958). See especially Chapter 3, "The Layout of Arguments."

[6] Several liberties have been taken with Toulmin's method in the analysis that follows. Toulmin's "layout" scheme permits more detailed and definitive analysis of arguments than the adaptation we use here for expository purposes.

Several options were open to Hill which he did not use. He could have marked out more explicitly the route his listener was to follow in thinking: by justifying the truth of his DATA through adding confirming evidence; he could have expressed his WARRANT in words so no one could miss it; he could have given different or additional reasoning and evidence as BACK-ING; he could have expressed his CLAIM in words and not left listeners to formulate it. These, plus what Hill did do, constitute the options that are open to any speaker when he undertakes to build rational justifications for any conclusion.

Now, what if we ask whether Mr. Hill proved his CLAIM about the segregationists' position? We shall certainly get very different answers from different listeners and readers, and this is the case with most rhetorical arguments. The kind of answer we would get in Hill's case would depend on (1) whether the person we consulted agreed that the segregationists' position did in fact depend on the *Plessy vs. Ferguson* precedent. (2) It would depend on whether our consultant supplied and accepted a WARRANT that would, for him, "register explicitly the legitimacy of the [logical] step involved and refer it back to the larger class of steps [making reliable analogies] whose legitimacy is being presupposed."[7] Anyone who accepted Hill's CLAIM as proved must have presupposed that to be a good precedent a legal decision must deal directly with evidence relevant to the situation in which it is being applied. To anyone who did not accept this general rule, Mr. Hill's CLAIM would seem unjustified. (3) Whether Mr. Hill proved his point would depend on whether the person we consulted agreed that Hill's unspoken WARRANT really applied to the DATA about which he implied a CLAIM. Thus, if we were to ask whether Mr. Hill proved his CLAIM, we should expect responses ranging all the way from "Not at all" to "Absolutely." Any respondent would be able to find some grounds for his answer. In such a jungle of differing judgments by listeners, composers of speeches must think carefully about how the majorities of their hearers are likely to reason.

---

[7] Toulmin, *op. cit.*, p. 100.

It appears that Mr. Hill believed he had few listeners who would question his assertion that the segregationists' case rested on *Plessy vs. Ferguson.* By leaving DATA unamplified and undefended, he acted as one ought to act when making a statement certain to be believed by all the listeners one really cares about. Hill may have thought that there were important listeners who would have doubts or misunderstandings about his it's-a-poor-analogy WARRANT. This would be a sensible reason for offering several pieces of reasoning and evidence as BACKING for the WARRANT. Apparently, too, he felt no one would miss the conclusion he was urging, for he chose not to state it. In general, the only good reasons for not stating one's conclusions in a speech are that the conclusions are obvious or that to assert them might force a listener too far too fast. Since Hill's position on segregation was well known, it was unlikely he was trying to be especially gentle with his audience.

We have made this extended examination of Mr. Hill's argument in order to put before you the kinds of choices and assumptions that are involved every time you formulate and support an argument. Ask yourself always what general idea it is that warrants or justifies or legitimizes making such a claim about these data. And ask what kind of knowledge listeners will need in order to see why the general, warranting idea you ask them to use justifies your particular thought movement from DATA to CLAIM. When you have located these three major points in argument (DATA, WARRANT, CLAIM) ask yourself which of these points are likely to seem troublesome to the important listeners. Now, bolster the trouble spots with additional reasoning, evidence, amplification, or all three. Your goal is to supply important groups of listeners in your audience with what they will consider sufficient justification for moving confidently with you from one position in thought (DATA) through a suitable bridge-forming idea (WARRANT) to a new position or outlook (CLAIM). Willing and accepting movement of this kind inside listeners is the proving which men call rational.

To proceed in this manner, producing whatever elements of argument are needed to impel your listeners to assent to your conclusions will require some general knowledge of people and considerable specific knowledge of the viewpoints of your particular audience. You also must know of the standards of rationality that various sections of the audience are likely to apply to your theme when you offer it. A good rule-of-thumb for developing arguments in speeches is: (1) satisfy yourself that you are right, then (2) build up your argument to the point where it will satisfy the most skeptical listener whose viewpoint you think might possibly change.

Any speaker must first be satisfied he is right about the legitimacy of the position he takes. Having settled that matter according to his own standards of rationality and ethics, he has to decide what it would take to satisfy those among his auditors whose viewpoints he can, practically, hope to change. For Mr. Hill to try to prove his case to segregationists would have been a waste of time. Hill, like any other speaker, had to define a segment of his total audience as the real audience for this bit of speech. This kind of decision determines how wide a range of standards it is worthwhile to try to satisfy. It means deciding upon the most demanding standards of rationality and sufficiency which your materials make it possible and desirable to meet. Ordinarily you may assume that anyone who neither doubts nor misunderstands your point will be more than satisfied by whatever proof suffices for doubters.

A mistake speakers make is to give only their own validations for ideas. Those who do this sometimes discover their listeners are unimpressed, especially if those who are or should be part of the real audience apply more demanding standards of justification than the speaker. Sometimes a speaker bores his hearers by trying to meet higher standards of rational justification than the listeners think necessary. To repeat: in rhetoric listeners set the logical standards and the standards of completeness in argument; speakers do not, nor do logic books.

There is considerable variety in the patterns of our reasoning and in the forms in which evidence occurs. Some of the variations will be examined under *Clarifying and Reinforcing Ideas* later in this chapter; others will be treated in Chapters 8 and 9 which deal with organizing speech materials. For detailed treatments of technical reliability and scientific or statistical validity in reasoning you should consult authoritative works on logic, argument, and statistical and experimental procedures. These matters are not treated here because we believe with the classical writers on rhetoric and public speaking that the applicable tests of rationality in public speaking are psychological and situational, not philosophical or mathematical. It seems to us that the formal rules of scientific or philosophical reasoning are far too abstract to be fruitfully applied in speaker-listener relationships where private rather than universal standards of validity and adequacy normally operate. Centuries of experience and numerous experimental studies indicate that in the logic of popular communication "One man's meat is another's poison." What constitutes sufficient rational proof of any idea depends on who is the audience. The very degree to which every speaker is, himself, a powerful proof or disproof of his ideas further indicates that the role of formal logic in popular communication is limited indeed.

The Speaker as a Justification of Ideas. Why should I listen to *you* on this matter? is asked often. Aristotle pointedly stated the reasons for the question:

> The character of the speaker is a cause of persuasion when the speech is so uttered as to make him worthy of belief; for as a rule we trust men of probity more, and more quickly, about things in general, while on points outside the realm of exact knowledge, where opinion is divided, we trust them absolutely. This trust, however, should be created by the speech itself, and not left to depend upon an antecedent impression that the speaker is this or that kind of man. It is not true, as some writers on the art maintain, that the probity of the speaker contributes nothing to his persuasiveness; on the contrary, we might almost affirm that his character is the most potent of all the means of persuasion.[8]

At a later point in his great work on the art of speech-making Aristotle added:

---

[8] From *The Rhetoric of Aristotle* trans. and ed. by Lane Cooper. Copyright, 1932, Lane Cooper, pp. 8–9, Bk I, Ch. 2. Reprinted by permission of the publisher Appleton–Century–Crofts.

As for the speakers themselves, the sources of our trust in them are three, for apart from the arguments [in a speech] there are three things that gain our belief, namely, intelligence, character, and good will. Speakers are untrustworthy in what they say or advise from one or more of the following causes. Either through want of intelligence they form the wrong conclusions; or, while they form correct opinions, their rascality leads them to say what they do not think; or, while intelligent and honest enough, they are not well-disposed [to the hearer, audience], and so perchance will fail to advise the best course, though they see it. That is a complete list of the possibilities. It necessarily follows that the speaker who is thought to have all these qualities [intelligence, character, and good will] has the confidence of his hearers.[9]

In the twenty-four centuries since these observations were made neither experience nor research has significantly modified Aristotle's explanation of how what-the-speaker-seems increases or detracts from his total influence. Some research suggests that perhaps the speaker's "character is the most potent of all the means of persuasion" in the short run only,[10] but no evidence has called into question the general assertion that the listener's confidence or lack of confidence in the speaker is the most potent complex of forces consistently working to justify or undermine the message.

Two reminders contained in our first quotation from Aristotle deserve special attention. First, the further removed from "exact knowledge" an idea or contention is, the more heavily listeners depend on their impressions of the messenger for indications of how safe it is to agree. Herein is an important rule of thumb for the practicing public speaker: *The less his listeners know about his subject matter, the more attention he must give to establishing himself as a messenger worthy of belief.* A second of Aristotle's important observations is: "This trust, however, should be created

---

[9] *Ibid.*, pp. 91–92, Bk II, Ch. 1.

[10] C. I. Hovland, I. J. Janis, and H. H. Kelley, *Communication and Persuasion* (New Haven: Yale University Press, 1953), p. 259. "In summary, the available evidence indicates that both positive and negative prestige effects tend to be lost over a period of time." However, subsequent research has raised doubt that this is invariably the case.

by the speech itself, and not left to depend upon an antecedent impression that the speaker is this or that kind of man."

It is not reputation alone that makes or mars a speaker's prestige. Everything revealed by the speech—knowledge, analytical power, organizational ability, verbal skill, delivery—plays a part in maintaining, strengthening, or weakening a listener's confidence in what is said. Each speaker shapes his prestige by every choice he makes or leaves unmade in research, composition, and delivery. This fact is far too often neglected by inexperienced speakers, and it has, until recently, been largely disregarded by social scientists exploring what the ancient Greeks called the *ethos* of speakers. One group of contemporary scholars has had this to say about the complex judgments people make concerning the credibility of those who address them:

> In order to understand these various effects and the conditions under which they occur, one is led to a fact which is obvious but has rarely been incorporated into investigations of communicator effects: Attitudes toward the communicator and the cues which elicit them operate in interaction with many other factors of the communication situation. These other factors include such variables as initial attitudes toward the content, cues as to the source's responsibility for the content, the congruence between what is said and prior knowledge about the source's position on the issue, the complexity of the question raised in the communication, the ambiguity of the proposed answer, and the vividness of the source.[11]

And even these authors have only begun to enumerate the variables that modify our impressions of the worth of a messenger and his message. Every choice you make or leave unmade in creating and presenting a speech can, potentially, generate proof or disproof of your message for some listener.

What must you establish about yourself in order to lend personal justification to what you say? Three things must be shown —or be already known—to your listeners. Cooper's translation of Aristotle expresses these as "intelligence, character, and good will." Hovland, Janis and Kelley infer from twentieth-century research

---

[11] *Ibid.*, p. 47.

that "expertness," "trustworthiness," and "intentions" are the qualities that determine how influential the source of a communication can be.[12] In short, if your qualifications are to justify what you say, you must establish in your listeners' minds that (1) you know enough about what you are saying to deserve a hearing (intelligence or expertness); (2) you are dealing with your material and your listeners candidly and honestly (character or trustworthiness); and (3) you have the listeners' interests in mind in all you say and recommend (good will or good intentions).

To see how these impressions are normally established, let us look at some examples illustrating various ways of achieving what we have called source justification. We shall first consider two instances in which well-known speakers strengthened their contentions by indicating that they were trying to think broadly, beyond the special ways of their professional interests. In each case, too, the speaker draws attention to his own fairness in managing ideas and in dealing with his audience.

Even the scientist and former President of Harvard University does not trade on reputation alone:

> I have purposely placed before you a false dichotomy—the Book of Job taken literally or dialectical materialism. I have already suggested, I hope, my own predilection; I would not repudiate the nineteenth-century optimism about the continued improvement, with the aid of science, of all the practical arts (including the art of human relations). I would not, however, subscribe to any "in principle" argument about what science can accomplish. I would be certain that for the next century, under the best conditions, the areas of uncertainty and empiricism would remain enormous. As to the Book of Job, I would subscribe to the answer that the universe is essentially inexplicable and I would interpret Job's vision symbolically, using this as one entrance to the whole area of inquiry that can be designated as the universe of spiritual values.[13]

---

[12] *Ibid.*, p. 35.

[13] James B. Conant, "Science and Spiritual Values," a lecture delivered at Columbia University in 1952. In his *Modern Science and Modern Man* (New York: Columbia University Press, 1952), p. 92.

By candidly warning his listeners that for emphasis he has over-drawn the conflict between spirituality and the scientific spirit, Dr. Conant encourages a favorable impression of his own integrity and, therefore, his trustworthiness as an interpreter and judge. And his caution also enhances his trustworthiness. That Conant, a scientist, will "subscribe to the answer that the universe is essentially inexplicable" is surprising, perhaps. If so, the statement may render his viewpiont all the more acceptable because, as a listener might say to himself, "A scientist would hardly say a thing like that unless he had very good reason. His training should make him give the opposite answer."

On April 5, 1906, President Theodore Roosevelt pleaded for moderation and regard for truth in the journalism of the "muck-rakers," some of whom had been carried far from fact by their zeal for exposing corruption. At one point in his "The Man with the Muck-Rake" speech Roosevelt said:

> It is because I feel that there should be no rest in the endless war against the forces of evil that I ask that the war be conducted with sanity as well as with resolution.
> The men with the muck-rakes are often indispensable to the well-being of society; but only if they know when to stop raking muck, and to look upward to the celestial crown above them, to the crown of worthy endeavor. There are beautiful things above and round about them; and if they gradually grow to feel that the whole world is nothing but muck, their power of usefulness is gone.[14]

Like Dr. Conant, Theodore Roosevelt conveys an impression of trustworthiness through the care he takes in defining his position, between sensationalism and complacency, while keeping himself on the side of reform. He not only implies this is a sane and sensible position, he declares its opposite is not very sane. He further asserts that he has adopted his position because he is against evil. His tactics in claiming credit for intelligence and trustworthiness are more direct than Conant's, but he is subtle also. His metaphorical imagery, borrowed from John Bunyan's

---

[14] In *American Public Addresses, 1740–1952*, ed. by A. Craig Baird (New York: McGraw-Hill, 1956), p. 214.

The Pilgrim's Progress, could evoke religious or spiritual attitudes of approval in some listeners. Finally, we should note that by casting doubt upon the intelligence and trustworthiness of those he is criticizing, Roosevelt goes a step beyond Conant. He seeks deliberately to detract from the trustworthiness of his opponents.

These are representative examples of the ways speakers seek to enhance their own images. It is worth recalling that Franklin Roosevelt, in the passage we quoted earlier, worked in like ways. To justify his contention that social action can remove the causes of social evils, it would have been as logical for him to point out that government action had "twenty or thirty years ago" brought sanitation to the slaughter houses of the country. His image as a speaker with warm and sympathetically humane intentions would not have been enhanced by that choice. It was enhanced, how-ever, because he chose to illustrate his point by referring to what governmental action had accomplished for crippled children—and his comments on this topic were doubly strengthened by the fact that he was, himself, a cripple.

There are other more obvious but nonetheless important steps a speaker can take to justify his message through justifying himself as its source. The late Ralph Zimmerman, an under-graduate at Wisconsin State College, Eau Claire, Wisconsin, did this impressively in a speech entitled "Mingled Blood." His opening words were:

> I am a hemophiliac. To many of you, that word signifies little or nothing. A few may pause a moment and then remember that it has something to do with bleeding. Probably none of you can appreciate the gigantic impact of what those words mean to me.

At a later point Zimmerman tellingly used his own disabilities as proofs in his explanation of the disease:

> If internal bleeding into a muscle or joint goes unchecked repeatedly, muscle contraction and bone deformity inevitably result. My crooked left arm, the built-up heel on my right shoe, and the full-length brace on my left leg offer mute but undeniable testimony to that fact. Vocal evidence you hear;

weak tongue muscles are likely to produce defective L and R sounds.[15]

Mr. Zimmerman's subject matter is exceptional but his method is not. He is only being more direct than Franklin Roosevelt. He offers the familiar proof: "Believe me because I have experienced it." That every listener could hear his weakly formed "r" and "l" sounds was perhaps more dramatic evidence of "I have been there" than displaying a piece of coal picked up in a mine, but both devices qualify the speaker by displaying evidence of his authority.

You probably have not the initial *ethos* of a Conant or a Theodore Roosevelt nor, we hope, the dramatic physical disabilities of a Zimmerman or Franklin D. Roosevelt, but the methods illustrated by these speakers are as open to you as to them. Your speeches ought always to acknowledge, as Conant did, the limits and the reliability of the ways you analyze and present your subject matter; this in itself gives you and your analyses strength and respect. It is as open to you as to Theodore Roosevelt to contrast the good sense of your positions with the lesser wisdom of other views. Allusions that associate you and your ideas with that which is intelligent, candid, and in your listeners' interests also are as available to you as to the earlier Roosevelt. And "I have seen it" or "I have been there" or even "I have read it" are claims to respectful hearing which you can use as efficiently as Ralph Zimmerman. All this is not pious exhortation. Student speakers constantly evince their intelligence, integrity, and good will toward listeners easily and without pretense.

Daniel R. Crary employed all the methods of source justification we have discussed when a senior at the University of Kansas. He spoke on population problems. A college senior is not normally an acknowledged authority on population, but you will have to agree that Mr. Crary gave his listeners ample reason to have con-

---

[15] Copyright by the Interstate Oratorical Association. For a full text of this speech see Carroll C. Arnold, Douglas Ehninger, and John C. Gerber, eds., *The Speaker's Resource Book*, rev. ed., (Chicago: Scott, Foresman, 1966), pp. 98–100.

fidence in him and in what he told them. At an early point in his speech Crary said:

> But the best conservative information, which is now available from United Nations demographers, says flatly that this increase in population, which has taken us nearly 2,000 years, is going to be *repeated*, not in 2,000 years, but in forty. The 1958 publication *Future Growth of World Population* from the U.N. states that the population of the world by A.D. 2,000 will be seven billion. I suppose we've all heard population-explosion statistics which are designed to scare us into subscribing to some socially beneficent endeavor or another, but the United Nations is not passing the hat or trying to scare anyone when it says this (and I quote): "With the present rate of increase it can be calculated that in 600 years the number of human beings on earth will be such that there will be only one-square meter for each to live on." Now this puts into question one of the rather old and often-used jokes, which goes: "If all the people of the world were laid end-to-end around the equator, they'd be more comfortable." But if the United Nations' facts are correct, in a few hundred years it may be decidedly more comfortable to stand, thank you. That is purely speculative, but the expectation that world population is going to double in the next 35 or 40 years is not just a speculative game played with almanac and slide-rule. Rather this incredible prospect is the logical implication of what we know to be the facts. And the results are already becoming clear.[16]

Mr. Crary draws to his own support the impartiality of the United Nations' scholars; he makes clear in words his caution in interpreting information; like Theodore Roosevelt, he rejects hat-passing and "scare," and purely "speculative" data; and he lets it be known that he is personally familiar with more kinds of information than he chooses to place before listeners as grounds for conclusions. Happily, too, he reveals his own humanity by touches of mild, relevant humor. All these resources and more are open also to you, as means of justifying yourself as a source and

---

[16] "A Plague of People," in Wil A. Linkugel, R. R. Allen, and Richard L. Johannesen, *Contemporary American Speeches* (Belmont, Calif.: Wadsworth Publishing Company, Inc., 1965), pp. 212–213. Used by permission of the publisher.

demonstrating that you are a messenger to be trusted, bearing a message that deserves a hearing.

Other methods of providing source justification can be illustrated briefly. Franklin Roosevelt's famous salutation, "My friends—" or his "you and I know" or any speaker's use of the pronouns "we," "us," "our" instead of "I," "me," "my" exemplify the many small expressions of good will and friendly identification with an audience that are open to anyone's use. Simply to use a cogent argument or to cite the best rather than a second-best authority hints that you, as speaker, have intelligence and knowledge. A dispassionate recital of arguments for or against the position you are taking can suggest to some hearers: "He's keeping his feelings under control and so is the more to be relied on." Demeanor, too, leads to source justification. Listeners prize conversational directness, general pleasantness, and unself-conscious action, voice, and diction because they interpret these behaviors as signs that no ulterior intentions are diverting the speaker's attention from his business with us, his hearers.

In Aristotle's shrewd observations lies what every speaker must remember if he is to give his message personal credibility: not reputation alone, but eveything the speaker does in his speech influences the trust his hearers will have in him and in his ideas. Whatever your qualifications to speak, your speech must show (1) that you know enough to deserve a hearing, (2) that you are dealing honestly with your material and with your listeners, and (3) that you have your listeners' interests at heart.

In this section we have been looking at the kinds of justification listeners demand as the price of acceptance and belief. Although we have discussed personal-interest justifications, rational justifications, and source justifications separately, these forces cannot be disengaged from one another in reality, as our excerpts from speeches will show if carefully studied. To extend a metaphor we have already used, to compose and deliver an ideal speech for a given occasion is to weave a fabric of thoughts—some having the color of reason, some the color of personal interest, and some the color of *ethos* magnification. The weaver of such a fabric creates the shadings of coloration that will satisfy those who must purchase his cloth—his *real* audience.

Clarifying and Reinforcing Ideas

How does one increase the chances that auditor-viewers will grasp spoken messages as they were intended to be grasped? In all forms of communication it is essential to assure that respondents will get the message. When you deliver a speech, what you say must be instantaneously intelligible, for review and recapitulation are impossible unless you provide them. Consequently the methods of clarifying and reinforcing thought are of critical importance to you.

It is customary when writing about public speaking to distinguish "proof" from the clarifying-reinforcing operations called "amplification." Though the distinction has been honored for centuries, the differences between the two kinds of content are fuzzy. Most ideas have to be justified in some degree before listeners will accept them. Sometimes this requires that reasons and evidence (DATA and BACKING) be furnished, sometimes that the source of the idea be rendered more credible. Any cluster of statements put into a speech for such justifying purposes will clarify as well as justify. But an attitude-awakening statement or a bit of rational justification may not, by itself, convey enough knowledge or allow enough time for a listener to apprehend fully what he is supposed to accept. Additional content, inserted primarily to clarify, to detail or reinforce other ideas, is what writers on the art of public speaking have long termed *amplification*. To restate, we have now to consider what tactics speakers use primarily to clarify, magnify, or otherwise enhance the likelihood that listeners will understand messages as they were meant to be understood. We shall speak of these as *amplifying* procedures or tactics, but we shall try to show also that they often yield justification as well as clarification and vivification.

Speakers amplify ideas by at least nine common methods

which are identified and briefly discussed below. Note that we are considering *methods* more than materials here; one kind of material can serve more than a single end.

INTRODUCING ANECDOTES

An anecdote is usually a brief narrative illustrating another idea with which it is connected. To clarify or emphasize the damage a storm can produce, you might tell the story of a family's experience in a tornado. Fables, parables, imagined episodes, or real incidents all provide anecdotal amplification and often, because of their narrative form, dramatization. The chief considerations in using anecdotes are that one needs to keep them short and sharply relevant to the points they are intended to clarify.

An anecdote, like any other example, offers some rational justification of what it illustrates and clarifies. Moreover, as a narrative, an anecdote can set events before hearers in a dynamic, vivid way; this makes it easier to enlist listeners' personal interests and attitudes for or against what is being clarified. Anecdotes contribute more proof by eliciting strong attitudes than by furnishing grounds for rational justification.

COMPARING AND CONTRASTING

Comparisons and contrasts also clarify and vivify. One may offer concise metaphors, similes, or antitheses, or compare and contrast extensive anecdotes, examples, whole arguments, or descriptions. Since we acquire many of our new concepts by comparing or contrasting the new with the old, these methods are especially valuable in clarifying because they use familiar learning processes. And since conflict and similarity are fundamentally interesting to man, all contrasting and comparing vivifies.

An important distinction is that a comparison or contrast, used primarily to prove, needs to be developed with much more attention to literal likenesses and dissimilarities than do comparisons and contrasts used merely to clarify. When Lincoln said, "A house divided against itself cannot stand," he used a metaphor to clarify his view of the divided country's crisis; he was not trying to prove that a nation is so like a family or "house" that precisely the same forces affect both. For his amplifying purpose it was enough to suggest a loose yet clarifying similarity; nonetheless, even this hint at a likeness could function as reasoned justification for Lincoln's view.

DEFINING

Defining may be accomplished in several ways. Ideas are commonly defined (1) by classifying them; (2) by differentiating them from other ideas that belong to the same class; (3) by exemplifying them; (4) by inferring their natures from the contexts in which they normally occur; (5) by referring to the etymological derivations of their names; (6) by explaining what they are not; (7) by describing or explaining them from some special vantage point (such as specifying what a musical note is if we view it as a complex of sound waves); (8) by specifying functions, as when a child defines an automobile as a thing to ride in.

The most formal kinds of definition are overused in public speaking. Particularly is this true of those "dictionary definitions" that classify terms and define them etymologically. Definitions that compare, contrast, or exemplify are far more interesting and easier to understand. Definitions involving classifications or derivations usually demand that the listener think abstractly, whether or not he has enough understanding to abstract. It is a good rule to offer classifying definitions only after other modes of amplification have been provided. The formal definitions will then sum up other clarifying material as in the first amplification below.

> To understand what a puppet is, think of a ventriloquist's dummy. [Example.] He's a doll of sorts, and a very agile one. [Very broad, hence easy, classification.] If you inspect his limbs you'll find they are specially devised to be moved by hidden hands or wires or strings. [Functional definition.] A puppet, then, is any form of doll with jointed limbs that are controlled

by some hidden means. [Classifying definition differentiating "puppet" from all other things in its class.]

The following amplification is less easy to take in at a single hearing and so is less well suited to speech:

> A puppet is any form of doll with jointed limbs that are controlled by some hidden means. Its limbs are specially devised to be moved by hidden wires or strings. It is a doll of sorts, and a very agile one, as you can see if you think of a ventriloquist's dummy.

These two explanations are the same in content, but the first proceeds from the specific (example) to the abstract. It carefully prepares the hearer for the final abstraction. The second explanation proceeds in the opposite order, immediately confronting the listener with the most difficult form of amplification and only afterward illustrating what the abstract definition meant.

Only occasionally do etymological definitions interest and genuinely clarify. It does not help very much to know that the English word *define* comes from the Latin *definire*, meaning "to limit." Better to comment that *define* means to "explain or set forth the limits of something." On the other hand, if you are trying to explain what *habeas corpus* means in law, the shortest, quickest, and most vivid way to do it is probably to tell your listener that the literal Latin meaning of *habeas corpus* is "You may have the body." In short, etymological definitions are always available to you, but they ought to be used or rejected according to the *practical* help they will give your particular audience. Discussion of derivations is not inevitably clarifying or interesting.

DESCRIBING

When Aristotle noted that all men like communications that set pictures before their eyes, he pinpointed the chief standard by which to judge the value of a description. Describing is a process of amplification.

While telling anecdotes, comparing and contrasting, and defining provide emphasis for special details of whatever is being talked about, describing usually sets the whole of something before a listener. Generally a unit of oral description should focus attention on significant rather than trivial aspects of what is being described; it should be free from ambiguity; it should clarify interrelationships or patterns that give the subject its special character, and it should be as pictorial as the content will allow.

Description can contribute rational justification to communication as well as clarity and liveliness. The way we see anything influences our judgment of its plausibility. Since a describer fits together the elements that go into his description, he will always imply that his is the best way of understanding what he describes. Observe the functions of clarifying, vivifying, and justifying in this description used in a speech by the historian, essayist, statesman, Thomas Babington Macaulay:

> If, Sir, I wished to make such a foreigner clearly understand what I consider as the great defects of our system, I would conduct him through that immense city which lies to the north of Great Russell Street and Oxford Street, a city superior in size and in population to the capitals of many mighty kingdoms; and probably superior in opulence, intelligence, and general respectability to any city in the world. I would conduct him through that interminable succession of streets and squares, all consisting of well-built and well-furnished houses. I would make him observe the brilliancy of the shops, and the crowd of well-appointed equipages. . . . And then I would tell him that this was an unrepresented district.[17]

Obviously Macaulay was clarifying the nature and extent of an unrepresented section of London. He was also making listeners see in vivid terms an unrepresented area; and for at least some of his listeners his enumeration of the city's features must have strengthened attitudes favorable to parliamentary representation.

EXEMPLIFYING

Exemplification is probably the most readily available and most useful of all modes of amplification. Whether factual or

---

[17] "On Parliamentary Reform," an address to the English House of Commons, March 2, 1831. In *Speeches* (New York: Hurst and Co., n.d.), p. 79.

hypothetical, examples can focus listeners' attention on just those features of his subject that the speaker most wants understood. All of us have said perplexedly, "Can you give me an example?" We seem to understand specific cases more easily than generalizations, and most of us gain more satisfaction from specific data than from abstractions. Exemplifying, whether as a part of defining or in the form of anecdote or as an element in description, is the speaker's ultimate weapon where clarification and vivification are his principal concerns.

Examples used primarily for the purpose of justifying need to be examined carefully to see that they really prove what they are intended to prove. We are all so used to reasoning from examples to generalizations that listeners sometimes take examples as purported proof when they were not so intended. The habit of trying to generalize from specific instances is so well established in our culture that you may now and then need to caution your audiences not to reason too far from examples you use primarily to clarify and vivify. It may clarify the meaning of tolerance to cite Prince Hal's amusement at Falstaff's habits, but you would be wise to caution your listeners against interpreting this example as meaning that tolerance of wenching and violence is your ideal measure of one man's regard for the rights of others.

QUOTING

Quoting some other source usually lends justification to what is said. If chosen carefully, quotations can also clarify matters. Whenever a speaker shows by quoting that he is not the only person in the world who holds the viewpoint he expresses, he directs justifying forces toward his listeners. But if quotations are used principally to amplify, they must do more than lend authority; they must express thought better than the speaker can express it. Benjamin Franklin's "A penny saved is a penny earned" may express one of the values of thrift better than you can ever express it. In that case the line is worth quoting as *amplifying* material. But if Franklin's observation had run, "Money not spent becomes as accessible a resource as earnings," you could invent a better way of expressing the same idea.

REPEATING AND RESTATING

Repeating and restating are substantial amplifying tactics. Listening is not a very efficient way to collect ideas; consequently, speakers have to give their hearers second and third chances to perceive and understand. Research on the usefulness of repetition suggests that with each of your first three repetitions of a given thought you further increase the likelihood that your listeners will actually grasp the idea. It appears that after the third repetition the gains achieved by each succeeding repetition diminish. There is also evidence that repetitions work more effectively when distributed. Apparently, however, this is not always true with restatement—phrasing a given idea in several different ways. Note the clarification and the emphatic force Macaulay gave his idea that Parliament might get no second chance to reform the representative system:

> Now, therefore, while everything at home and abroad forebodes ruin to those who persist in a hopeless struggle against the spirit of the age; now, while the crash of the proudest throne on the Continent is still resounding in our ears; now, while the roof of a British palace affords an ignominious shelter to the exiled heir of forty kings; now, while we see on every side ancient institutions subverted and great societies dissolved; now, while the heart of England is still sound; now, while old feelings and old associations retain a power and a charm which may too soon pass away; now, in this your accepted time; now, in this your day of salvation, take counsel, not of prejudice, not of party spirit, not of the ignominious pride of a fatal consistency, but of history, of reason, of the ages which are past, of the signs of this most portentous time.[18]

Here the tightly packed, paralleled restatements of the time-is-running-out theme make Macaulay's meaning unmistakable and

---

[18] *Ibid.,* p. 91.

the idea impressive. A safe general rule for amplifying through repetition and restatement is to *distribute* repetitions of an idea but to use restatements both sequentially and distributively.

Any repetition—whether in the same or in different terms —increases the probability that it will be perceived by a listener. Even unvaried repetitions tend to make listeners accept what they hear as true. In both repeating and restating, the method that clarifies tends also to justify. And if one variously rephrases content so as to awaken strong attitudes—as Macaulay did—a great deal of personal-interest justification can be built into speech even though repetition and restatement are essentially amplifying procedures.

QUANTIFYING

Statistics clarify and often support or prove because they express quantity in the language of numbers. Therein lie the strengths and weaknesses of statistics as amplifying materials.

The danger of highway travel can be variously expressed. One can dramatize it through anecdote or example; one can compare it to the danger of air travel; one can describe congestion and consequent dangers. One can also express this danger statistically; but now one shifts from word symbols to numerical symbols. By this shift we gain much in precision, but we lose much in imagery. We may say there were 500 traffic fatalities in Powhatan County which has a population of 1,500,000 people. This is a precise expression of traffic dangers in that county. But to get this precision, the conditions under which 500 people died, all the consequences of their deaths, and much other information have to be dropped out of the story. We have chosen to represent people and things by numbers. Moreover, the language of numerical expression has specialized rules—a kind of special grammar. What is it the numbers represent? Considering what they represent, and how the counting was done, what may or may not be inferred? What kinds of statistical manipulation are allowable, given these numerical representations of reality? Such are the normal questions any use of numbers raises. Unless the speaker tells his listener how his statistics may and may not be interpreted, given the accepted principles of statistical manipulation and expression, his statistical amplifications may confuse or even mislead. This means statistics alone are not very useful to a listener; auditors require numbers plus analysis of their meaning.

Even with their limitations, statistics are invaluable amplifying materials wherever quantitative attributes and relationships have to be clarified. Because they are so valuable for these purposes, it is all the more important for you to remember (1) that you must often compensate for the dryness of statistics, and (2) that it is usually not enough merely to supply statistics—you may also need to explain their alternative interpretations.

To compensate for the abstractness of statistics and to focus attention it is well to round off figures (let 1611 become "slightly over sixteen hundred"). It is also useful to present any series of statistics visually as well as orally. Note that concentrated clusters of statistics become confusing. Distribute them if you would hold attention. Finally, because statistics can only express quantitative attributes and relationships, it is well to amplify them further by using imagistic materials.

Quantitative precision is exceedingly important in clarifying; so is realism. Both should be thought of in preparation and presentation of statistics. It is when realism and vividness are neglected in the presentation of statistics that listeners think, "There are too many dry statistics here."

USING AUDIO-VISUAL AIDS

Rightly introduced and used, audio-visual aids become valuable amplifying materials which can lend clarity, vividness, and personal-interest or rational justification to what is said. The proper reasons for introducing aids of this sort are to save or reinforce words, to bring ideas closer to reality, to render the abstract concrete, and to enhance attention through introducing change or movement. Too often speakers associate only charts and graphs with visual aids. The raw materials for audio-visual reinforcement are much more numerous, including photographs, maps, charts or graphs, models, mock-ups, blackboard drawings, assistants who help with demonstrations, sound movies, television kinescopes, musical instruments, and disc and tape recordings. And the most versatile and convenient audio-visual aid any speaker has at his disposal is himself—a fact he should never forget, lest his best resources be neglected out of fascination with gadgets of inferior potentiality.

One basic principle should be observed in deciding whether to amplify ideas with audio-visual aids: Unless the aid is less complicated than the idea being clarified it will confuse or distract attention. More specific considerations are important too. Any aid must be relevant and well timed. Your listener demands as the price of his attention that whatever aids you use be: see-able or hearable or both, understandable, and interesting. The speaking situation will determine what is tasteful and appropriate, and what physical properties the aid must have to be seen, heard, and understood. You must determine the worth of a given audio-visual aid. You (or someone available to help you) must be able to manage and control your aids without disturbing the intimate relationship you need always to maintain with your audience during a public speech. There is nothing intrinsically wrong with an hour-long documentary film or a twenty-minute segment of an opera, but a public speech cannot *contain* either because the speaker cannot maintain a continuing association with his hearers.

There seems almost no end to the ways in which audio-visual aids can be misused in public speaking situations; almost all misuses grow out of disregard for the fact that audio-visual aids potentially endanger the speaker's own mastery of purpose, audience, and occasion. "Who is in charge?" is always a pertinent question when audio-visual aids are brought in. The following true story presents a set of extreme circumstances, but it illustrates how and why unsophisticated use of audio-visual amplification can turn a public speech into something very different.

The student's chosen subject was "The Treatment of Snake Bites." Having introduced his subject, he startled his audience by releasing a white rat from a cardboard canister. The speaker announced the rat's name was Maudie, and whipped out a hypodermic needle. Plunging the needle into Maudie, he explained that he was giving the animal an injection of snake venom. Maudie would expire within a few seconds. Meanwhile, he would explain what steps a human being should take if bitten by a poisonous snake. To clarify these steps the speaker now drew grease-pencilled lines and circles on his forearm to indicate where incisions should be made in cases of snake bite. But Maudie was dragging herself about, gasping her last in full view of everyone. Naturally, her troubles drew even the speaker's attention away from his explanations. He interrupted himself to comment: "Oh, yes. Bleeding at the mouth—quite natural at this stage." The speech, of course, was a failure, as any thoughtful person could have foretold from the moment this speaker decided to introduce poor Maudie as an "aid."

Quite apart from the charges of cruelty and bad taste with which listener-spectators had every right to counter this speaker's claims to good sense and good character, the poisoning of a rat was foreseeably irrelevant to his purpose. It would set in motion forces he could not control, and it was predestined to direct attention away from his message. Movement, attitudes of revulsion, surprise, the life-death contest, grim realism, suspense, and like forces would be at work to grip audience attention. No comparable forces would be working for the speaker's message—however good his grease-pencil drawings or his exposition of them. Any speaker who introduces charts that are too detailed or passes items through the audience while he talks or involves himself with overly complicated mechanisms makes the same fundamental mistake as Maudie's executioner: he abdicates his proper position of command.

We do not intend to discourage the use of audio-visual aids in public speech. What we want you to see is that audio-visual materials used for their own sakes can overwhelm speaker and speech. "A picture is worth a thousand words," it is said. But if pictures or other non-speech content can convey one's entire message, the speaker ought to send the pictures and omit the speech. Where speech can convey the message best, one then should speak—introducing audio-visual materials of other sorts only as incidental aids at those points where they communicate better than speech.

Without doubt, audio-visual resources can be exceptionally effective means of clarifying, vivifying, and proving. The variety of these resources multiplies as graphic and acoustic technologies advance, and we cannot possibly illustrate and discuss their full potentialities. However, to stimulate your consideration of what may effectively aid your speech, we offer a partial list of audio-visual materials which public speakers have successfully (and unsuccessfully) used:

The object itself
Models: complete, cut-away, mock-ups
Motion picture film clips
Photographic slides
Photographic enlargements
Maps
Blackboard or other sketches, diagrams, outlines
Graphs: bar graphs, pie graphs, pictorial graphs
Schematic representations: organizational charts, genealogical charts, etc.
Sound tapes and disc recordings
Video tapes
Other people: as demonstration assistants, examples, etc.
Staged scenes

The list could be further extended. The point to understand is that any device whatever which will present an idea to the five senses—sight, hearing, touch, taste, and smell—can clarify, vivify, and prove what you want to tell chiefly through speech.

A few *do's* concerning the effective use of audio-visual resources deserve to be remembered as important guide lines:

1. Introduce external resources at any point where your best verbal-personal presentation is likely to fall short of complete clarity.

2. Always verbalize what it is your listeners are supposed to see, hear, and understand from any audio-visual resources you introduce as aids.

3. Where more than a few seconds are to be devoted to an aid, let your hearers know what they are to learn from it *before* introducing it; then, restate what should have been learned *after* using the aid.

4. Design or edit all audio-visual aids to eliminate as much as possible any material irrelevant to your immediate purpose. Eliminate whatever might send thoughts in directions you do not wish to take.

5. Use your aid where you need it, then get it out of sight and hearing so your audience cannot dwell on it when you want them to attend to something else.

6. If possible, pretest sight lines and sound levels from all positions in which listeners will be during your speech. And pretest the workings of your aid.

7. Give *your* attention to the audience when using audio-visual aids, not to the devices themselves. You are still presumably the chief messenger and your listeners need your attention even though they are receiving part of your message through another source.

8. Always prefer the simplest possible form of audio-visual stimuli capable of doing what you need done in reinforcing and clarifying your speech content. For the same reasons, keep machinery to the minimum that the task to be done will allow.

The most important advice for all public speakers who take advantage of audio-visual resources is: *keep yourself in charge* and *maintain the closest possible personal relation with your hearers.* You are still the speaker!

In summary, audio-visual resources are exceedingly effective means of clarification when judiciously conceived, planned, and used. Ill-conceived or ill-used, they supplant rather than supplement the speaker. Where statistics must be given vitality, audio-visual aids have so much potential power over listeners' attention that their influence must be carefully modulated if they are to be constructive, clarifying forces in public speaking. A graph may be so interesting its meaning is obscured.

We cannot say in a textbook: "Take your pen in hand and compose your speech in precisely the following manner." We can only say: "When you compose any speech, these are the rhetorical resources and tactics available for meeting the demands of your particular subject matter, audience, and occasion." That is the kind of counsel about speech composition we have tried to present in this chapter.

Looking for the resources available to the composer of any speech, we have indicated the characteristics a good speech subject must have and how promising subjects may be found. In considering how needed features can be built into any speech we examined ways of giving purposiveness, personal-interest justifications, rational justifications, speaker justifications, and nine other ways of clarifying, vivifying, and indirectly proving. Exactly how you will need to blend these methods and materials depends, in part, on the specific purpose you have chosen. In the next chapter we shall deal with special ways of managing ideas in informing, inquiring, reinforcing, persuading, and entertaining.

Exercises

WRITTEN

1. Before beginning other preparation for your next speech write out a "Choice of Subject" paper containing the following information: (a) an exact statement of your proposed speech subject; (b) an exact statement of your specific purpose; (c) a brief essay explaining why your subject and purpose are timely, significant for you and your audience, amenable to oral presentation, and manageable in the time available.

2. Evaluate each of the following statements, indicating how well each meets the criteria for good expression of a specific purpose. Properly rephrase any statement you find unsatisfactory in wording.
   a. Don't adopt the sales tax.
   b. This is a speech to clarify the processes by which committee chairmen are chosen in the United States Senate.
   c. I want to explain that women ought to receive the same pay as men when they perform the same jobs and that in general their equality with men should be universally recognized.

    d. Economic and social effects of the growth in the United States' tourist industries since 1960.

    e. It takes study to appreciate the art of motion pictures.

3. Identify and evaluate (a) the kinds of justification and (b) the forms of amplification used in the following excerpt from Leonard Bernstein's lecture, "The World of Jazz":

But I find I have to defend jazz to those who say it is low-class. As a matter of fact, all music has low-class origins, since it comes from folk music, which is necessarily earthy. After all, Haydn minuets are only a refinement of simple, rustic German dances, and so are Beethoven scherzos. An aria from a Verdi opera can often be traced back to the simplest Neapolitan fisherman. Besides, there has always been a certain shadow of indignity around music, particularly around the players of music.

I suppose it is due to the fact that historically *players* of music seem to lack the dignity of *composers* of music. But this is especially true of jazz, which is almost completely a player's art, depending as it does on improvisation rather than on composition. But this also means that the player of jazz is himself the real composer, which gives him a creative, and therefore *more* dignified status.[19]

ORAL

1. Prepare and deliver a one-point informative speech in which you use at least four different forms of amplification.

2. Prepare and present a short speech on some aspect of a subject you know your classmates disagree about. Try to build enough rational justification into your speech to satisfy a skeptical listener. After the speech, invite a listener who agrees with you and one who still disagrees with you to evaluate how well you proved your point. Conduct a class discussion of their evaluations of your proof.

3. Present an oral report on an advertisement or advertising campaign. Discuss the ways in which personal-interest, rational, and source justifications are used in this advertising.

---

[19] From Leonard Bernstein's televised lecture "The World of Jazz," in *The Joy of Music* (New York: Simon and Schuster, 1959), p. 97. Used by permission of the author.

Invention

in Relation

to Purposes

This chapter concludes our consideration of the discovery and
selection of what to say in a public speech. In Chapters 5 and 6
we tried to generalize about all speeches and all speakers. But
your specific purpose affects your choice and management of
what to say. Here, then, we shall examine how each of the normal
objectives in speaking (to inform, to induce inquiry, to reinforce,
to persuade, to entertain) influences your choices.

Speaking to Inform

There are times when speakers are fully satisfied if their hearers
understand what is said. Then we tend to think of the talk as
wholly informative. We could as easily call it explanatory or
expository. A teacher's lecture and a physician's explanation of
how a disease must be treated are examples of this kind of discourse. Whether understanding is a speaker's over-all objective
or the objective of only a part of his talk, the aim of informing
requires him to find particular kinds of material and use them in
special ways that meet the distinctive standards listeners always
impose when asked to accept knowledge understandingly.

    What kinds of content are especially appropriate when you

set out to inform? Any material clarifying such attributes and relationships of a subject as are listed on page 115, excepting the attribute of desirability, will be potentially informative. Also, whatever clarifies any of the five relationships listed on page 115 will be potentially informative. But material that concerns the desirability of anything is never purely informative. It implicitly or explicitly raises questions about debatable matters: "goods," "bads," "betters," "poorers." In other words, any material that affirms or denies desirability forces speaker and listener into the realm of persuasion and however informative, talk about desirabilities must always be persuasive as well. The result is that the speaker who raises questions of desirability must meet the standards of persuasive speaking as the purely informative speaker need not.

The standards peculiar to informative speaking are: (1) *accuracy*, being true to fact in both detail and proportion; (2) *completeness*, being comprehensive enough to cover the subject promised by the specific purpose or in any sub-section of the speech; and (3) *unity*, providing knowledge that will be intelligible as a whole. Like many other propositions about oral communication, these standards of good informative speaking grow out of the demands of the audience. When a speaker indicates he wants to make us understand, listeners begin analyzing what he says for its "truth," for whether there is enough detail to permit understanding, and for whether what we are told adds up to any significant whole.

The speaker who undertakes to explain how a tape recorder works will err if he alleges that all tape recorders use vacuum tubes for sound amplification (many use transistors); he will err in a different way if he neglects to discuss the play-back systems most recorders have; and he will err in another fashion if he does not make it clear that the entire mechanical system exists to preserve and repeat sound. If the speaker makes all three errors, he will have violated all the basic demands listeners place on those who inform. His listeners may not reject him as a person for his error of fact, his omission, and his disregard for the total meaning of his material; but they will not understand tape recorders unless they understood them before. The speaker did not put into his discourse those things that must be there if talk is to inform or teach: accuracy, completeness, unity.

When you set yourself the task of informing you take on an assignment in clarifying and amplifying. In informing, proving by direct argument is not your primary business.

It is easy to become imprecise about what one is clarifying and amplifying. Imprecision will surely confuse a listener. If you write out your specific purpose, then examine it carefully to see that your statement expresses all, but no more than, you want your listeners to understand, you will seldom confuse yourself or your audience by having an imprecise purpose. A very good practice is the following. Write the words: "When I finish my speech I want my listeners to understand *that. . . .*" Insert after "that," a single clause completing the sentence and expressing what you want to accomplish. "When I finish my speech I want them to understand *that* the Battle of Gettysburg was a battle of maneuver rather than firepower," is a precise subject sentence. "When I finish my speech I want my listeners to understand the Battle of Gettysburg" is useless as a subject sentence because it gives the speaker no focus and promises the listener no clear boundaries for the knowledge to be presented.

Even if audiences did not insist that informative speakers be explicit about their purposes, your own convenience would justify taking great care in phrasing subject sentences. Without an exact expression of specific purpose you are likely to try to cover too many points, you will tend to gather material you cannot use, and you will have frustrating difficulties in organizing your materials. You need to be precise in formulating your subject sentences in all forms of speaking, but especially in informative speeches because your listeners' expectations will be especially exacting and you will be tempted to speak too discursively.

Maintaining interest is often difficult in informative speaking, when one must from time to time explain abstractions, static things, or technical matters. Such content lacks inherent power to command attention. The material does not exhibit activity, vividness, familiarity, conflict, vitality, or humor, so you must arouse interest through choosing special materials, through style, and through delivery.

When subject matter of the kind we are talking about has to be discussed, you will have to search out justifying and amplifying materials that have the interest-enhancing qualities the topic itself lacks. Specific examples, comparisons and contrasts, brief narratives, real and figurative analogies are especially useful. So, too, are all facts that are close to the experience of your listeners —even facts that appear threatening.

The anatomy of the housefly does not seem a subject on which to build an engrossing speech, but a student speaker did just that by finding concrete and threatening amplifying materials. The housefly is hairy. This unexciting fact assumed significance when the speaker amplified it by saying that the fly's body hairs are easily befouled as he moves around filth, and the same hairs as easily pollute human food when the fly later alights on it. The fly's digestive system is not universally arousing, but the speaker centered her exposition on the fact that the insect's digestive system is not capable of handling dry matter, thus it is necessary for him to salivate or regurgitate on dry food in order that he may wet it and make it edible. In explaining the mouth, legs, and wings of the fly the speaker used visual aids and other attention-compelling methods. That exposition of the housefly's anatomy did not lack for attention or understanding. Our discussion of Bob Barth's speech on jet engines (see Chapter 5, pp. 136–137) illustrates comparable ingenuity in locating the kinds of information that compensate for remoteness, technicality, or plain dullness of subject matters which must be lucidly explained.

Speakers often neglect another opportunity when explaining difficult subjects. It is the opportunity to treat the subject matter *as if* it were other than it literally is.

No one has ever seen a sound wave. Sound waves do not behave precisely like the water waves we call ripples. Nonetheless, it is customary to explain part of the behavior of sound waves *as if* the waves acted as ripples spreading outward when a stone is dropped into water. There are many aspects of sound that cannot be explained properly by this *as-if* treatment; nevertheless, the treatment will serve as long as we confine our attention to specific aspects of how sound waves spread out from their source. The whole point of hunting for *as-if* treatments is that people build new knowledge upon the knowledge they already have— through comparison and contrast. Some aspects of a steel rolling mill can be made both clear and interesting if we think of the steel *as if* it were dough and the mill *as if* it were equipped with kitchen rolling pins. One must be careful that listeners understand that an *as-if* treatment is not a discussion of actuality; yet, informative speakers are well advised to search more often than they do for such potentially useful ways of explaining. It is worth remembering that this method of thinking and explaining has become standard in scientific communication because many concepts can only be expressed in *as-if* terms or through mathematical symbols.

We have been discussing informative speaking *as if* information-giving really existed completely apart from inquiry, reinforcement, persuasion, or entertainment. It seldom does, but we can talk clearly of only one thing at a time. Clear explanations persuade us to believe; they encourage us to seek more knowledge; they reinforce our feelings; and they are often entertaining in the sense that new learning is pleasing. Good informative speaking frequently persuades. When Winston Churchill explained the battle-front situation to the British people during World War II, he was at the same time persuading and encouraging them to stand firm against Britain's enemies. President John F. Kennedy's broadcast explaining the steps his government had taken in the Cuban crisis of 1962 both clarified the United States' actions and encouraged support for those actions. Speakers too often forget that the strongest persuasion is often simply a clear exposition of how or why the facts are as the speaker knows them.

To summarize, informing is one of the purposes that may dominate a speaker's effort at communication. When it does, it is particularly important that he carefully specify to himself (perhaps to his auditors also) exactly what he wants understood. Information about any characteristic of what he is explaining is potentially useful, except that propositions about desirability automatically involve him in persuasion as well as informing. Accuracy, completeness, and unity are the qualities that justify what is said. Informing is thus an enterprise in clarifying and amplifying rather than proving. For these ends, comparisons, contrasts, reference to the familiar, exemplification, narratives, and analogies are especially useful kinds of material because they tend to contain the factors of attention. When the subject matter to be explained is not inherently interesting, make special efforts to introduce factors of attention. If the right kinds of material are found, are carefully developed in ways we have suggested, and are made to convey a unified view of what is being explained, the speech will induce understanding and stimulate interest, belief, and personal satisfaction in listeners.

Speaking to Induce Inquiry

Do speakers ever address audiences without having "the answers"? Unquestionably, though when this happens the audience is likely to be small and select. An executive or a chairman presenting a problem to his staff or committee often finds it necessary to set forth the problem before requesting the discussion through which it will be solved. A more formal example of speaking to induce inquiry might be seen when a city manager describes to a mass meeting the nature of his city's water-supply crisis and presents the alternatives from which the city must choose its solution.

If discussion is a subject of study in your classroom group you will observe that inducing a spirit of inquiry is the primary goal of group chairmen in their opening remarks. Ideally, many remarks made in reflective discussion also will be intended to provoke inquiry. A public speech to induce inquiry is simply a formal presentation of considerations which, under different circumstances, might have formed the agenda of an inquiring discussion group.

Look about you, and you will see far more formal speeches to induce inquiry than you thought. A fraternity member may observe that the porch of the chapter house is deteriorating. He may want to introduce the problem at a business meeting. Not having the answers himself, he may choose to discuss the problem and several possible ways of doing the necessary repair work. A speaker might be perplexed about what attitude we should take toward conscientious objectors, and so wish to set off discussion of the topic. These speakers are not informants in the usual sense, nor do they want to persuade about anything except the need for reflection. Their objective is to set out the conditions within which a solution must be found and to challenge listeners to evaluate and select a desirable solution. The challenge may be for private thought or for public discussion in the open forums that often follow such speeches.[1]

The subject sentence of any speaker who undertakes to induce inquiry is stated well when it expresses the precise question he believes his listeners can and will attempt to answer. Such a sentence might be stated, "When I finish my speech I want the audience to be prepared and motivated to answer the question, '. . . . .?' " The words, "be prepared and motivated," represent key aspects of the inquiring speaker's assignment. Whether he puts these words in a formal statement of purpose or not, his function is always to pave the way for a search for answers. To do this he must explain the problem and, insofar as he can foresee, suggest directions in which a solution might be looked for. These parts of his task are primarily informative, but unless he can also answer his hearers' ever-present question, "Why should I care?" little will result from his speech. Whoever undertakes to induce inquiry must accept the dual responsibility for preparing and for motivating his audience to try to solve a problem.

---

[1] Exposition of this kind of speaking may also be found in J. H. McBurney and Ernest J. Wrage, *The Art of Good Speech* (New York: Prentice-Hall, 1953), Ch. 13, "The Methods of Inquiry." Recognition that formal speaking of this kind does occur can be found in the writings of Cicero and Quintilian and even in the works of lesser but earlier authors. Our discussion of this topic draws upon many of these sources and, at several points, goes somewhat beyond what has heretofore been said.

The fact that men who make speeches to induce inquiry do not "know the answers" too frequently keeps them from even identifying the proper questions! Men often are sensitive to difficulties and have standards or goals by which to measure solutions, yet possess no clear idea of what question needs solving. The agriculturist and writer, Arthur Young, observed this state of mind among the revolutionists in France in 1792:

> I have been in much company all day, and cannot but remark, that there seem to be no settled ideas of the best means of forming a new constitution. . . . In these most interesting discussions, I find a general ignorance of the principles of government; a strange and unaccountable appeal, on one side, to ideal and visionary rights of nature; and, on the other, no settled plan that shall give security to the people for being in future in a much better situation than hitherto; . . .[2]

Mr. Young identified one of the great sources of difficulty in the French Revolution: most of the leaders formulating and debating revolutionary measures simply lacked the political wisdom or experience to formulate political questions. They framed, discussed, and debated philosophical propositions instead. Some excesses of the period followed from this fault, for philosophical propositions are not best settled by popular discussion and debate.

The campus speaker who sets as his purpose, "To prepare and motivate the student council to answer the question, 'What is student government for?' " is in the same difficulty as the French leaders. He is aware of a general problem area, but he has not identified any precise question with which to begin a practical inquiry into the topic. No speaker can, in his normal time allotment, lay out the entire subject of student government as an area for inquiry and at the same time indicate the many directions in which we might look to find fractional answers to why student governments should exist. But a practical question for inquiry might be, "What role, if any, should student government have in regulating student conduct?" Another inquiry might investigate "What administrative functions within the university can be

---

[2] *Travels in France.* Quoted in *The Debate on the French Revolution, 1789–1800,* ed. by Alfred Cobban (London: Nicholas Kaye, 1950), pp. 51–52.

usefully delegated to student government?" These are questions for which we might get answers from an audience; from unduly philosophical queries we can only expect aggravating controversy.

It is essential, then, that the subject sentence for a speech to induce inquiry stipulate in precise language a question that the listeners potentially can answer, given their available time and knowledge. Problems or questions need not be *completely* answerable to be worthy of inquiring consideration. If it seems that your listeners can progress toward an answer, you are justified in asking them to make the attempt.

With a single exception, preparing to speak to induce inquiry is like preparing to speak to inform. The exception is that *desirability* is a topic that must be treated in any inquiry into a question involving policies. An informant has little use for materials relating to *desirability*. Whether student government should regulate conduct finally becomes a question of whether such regulation would be desirable. So it is with most questions about courses of action or human values. The desirability of the action or what is to be judged is a topic that must be explored in settling such questions. Where the question is to determine a fact or truth or falsity, desirability is seldom discussed.

The distinctive pattern of organization into which main ideas fall in a speech of inquiry is discussed in Chapter 8 (pp. 238–240). The divisions of an inquiry also constitute useful guides to the materials needed in developing speeches of this kind.

Inquiring speeches normally begin with discussion of a problem and proceed toward solutions deserving consideration by reasonable people. This kind of thought movement is not inherently interesting. The speaker, and therefore the listener, moves in thought from point to point with judgment suspended. Even at his close, the inquirer may or may not have revealed a preferred solution. There are, thus, few natural climaxes in the communicative experience. There is no inherent sense of energetic progress toward satisfying release from the tensions involved in wrestling with the uncertain. In return for asking his listeners to defer judgment and to sustain the tensions of inquiry, the inquiring speaker ought to repay them by using the most interesting clarifying and vivifying materials available to him. He ought to use those amplifying tactics that do most to aid his auditors in grasping his message (see Chapter 6, pp. 170–182).

An inquiring speaker assumes a special leadership role. He presides over a collaborative search for a "best choice"—possibly even for the truth. In this role he must be exceedingly careful to demonstrate his own knowledge of the subject, his impartiality concerning the decisions he is asking his listeners to make, and his candor in dealing with both content and listeners. Few tactics are more resented than attempts to maneuver audiences toward a preselected conclusion under the pretense of inviting them to inquire freely.

Questions, not propositions, stimulate inquiry; so, the subject sentences of speeches to induce inquiry ought to contain clear expressions of potentially answerable questions. Where the issue for inquiry concerns a matter of policy, *desirability* and all the other attributes and relationships we commonly talk about can suggest aspects of the problem and of solutions that may deserve discussion. Because of their inductive character, speeches of inquiry usually need to be specially enlivened by the most interesting amplifying tactics that are available and relevant. Those who try to induce inquiry assume the roles of informant and leader; therefore all they do and say must show their personal qualifications for these roles.

Speaking to Reinforce
Beliefs and Feelings

From time to time we speak without intending to establish new beliefs or reverse our listeners' feelings. We often talk simply to reinforce existing beliefs and feelings. We speak of the values of education on a commencement day; we assure a friend that he is right in asserting that Joe DiMaggio was a better baseball player than Mickey Mantle. The aim of such talk is to make the listener believe something more than ever.

Speeches that reinforce beliefs and feelings are a kind of persuasion. The reasons for considering them apart from what we shall later refer to as "persuasion" are that the materials one needs for reinforcement are unique and the modes of development by which speeches reinforce always amplify more than prove.

Whether his subject is education, physical fitness, or nuclear weapons, a speaker who wishes to reinforce beliefs or feelings tends to limit his search for major ideas to what his hearers already know; and he treats these ideas in ways that are familiar to the listeners. Reinforcing beliefs and feelings, speakers locate their themes by studying the knowledge and attitudes their listeners already possess and develop those themes according to the value systems the hearers already accept. The kind of speaking we are now discussing allows speakers the least intellectual freedom of any customary mode of speech making. This is precisely why speeches to reinforce can be found in all societies no matter how totalitarian their control over men's minds. Even where freedom to change people's minds and freedom to disseminate information disappear, there always remain some approved values which may be extolled and some rejected values to be deplored.

Although the speaker who seeks to reinforce beliefs and feelings is severely limited in what he may use as basic content, his purpose and what he says often have important social functions. Through such speaking, organizations are unified, religious congregations are sustained, and social and political virtues such as civic pride and mutual respect are maintained as active forces. Indeed, the shared values that bind us into social groups form the subjects of most of the important reinforcing communication that occurs. Without reinforcement through public speeches and other media of communication, social bonds would begin to atrophy and any society would begin to drift toward anarchism.

The audience, then, determines on what subjects a speech of reinforcement may be made. Whatever the audience already believes or disbelieves and whatever values they hold in high esteem or plainly reject can become subject matter for speeches of reinforcement. (One can reinforce disbelief or rejection as readily as belief or acceptance.) But not every existing belief or disbelief is appropriate for discussion at any time. Those who attend graduation exercises indicate by that act that their beliefs about education are just then of high importance; hence, the commencement occasion determines that beliefs about education are to be reinforced rather than, say, beliefs concerning what splendid communities the listeners live in. Many parents attending commencement exercises will also be members of business and political groups, but during commencement ceremonies they are unlikely to be strongly conscious of these associations and unready to hear commercial and political values extolled. But the next meeting of the business men's club or political association is likely to be an occasion for a speech reinforcing just such themes. Thus, audiences' beliefs and values define the subjects available to all who speak to reinforce, but the range of these subjects is always further narrowed by the special expectations listeners adopt on specific occasions.

The occasions that call for speeches of reinforcement are generally ceremonial (anniversaries, religious or other observances, ritualistic meetings) and those dedicated to arousing and exhilarating (rallies, pep meetings, "kick off" meetings).

When you have identified what topics are allowed you by the demands of your audience and occasion and when you have selected a speech subject from these options, your next problem is to state your subject sentence in a way that will guide you in research and composition. We have discussed this matter generally in Chapter 6. Here, we need only add that you can help yourself and your listeners if you adopt the following formula for writing subject sentences of this type. Write the words, "When I complete my speech I want the audience to (believe, feel) (more, less) strongly *that* ...." When you compose a clause to follow the word, "that," express the *single* proposition you expect to reinforce. Your finished subject sentence might read: "When I complete my speech I want the audience to believe more strongly that Centerville can be made a popular tourist center."

There are no fundamental differences between these subject sentences for speeches of reinforcement and comparable statements for other persuasive speeches, except that the purpose of a speech to reinforce always indicates that a *degree* of existing belief or feeling is to be changed. If the citizens of Centerville had no previous idea their city might be made a tourist center, the subject sentence we have just used for illustration could not sensibly include the term "more strongly." Without this expression of degree, the sentence would become a statement that defined creation of a new opinion as the objective of speaking.

Except for the limitations we have discussed, the reinforcing speaker's search for ideas differs little from the kind of searching we have discussed in Chapter 5. Any of the attributes we commonly assign to things and people and any of the relationships we commonly assert or argue (see p. 115) can suggest potentially discussable themes for justifying greater or less belief or feeling. There are, however, two special bits of advice that can help you when you aim to reinforce.

The first comes from Aristotle's *Rhetoric* and concerns how ideas are made impressive. Aristotle's advice was that a belief or feeling can be made impressive by connecting it with some familiar "good" such as justice, courage, temperance, grandeur, magnanimity, liberality, gentleness, prudence, or wisdom. His reasoning was that ideas are more or less impressive depending on how much they contribute to or are consistent with these qualities which we all admire. The other item of special advice is: it is better to keep the train of thought simple and uncomplicated than to try to render a central idea impressive in many different ways. Enlargement of the idea to be reinforced is preferable to multiplying its features. In his famous funeral oration commemorating the bravery of Athenians who had died in the first year of the Peloponnesian Wars, Pericles expressed the pith of his whole discourse thus:

> Taking everything together then, I declare that our city is an education to Greece, and I declare that in my opinion each single one of our citizens, in all the manifold aspects of life, is able to show himself the rightful lord and owner of his own person, and do this, moreover, with exceptional grace and exceptional versatility.[3]

---

[3] Thucydides, *The Peloponnesian War*, trans. by Rex Warner (Baltimore: Penguin Books, 1954), p. 119.

His whole address, as Thucydides reports it, merely amplifies these tightly related thoughts concerning the city for which the dead had fought. A lesser speaker might have insisted on discussing the way the heroes died, the justice of the war, the qualities of victories and defeats, and the gratitude of living Athenians—all in a misguided effort to enlarge his listeners' feelings of gratitude to the dead. Pericles wisely chose a single theme and amplified it: Athens' worth ennobles its fallen soldiers.

What makes a speech to reinforce distinctively successful? What you must strive for are freshness and originality in amplification of familiar ideas. To succeed, you will need to offer hitherto unperceived connections between the familiar belief and such "goods" as Aristotle suggested you use. Or, you can point out unobserved attributes of propositions your listeners already believe in. This is what Lincoln did at Gettysburg when he contended that the *substance* of the ceremony was not really to dedicate a burial ground but to "dedicate ourselves." He thus reinforced the feeling that the cemetery was a meaningful national monument by adding a new attribute to the dedication process. Winston Churchill, in a moment of reinforcement during a World War II address, similarily enhanced the admittedly impressive achievement of British aviators in the Battle for Britain. He linked the airmen's small number (*degree*) to the large number (*degree*) of those indebted to them: "Never in the field of human conflict was so much owed by so many to so few."[4] A speaker less adept at reinforcing feelings might have been content to speak in a more usual vein of the airmen's courage. Mr. Churchill did that, but he found another, less familiar attribute of their achievement and thus produced a fresh thought we still quote a third of a century later.

In summary, speaking to reinforce beliefs and feelings is in some ways a confined and confining enterprise. The commitment to reinforce is a commitment to work with subjects already known

---

[4] Speech in the House of Commons, August 20, 1940, quoted in *Voices from Britain*, ed. by Henning Krabbe (London: George Allen & Unwin, 1947), p. 59.

to both speaker and listener. This kind of persuasion is usually ceremonial. Purposiveness and clarity are no less important when reinforcing belief or feeling than in other kinds of speaking; yet, perhaps because they work so much with familiar ideas, speakers aiming at reinforcement are often less precise than they should be in framing their purposes. The search for materials parallels the search for other kinds of speech materials with two deviations: (1) reinforcement requires that subject matter be rendered impressive, hence amplifying is chiefly needed rather than generating new rational justifications; and (2) hitherto unthought-of attributes and relationships are the chief sources of that originality which alone can give vigor to reinforcement and authority to the speaker.

Speaking to Persuade

We now turn from a special form of persuasion to the typical problems of persuasive speaking, in which the speaker aims at altering beliefs, attitudes, feelings, or behavior.

The only realistic standard of excellence in persuasive speaking is: Did the speaker engender as much change as the circumstances, including his own sense of responsibility, permitted? Speakers often wish for changes they cannot completely achieve. They must then settle for less than their desires. Norman Thomas was a constant spokesman and political candidate for the Socialist Party in America for nearly three decades. Though he was never elected to office and won but a tiny proportion of his hearers to his party, he has been repeatedly credited with popularizing political and social reforms later adopted as their own by Democrats and Republicans. It would be absurd to say that such a persuader's achievements were negligible or his public persuasion unsuccessful because he won no office. The only fair question to ask about Mr. Thomas' powers as a persuader is: Did he engender as much change as the unfavorable views of his audiences and his own sense of responsibility permitted? In the absence of extensive rhetorical and sociological research, the general answer must be that Norman Thomas' persuasion was at least creditable, despite his failures at the polls. It is not the *absolute effect* of a persuasive speech that testifies to its excellence, but *the comparison between the actual effect and what was reasonably possible considering all the circumstances.*

What special demands does persuasion place upon you, in addition to the demands characteristic of all public speaking?

Justifying, as well as amplifying, is essential in any attempt at altering beliefs and feelings. And both must have motivational importance for the audience. This ought to be true of all content in all speeches, but it is crucial in persuasion. If hearers are to alter their viewpoints or feelings, their own interests must supply especially strong justifications for change. This point was forcefully expressed by the Scottish rhetorician, George Campbell. His language and psychological theory now seem quaint, but his general point concerning persuasion is unmistakably sound:

> . . . when persuasion is the end, passion also must be engaged. If it is fancy which bestows brilliancy on our ideas, if it is memory which gives them stability, passion doth more, it animates them. Hence they derive spirit and energy. To say that it is possible to persuade without speaking to the passions, is but at best a kind of specious nonsense. The coolest reasoner always in persuading addresseth himself to the passions some way or other. This he cannot avoid doing, if he speak to the purpose. To make me believe it is enough to show me that things are so; to make me act, it is necessary to show that the action will answer some end. That can never be an end to me which gratifies no passion or affection in my nature. You assure me, "It is for my honour." Now you solicit my pride, without which I had never been able to understand the word. You say, "It is for my interest." Now you bespeak my self-love. "It is for the public good." Now you rouse my patriotism. "It will relieve the miserable." Now you touch my pity. So far . . . [is it] from being an unfair method of persuasion to move the passions, that there is no persuasion without moving them.[5]

A twentieth-century psychologist might reject Campbell's technical distinctions among fancy, memory, and "passion," but he would

---

[5] *Philosophy of Rhetoric*, ed. by Lloyd Bitzer (Carbondale, Ill.: Southern Illinois University Press, 1963), Bk. I. Ch. 7, p. 77. Originally published in 1776.

agree that there is no changing the attitudes or feelings of man-kind without engaging the drives or desires that Campbell called "passions." The modern psychologist would agree with Campbell that "the coolest reasoner" must certainly fail to change men's views unless aided by their feelings. This necessity of enlisting active drives and desires is one of the special demands the per-suader's aim imposes on you.

In order that active drives toward belief and action may operate within hearers, it is sometimes necessary for a persuasive speaker to refrain from expressing all that he himself believes. He may even avoid asking for all the opinion change he would really like to attain. The reason is that what men cannot yet understand, what they are not intellectually or emotionally ready to receive, is more likely to trouble them than persuade them. St. Paul's sermon on Mars Hill (pp. 128–130) illustrates how audi-ences' limitations affect what persuasive speakers dare say. Paul deliberately claimed less for his religious doctrines than he might have had his audience of Athenian philosophers been intellectually and emotionally ready to examine his teachings without bewilder-ment. Most persuaders find themselves in comparable situations where they dare not claim all they would like to claim for fear of losing their chance to change *some* beliefs. It might be argued that St. Paul, himself, pressed a mite too far for his hearers when he introduced the doctrine of resurrection of the dead at the close of his sermon. We are told, "Now when they heard of the resur-rection of the dead, some mocked; but others said, 'We will hear you again about this.' "

When he prepares for persuasive speaking, any speaker must also be cautious against being misled by biased sources. All subjects about which we seek to persuade one another are in some degree controversial, and this means there are many sources of informa-tion so strongly committed to one side of the controversy they cannot give us a whole view of the issues and evidence. One does not expect to receive the whole story about a labor dispute at either the labor union headquarters or from officials of the dis-puting corporation. Nor is one likely to get all the facts from hearing the witnesses for only one side in a court case. Less obvious but equally biased sources of information abound on almost all controversial issues.

You need to consult both sides in your research: read *The Nation* and *The National Review*, if your subject involves liberal-conservative controversy in politics; see that you get the positions of union and management, if your subject concerns a labor dispute. Getting both sides will not necessarily give you the whole story. You are likely to come away from this kind of investigation with a good deal of extraneous information. But you will know where opponents on the question differ and where they agree. Where they agree, you may probably accept; where they disagree, you must search for more facts by firsthand investigation and by consulting the most impartial sources available. Using both modes of research you will ultimately acquire a reliable body of material for the construction of arguments.

What we have just said may sound idealistic, but it is practical too. Of all speakers, the inquirer and the persuader must be most jealous of their reputations for integrity. Persuaders, like inquirers, presume to lead and advise. Thereby they place their own reliability at issue. You do not readily accept the advice of people who know less about the matter than you do. So it is with all persuadees. What they especially want from their advisers is consistent evidence that the adviser fully understands and reasons well about the matter at issue, and counsel in their own best interests. A persuader must meet both demands. The salesman who shows he knows his own product but no other becomes a "salesman" only; the salesman who shows he knows his competitors' products well enough to tell you why his is better becomes a persuader in the full sense—a counsellor. Persuasion that recognizes and successfully refutes opposing positions tends to have more durable influence on audiences than purely one-sided presentations. The only exception, experimental evidence indicates, is where the audience already agrees or where it will never be exposed to the other side of the question.[6] These are hardly the typical circumstances of important persuasion.

---

[6] See, for example, C. I. Hovland, I. L. Janis, and H. H. Kelley, *Communication and Persuasion* (New Haven: Yale University Press, 1953), pp. 105–111.

What we have just said about the importance of recognizing opposing views in persuasive speeches implies that effective persuasion normally involves both constructive and refutational discourse. Constructive argument builds up the persuader's side of his subject; refutational argument challenges or otherwise exposes weaknesses in contrary views. The technicalities of developing these two sorts of arguments are better studied in courses devoted specifically to persuasion and argumentation. As a beginning student of public speaking, you can carry out your work if you follow these guidelines in developing constructive and refutational arguments:

1. No matter what motivational justifications you offer for your position in persuasion, you must satisfy your listeners that you have not taken up your position irresponsibly. You must give some kind of evidence that you have taken it for sensible and essentially rational reasons. (Concerning the development of rational supports see Chapter 6, pp. 154–161.)
2. You need to show your listeners why the position you have adopted is more sensible and responsible than other positions they may have heard of (or may hear of in the future). This usually means you must give your audience both rational and self-interest justifications for rejecting alternatives to the position you endorse.
3. The ultimate justification for any position you endorse will be, for your audience at least, your constructive proof that your position is better for them. Hence, the bulk of persuasion is constructive.[7]

One final matter that deserves comment here concerns the nature of persuasion itself. What chiefly distinguishes the persuasive speaker from the informant, inquirer, or entertainer is that his *primary* test in choosing available materials for proof or amplification is always, "Has this piece of potential speech material enough promise or threat for my listeners so I may expect their outlooks to shift a bit because I have used it?" The persuasive speaker is unusually sensitive to George Campbell's previously quoted reminder: "That can never be an end for me which grati-

---

[7] For an excellent, detailed treatment of these responsibilities in argumentation see Douglas Ehninger and Wayne Brockriede, *Decision by Debate* (New York: Dodd, Mead, 1963), especially pp. 81–95 and 252–266.

fies no passion or affection in my nature." The informant, the inquirer, or the entertainer may select and use speech material solely because the material is a logical part of what he is talking about; the persuader, however, dares not stop his search until he finds materials that will make a psychological contribution toward altering human experience.

Speaking to Entertain

When a public speaker makes it his purpose to entertain, he commits himself to a speech that will hold attention agreeably by diverting listeners' thoughts from matters of high seriousness to less demanding things. Often, though not invariably, he adopts the task of providing amusement. Another way of defining an entertaining speech is to say it is a speech that so completely interests the audience they have almost no sense of working to acquire its full significance.

Notice that both definitions of *entertain* imply that entertainment may be amusing but is not invariably so. We all recognize that a first-rate travelogue can be entertaining but not necessarily amusing. Likewise, many narratives and descriptions entertain us with varying uses of humor. The public speaker who is asked to give "an entertaining speech" should recognize that he may elect either a humorous or a sober subject and still hope to entertain.

Any subject—any theme—that will hold attention agreeably and in a diverting rather than highly serious way is a potential subject for an entertaining public speech. It is not the topic that distinguishes the entertaining speech from others we have discussed in this chapter. The *treatment* of the subject matter is the distinguishing mark; the treatment must hold attention agreeably.

Typical occasions for speeches of entertainment allow extraordinary latitude in choosing speech subjects. These occasions are usually either convivial gatherings or those where no stronger motivation than casual curiosity has brought the audience together. The audiences chiefly wish their speakers to reinforce the convivial spirit with diverting experience to be shared by all. Almost any subject in suitable taste, that can by any stretch of reason be connected with the common bonds joining the auditors, will meet their demands.

On many occasions, casual curiosity is the chief reason for the listeners' presence. Unless the speaker is known as a humorist, such occasions usually call for light, straightforward treatment of whatever subject the speaker is qualified to discuss. To see the difference between the demands of these occasions and audiences and those that confront informative speakers, consider two familiar situations. The Rotary Club invites the public to an evening meeting at which Mr. So-and-So will talk about his recent visit to India. A sorority announces that Miss Blank who won a gold medal in Olympic competition will speak to the public. Plainly Mr. So-and-So's trip and Miss Blank's Olympic achievement prescribe each speaker's general subject, but how will the subject matter be treated? The expectations of the audiences that will attend the meetings will usually dictate that the speakers prepare divertingly informative talks. Few listeners will be deeply informed or consumingly interested in either India or Olympic competition. Many will come just to see the traveler or the champion. The tasks of the speakers, then, will be to present their special information in popular terms to satisfy their listeners' casual curiosity. This usually means giving special prominence to whatever is most colorful, most human, most tantalizing about the subject. Whatever discourse has these characteristics is almost certain to be entertaining. It may not be as objective or as comprehensive as a less entertaining speech on India or Olympic competition prepared with a purpose of informing.

From what we have said, one may draw several important inferences. *Speeches that entertain differ from other speeches primarily in the way subject matter is treated.* The more agreeable and diverting the amplification and delivery of ideas, the more entertaining a speech will be. The difference between informing, inquiring, and persuading on the one hand and entertaining on the other is chiefly a difference of manner, not of matter. A second inference is that *to be entertaining a speaker must regard the pleasure of his audience more highly than the logic of his subject.* This does not mean that to be entertaining one must be inaccurate; on the contrary, accuracy at least in some details is essential to entertainment. What arrests us is usually some disproportion of attention to specific details: detailed attention to the colorful garb of Indian women (without much attention to, say, the social significance of their dress) or ludicrously detailed attention to the rigors of training for Olympic competition (without much attention to the results of it). The entertaining speaker must remember that the interesting *parts* of his subject are often more important than the *whole.* It is in this sense that he sacrifices the logic of his subject to the pleasure of his audience. A third inference to be drawn about speaking to entertain is that *while good humor is always entertaining, entertainment does not necessarily hinge upon the presence of humor.* This inference has been amplified by our earlier examples.

Since it is the *treatment* of material rather than the subject matter that makes a speech entertaining, you will want to give special attention to stylistic resources in developing any speech to entertain. (See Chapter 10, pp. 274–313.) However, to create entertaining language, you first find ideas that lend themselves to entertaining treatment. Once again, a review of the attributes things and people may possess and the relationships that may exist among these attributes (p. 115) can suggest potentially entertaining thoughts. Any attribute of anything has potentially humorous possibilities if examined in enough detail or distorted in some fashion. The cartoonist, Rube Goldberg, spent a career reducing the attributes of *possibility* and *feasibility* to absurdity. He depicted fantastically complicated and transparently unreliable machinery for waking people in the morning or closing windows against rain. George Bernard Shaw played trenchantly but amusingly with the attribute of *degree* and with *causality* when addressing students at the University of Hong Kong:

> That war [World War I] was made by people with university education. There are really two dangerous classes in the world. There are the half-educated, who have destroyed one-half of

civilization, and there are the wholly educated, who have nearly completely destroyed the world.[8]

The Reverend Richard Whately, Anglican Bishop of Dublin and also an able rhetorician, developed an entertaining refutation to arguments denying that Jesus lived by applying the tests of *possibility, causality,* and *existence* too strictly to the life of Napoleon. He thereby "proved" that Napoleon could not have lived.[9] Mark Twain once addressed the Lotos Club in New York City soon after returning from England where he had been awarded an honorary doctorate by Oxford University. Members of the Lotos Club insisted Mark Twain put on and display the red-grey academic gown worn by Oxford doctors, which he did. Then he toyed with the gown's attributes of being red and being a "gown":

> I like that gown. I always did like red. The redder it is the better I like it. I was born for a savage. Now, whoever saw any red like this? There is no red outside the arteries of an archangel that could compare with this. I know you all envy me. I am going to have luncheon shortly with ladies—just ladies. I will be the only lady of my sex present, and I shall put on this gown and make those ladies look dim.[10]

Any subject—idea, object, or person—possesses diverting attributes and diverting relationships to other ideas, objects, or persons. These are what the entertaining speaker seeks in his preparation. Locating them is the first step toward treating the subject in an entertaining manner.

Three lesser and interrelated points must also be made concerning the content of speeches that entertain. They can be stated briefly, but their importance is considerable.

---

[8] "Universities and Education," delivered February 12, 1933. Reported in *The New York Times*, March 26, 1933. Note Shaw's exaggeration—one of the most common techniques for creating humor.

[9] *Historic Doubts Relative to Napoleon Bonaparte* (1819).

[10] Last "Lotos Club Speech," January 11, 1908. From the text and incidental remarks as published in *The Family Mark Twain* (New York: Harper and Brothers, 1935), pp. 1175–1178.

1. *Only in entertainment is it sometimes advantageous to make no sense.* Sometimes the nonsensical bears just enough similarity to the sensible to amuse us. Here lies much of the fun of Lewis Carroll's *Alice in Wonderland,* and comedian Danny Kaye's outrageous double talk.

2. *What entertains in speaking is that which is quickly and easily understood.* Private jokes or asides and private experience are not entertaining. In entertaining speech all meaning is public —familiar and easily grasped. Even nonsense must contain a semblance to sense, or the response is not amusement, only bafflement. It is true that working puzzles can be entertaining, but puzzling speech is not. The reason is that speech moves swiftly through time leaving listeners no opportunity to work the puzzles as they appear.

3. *An entertaining speaker may properly disregard or even do violence to the natural logic of his subject, but he will please his hearers best if his speech has some kind of thematic logic.* This will give the audience the satisfaction of having been pleased by *something,* not just some *things.* Even the night club gag man recognizes this audience demand for structure in entertainment. If artful, he will separate his mother-in-law jokes from his insurance-company jokes, giving each group the status of a thought unit within his patter. As though further adapting to the preferences of modern audiences, more and more comedians now develop entire monologues around single themes treated humorously. In so doing, they emulate the practice of the best among entertaining speech makers.

The basic test of a speech to entertain is: Did it divertingly please the audience? Achieving this goal does not depend upon what subject you choose or on whether you are funny or serious. It depends upon whether you ply your listeners with colorful, humanly interesting, tantalizing ideas about some subject concerning which they already knew something or are mildly curious.

Entertainment can be used without being the dominant objective of a speech. Comprehensive speeches of serious intent certainly can contain subordinate units of entertainment, provided they do not becloud the central content of otherwise serious speech.

In closing our three-chapter survey of how content for speeches is discovered and selected we have examined the special opportunities and difficulties that arise when you set out to inform, induce inquiry, reinforce beliefs or feelings, persuade, or entertain. We have seen that some of these special purposes limit the range of ideas from which you may draw content, and that each kind of purpose imposes its special manner of treating ideas after they are found. If any generalization is to be drawn from our survey in this chapter, it must be that you cannot be wholly successful until you have determined your specific purpose in speaking. Without understanding your task in communication, you cannot know what materials are useful to you nor can you know precisely how to treat them.

It would be an error to infer from what we have said here that mixed purposes never occur in good speeches. Informing, persuading, and entertaining, for example, can all be found in almost any first-rate speech. But if the speech is first-rate, one purpose will dominate the whole composition, nor will there be any confusion about which purpose dominates any *part* of the speech. If your primary intention is to persuade, your informing sections will have the features of informative speaking but will plainly serve your dominant persuasive intention by providing a base for it. Entertaining sub-sections will provide momentary diversion without distorting your information-giving processes or demeaning the importance of your persuasive content.

Exercises

WRITTEN

1. Write a brief essay on differences between speech materials that "prove" propositions and those that "amplify" ideas.
2. Choose a general topic such as "The Cost of Living" or "Clothing" and outline three different kinds of speeches that could be given on some aspect of the topic. For example, outline a

persuasive, an informative, and an entertaining speech on "The Cost of Food Is Rising."

3. Read a speech of your own choosing and write a critique in which you:
    a. Identify what seems to have been the speaker's dominant purpose in speaking.
    b. Identify any sub-sections of the speech in which the purpose of communication seems to have shifted temporarily (e.g., from a dominant purpose of informing to a subordinate purpose of entertaining or persuading).
    c. Evaluate the speaker's success in making shifts from primary to secondary aims and back to his primary aim. (Did he indicate to his listeners that he was shifting purpose? Did he indicate why he was doing this? How successful was he in keeping his dominant purpose clear despite temporary shifts? Was the total impact of his speech strengthened or weakened by temporary changes in purpose? If weakened, how might this effect have been avoided?)

ORAL

1. Prepare and present an oral report on the kinds of content used in some speech of entertainment you have read or heard. Indicate also what special treatment was given to this content. (Speeches by Mark Twain, Will Rogers, or speakers of their kind might be chosen for study in connection with this exercise.)

2. Prepare and present a brief talk on why it is unwise for those who speak to inform or to induce inquiry to color their speech content with personal opinions or value judgments.

3. Prepare and present an informative talk in which you assess why some allegedly good speaker failed in a major attempt at persuasion. (William Jennings Bryan, Norman Thomas, Adlai Stevenson, Richard Nixon, or Barry Goldwater might be examined as presidential campaign speakers; or Winston Churchill's "Sinews of Peace," delivered at Fulton, Missouri, March 5, 1946, might furnish a case study for use in this exercise.)

—◦◦⦃ 8 ⦄◦•— *Disposition:*

Organizing Materials

Therefore when the point for decision and the arguments which must be devised for the purpose of reaching a decision have been diligently discovered by the rules of art, and studied with careful thought, then, and not until then, the other parts of the oration are to be arranged in proper order.

Cicero, *De Inventione*[1]

In his book *The Image*, Kenneth E. Boulding points out that the dominant view of physical processes postulates that there is an omnipresent tendency "for things to run down." He continues, "The end of the universe, according to this picture, will be a thin, uniform soup without form. It is toward this comfortless end that all physical processes are moving." By contrast, Boulding insists, the record of history exhibits another tendency, "the tendency for the rise of organization." In support of this view he points out:

> It is the capacity for organizing information into large and complex images which is the chief glory of our species. . . . Our image of time . . . goes far beyond that of the most intelligent of lower animals, mainly because of our capacity for language and for record. . . . Closely associated with the time structure of his [man's] image is the image of the structure of relation-

---

[1] Cicero, *De Inventione*, trans. by H. M. Hubbell (Cambridge, Mass.: Harvard University Press, 1960), p. 39, Bk 1, Ch. 14.

ships. Because we are aware of time, we are also aware of cause and effect, of contiguity and succession of cycles and repetition.[2]

The organization of an oral message is the application of this distinctive human capacity for organizing our environment to accommodate our views to those of other people. This is more easily said than done.

The thought of a swimming pool, in your mind, may be veritably encrusted with what are *for you* related memories of friendships made while relaxing beside the pool; pleasing sensations of cool water on hot days; and, perhaps, of cook-outs and song after sunset. But you can never implant this cluster of remembrances instantaneously in anyone else's mind. The elements of the cluster must be detached from one another. They must be verbalized in some sequence that will enable someone else to create out of his own experiences a cluster of images and sensations comparable to your own. You must verbalize so that connections in the cluster are revealed and so that the sequence emphasizes these connections. Certainly, the more special or private the relationships you perceive, the more difficult it will be for you to convey those relationships in familiar, public terms. Some thoughts and sensations are so highly personal that we almost never succeed in communicating them. One reason is that we cannot, through language at least, line up the aspects of these sensations in any way that exhibits all of them in precisely the interrelationships that make them distinct as experience. Try, for example, to express in words what it feels like to swallow a mouthful of ice-cold water on a day when it is 100° in the shade and you haven't had a drink for three hours. This is a problem for poets, not artisans in public speaking.

Demands for Organization

Happily, most matters about which we normally make public speeches can be verbalized in structured forms that meaningfully

---

[2] (Ann Arbor: University of Michigan Press, 1956), p. 25. See Chapter 2, "The Image in the Theory of Organization." Used by permission.

convey their internal nature and significance. As Boulding says, the fact that man has a conception of the relationships we call time, cause, effect, contiguity, cyclical succession, and repetition makes it possible to communicate at least the basic natures of the thoughts we acquire. Even listeners whose perceptions are not efficient can see connections and relationships if speakers organize their thoughts with careful regard for the patterns all men are accustomed to perceiving. A speaker must invariably remember, however, that (1) listeners do not take in as much detail as readers, so he must show relationships among ideas plainly—sometimes obviously; (2) the object of all effort to organize ideas for public speech is to transform the shape of what the speaker thinks into shapes that a particular audience will be able to recognize; (3) as Cicero indicates in the quotation at the head of this chapter, it is foolish to try to organize the ideas of a speech before most of those ideas have been located and the specific purpose of the speech has been identified.

Audiences insist that they be able to understand what a speaker says. Much of their insistence is an expression of man's unique wish to reduce chaos through organization. This need is satisfied by such perceptions as seeing the interrelationships among ideas; seeing which ideas are primary and which are subsidiary; detecting the rationale behind the over-all pattern of a speech. Whoever departs from the order of thought anticipated by his audience, or from an apparently logical order of thoughts, had better explain why he does so, otherwise his hearers will find the flow of thought chaotic and possibly suspect the speaker of deliberately trying to mislead. When listeners cannot make sense of what they hear, the chances are that the speaker is losing his way and is in danger of losing his audience.

Listeners also lose interest in what is said to them when discourse does not seem to be advancing toward a psychologically meaningful goal. Just because they are human beings with a need to organize, listeners demand progression and a sense of constructive variety which produces cumulative, psychologically satisfying effects. A speech, then, must build, point by point. Somewhere a climax must be reached. This high point is usually near the end of the discourse, but it may and sometimes does occur earlier.

In either case it is psychologically satisfying if points along the way are given time, detailed development, and intensity which indicate their relative weights within the total structure. Listeners anticipate that somewhere in your speech, all the necessary facts and opinions will be in, all arguments will have been developed to the point of acceptability. They expect, in short, that all roads will lead to Rome. In this they are simply displaying the chief glory of their species.

Not every decision about the organization of oral communication derives from the nature of audiences. A speaker does well to evaluate his own response to the structure of his ideas. If his proposed pattern for organizing his discourse is so complicated he cannot maintain his grasp of it, he probably has made a poor choice of organizational procedures. Weak organization is often a main cause for a speaker's lack of confidence in himself and his materials. Patterns of thought which seem natural are most easily remembered. Only when the speaker is satisfied that each piece of supporting material is properly placed is he able to proceed with assurance.

Speech materials often impose specific patterns of organization upon both audience and speaker. Once material is discovered and gathered, it requires sorting. Such sorting may show that anecdotes, questions, examples, and statistics need to be grouped by topic or argument, spatially or chronologically.

As he moves through the period of invention which we have discussed in Chapters 5, 6, and 7, the speaker may envision the proportionate weight in time he would like to give to a particular point, yet when he assembles his data to give them place and relationship, he may find no support for his pet hypothesis. He may be startled to find that he still has little to say of this matter by way of amplification or support. Then he has the choice of discarding the seemingly weak contention or of backtracking to search out further support. The second procedure will not help if he has thoroughly researched his subject in the first place.

More often, a speaker finds he has too much material for the available speaking time. Upon sifting and sorting his data he may discover that he has support for twelve or thirteen main ideas.

He may then discard those ideas which are least fruitful, those least likely to gain audience acceptance, or those least necessary to his purpose. On the other hand, he may decide to regroup and reorganize his material. Very often when material seems to yield too many main points the problem is that broad ideas are being mistaken for lesser ones which should serve as support or amplification.

The processes of elimination or reorganization may seem painful. You may find you have to cut your speech until the very moment of delivery. Should you discover that your speaking time has been encroached upon by unforeseeable circumstances, you must sacrifice still more material without destroying form. Such was the case when Franklin Roosevelt found it necessary to cut his 1932 speech accepting the presidential nomination. The plane in which he flew from Albany to Chicago was hours late, which meant that he would appear before an audience wearied by waiting to hear him. He wisely decided that the speech would have to be shorter than he had planned. Samuel Rosenman, who assisted him with the speech, writes:

> With each radio report, we were falling further and further behind schedule; and more and more paragraphs came out of the acceptance speech. This lopping off of material on which we had worked so long and so hopefully was a painful process. I know that there were some jewels dropped on the airplane floor that day. It is likely, though, that the cutting process hurt us more than it did the speech.[3]

Such may be your feeling as you discard materials. Yet, rejection and red-pencilling will often result in conciseness and sharper focus. To drop a quotation or fact does not always mar the whole message. Often we use too many words or amplify too much. The tightening that comes from excision will usually enhance the speech and add to its organic unity.

Should you choose to regroup your materials, you will find you need to discover a new rationale, a new set of topics. Often

---

[3] Samuel I. Rosenman, *Working with Roosevelt* (New York: Harper & Brothers, 1952), p. 75.

this regrouping is less difficult than it at first seems. Many good speakers insist that the fewer the points in a speech, the better. If you are giving a short speech, you ordinarily ought to assume that you have time to develop three or four main points at most.

You may find that by slicing your material another way those twelve or thirteen points will fit under three or four main heads. What seemed main points may in reality be only sub-points or may be made to operate as sub-points with good effect. Again you will keep the audience in mind if you proceed wisely, for you will realize that two or three points acceptably substantiated are more valuable in achieving your purpose than a half-dozen points lightly touched and dropped.

The arrangement of main points according to strength also deserves serious consideration. When you have decided upon three or four points to be amplified or supported, questions arise as to placement. Knowing that audiences are likely to pay closer attention and to be least tired during the early part of a speech argues for putting your strongest point first. But knowing that listeners are most likely to remember the ideas they have heard most recently argues for placing your strongest point last. Despite numerous experiments, the bases on which you should choose between these alternatives remain unknown.[4] All you can be sure of is that the first and last positions in any series are more impressive than the others. Therefore, it is sensible to place ideas of lesser importance in the intermediate positions. Experienced speakers employing three points favor placing them in 1-3-2 or 2-3-1 orders of strength. In dealing with four points they favor 1-3-4-2; 1-4-3-2; 2-3-4-1 or 2-4-3-1 orders of strength. Your final decision ought to rest on whether special features of content or situation lead you to judge primacy or recency most important in eliciting the response you want from your particular audience —and at what moment you want or need the response.

The materials of a speech may, upon occasion, dictate a particular structural pattern. Speeches explaining procedures exem-

---

[4] See Ernest Thompson, "Some Effects of Message Structure on Listeners' Comprehension," *Speech Monographs*, XXXIV (1967), 51–57.

plify such dictation. A demonstrator can hardly demonstrate at whim. A vacuum cleaner cannot pick up lint before it is turned on, and a picture cannot be painted before the colors are mixed. A chemistry professor performing an experiment before a class must follow the order the experiment dictates. He cannot depart far from this pattern without being off on a tangent. In all these cases the path of development is determined mainly by the material.

While we usually think of organization or disposition with respect to the over-all pattern of a speech, the principles of clear organization also operate within the various points of a discourse. If you use narrative, chronological order is almost inescapable. Interruptions of narrative for expression of personal opinion are almost always out of place for they divert attention from the main movement of thought. Yet, there may be circumstances where spontaneous insertion of definitions or other clarifying detail is necessary if you are to adapt to the audience. The questions to be asked about any break in an established order of ideas are: "Is this departure relevant? Will this deviation from the thought pattern help to achieve my purpose?"

Occasions and settings influence organization of ideas less often than do audience, speaker, and material. The occasion may necessitate initial acknowledgments or personal greetings, but these are really audience adaptations. The setting may also narrow your choice among over-all patterns under certain circumstances. For example, a Washington's birthday celebration may call for a eulogy of George Washington. Speakers have found that eulogies are successful when the praise of the man is set forth by recounting incidents in his life or when the speech is organized around his traits of character. More obvious structural adjustments made for the sake of the occasion can be seen when speakers depart from a pattern because the occasion itself is unexpectedly changed by some distracting occurrence such as the rattle of jack hammers outside the window, a sudden failure in the lighting system, or the unexpected appearance of an important personage. But even here, the modification is as much a matter of audience adaptation as of adaptation to the occasion.

So we can see that the disposition of ideas, their orderly arrangement, is not random. Organizational choices are wisely made only after careful consideration of the audience's expectations; the speaker's capabilities; the nature of the data used to achieve the speaker's purpose; and, incidentally, the circumstances prevailing at the time of delivery.

Main Components of a Speech

As Plato noted in the *Phaedrus,* a speech is like the human body in that it has a head, a torso, and feet—meaning an introduction, a body, and a conclusion. In most cases the body, often called the "development" or "discussion," is the largest of the three parts. The conclusion is normally the smallest. Introductions may vary in length or may under certain circumstances be omitted altogether. The proportions of these parts depend upon the subject matter, the occasion, and the speaker himself, but most often they depend upon the audience's expectations and motivations. To carry Plato's analogy further, a speech also contains the equivalents of neck and ankles, which link the three main portions. These linking parts are major transitions. Normally, then, as in other works of art such as plays, poems, musical compositions, a speech has a beginning, a middle, an end, and transitional elements. We shall consider these separately.

INTRODUCTIONS

The introduction to your speech should fulfill demands made by all of the elements in public speaking. Since it is a beginning, it must (1) attract the initial, favorable attention of the audience; (2) provide necessary background for the audience so they may comprehend the remainder; (3) be suitable to the occasion; and (4) contribute to your ease during a crucial period of adjustment. In addition, the introduction ought to be coordinated with and must relate to what follows. It is not a preamble or prelude without relation to the rest of the speech.

At the outset, you must gain attention in such a way that your listeners will want to go on listening. Any of the methods for achieving attention may be employed, but the most useful ways to draw attention are by referring to something familiar or something novel. You may start with a reference to the occasion, to its purpose, or to other features about which the audience already knows. You may begin with greetings, a familiar quotation, an anecdote, or analogy. Tradition may dictate what you will say at the beginning. Or you may need to awaken the audience by sharpening the focus of their attention. Where this is so, unusual facts, strange stories, shocking or startling assertions, unfamiliar statistics, telegraphic headline fragments, or kaleidoscopic elements of a situation may enable you to create curiosity or suspense. Reference to your own interests and needs, especially if they are similar to those of your audience, may create common ground and cause your audience to want to listen. A modest statement of your qualifications for speaking on the subject you have chosen may also make your listeners want to hear more.

Most audiences want to be given reasons for listening. They are always ready to ask, "Why should *I* listen? What's in this for *me?*" And, often, they want directions about what to listen for. They want to be invited to pay attention. The ways in which you may touch off an audience's powers of concentration are limitless, yet none is truly useful unless it will at once seize attention and favorably dispose your audience to what follows.

It is often essential for you to provide background knowledge your hearers must have from the outset. It may be necessary for you to provide preliminary information about new materials, details you will use in amplification, or the relationships between main points and your central proposition. Such basic information may be new or it may be old. It may be provided by way of review. Such information will furnish a context for what you are going to say.

You may find it necessary to define unfamiliar terms to be used later in your discussion or to define familiar terms to insure that the audience understands special meanings you assign to them. A short, historical review of facts may help. In persuasive speeches where argument from precedent is involved but not as a main point, where your subject is one that listeners have not thought a great deal about, it is especially useful to employ such a history of the question.

Definitions and histories are sometimes supplemented or replaced by a statement of those matters you will or will not deal with in the body of your speech. Items so singled out because you intend to pass them over or because they seem irrelevant are often called "waived materials." You simply state that you will not consider them and give your listeners your reasons. Iteration of main points to be developed later by amplification or support is sometimes called "initial partition," especially useful when your audience needs to know the path you intend to take. Of course, you would not offer such statements if you wished to preserve suspense or feared that revealing your entire plan so early might make some listeners defensive. Initial partitioning is not a useful introductory tactic in speeches developed inductively or in those designed for unfriendly audiences. In such speeches even the subject sentence is often withheld until the end.

In speeches constructed on a deductive pattern you ought to include the subject sentence of your speech as a final item of the introduction, or as an initial item in the body of the speech. As we have already said, the subject sentence is delayed in most indirect sequences. Wherever it appears, it ought to be carefully expressed in a single, economical, unambiguous sentence as was pointed out in Chapters 3 and 6.

Not all the items we have mentioned will be included in any one speech introduction. Your time limit and what your listeners need to know before you proceed will dictate how much and what kinds of orientation materials you will offer.

The introduction is the one part of the speech which, given the right circumstances, may be omitted altogether. It is not necessary if an audience is already attentive and interested in your subject, if they expect you to speak, if they already possess the background information, if they are highly motivated, or if the occasion exerts no special pressures. College professors often dispense with introductions after the first few lectures. They judge their audiences oriented and motivated and so introductory remarks become superfluous. You, however, should use caution in deciding to omit an introduction. Rarely can an introduction be omitted when speaking to an audience for the first time; never, when your audience is not entirely ready to pay attention from the very outset.

THE BODY OF THE SPEECH

The body of a speech comprises (1) the main points, (2) the material which supports or amplifies these points, and (3) transitional phrases or sentences.

Earlier we discussed the sorting and sifting of materials by which you arrive at main points and determine their psychological weighting and placement for the purpose of achieving climax. When these stages of preliminary analysis have been completed and you know your main points you next word the main ideas.

Where possible, main points ought to be worded in parallel phrasings to provide balance in structure. They should also be worded to elicit the responses the speaker seeks from his audience. Main points for informative speeches to relate, relay or review should be simple, clear assertions. In speeches of inquiry the main points are often worded as questions which are then answered with information or explored. Main points for persuasive speeches should be assertions slanted in wording to express the speaker's point of view and to support the main proposition embodied in the subject sentence. Main points should be "contentions" or "reasons" closely linked to the subject sentence so that they become the foundation stones upon which the core idea rests. Main points for speeches of reinforcement are framed in essentially the same way as those for speeches of persuasion. For speeches designed to entertain, main points again take the form of assertions.

In all cases determination of the final form which your main points will take rests upon the interrelated demands of the material, the audience, your habitual mode of expression. The ways in which these main points are arranged into patterns will be discussed later in this chapter.

TRANSITIONS[5]

Since your listeners cannot easily review what you have said after it has been spoken, as they might turn back and re-read the pages in a book, you will need to provide careful transitions if your speech is to be clear at all points. Transitions are words, phrases, sentences, or groups of sentences which join ideas together. If clear and smoothly worded, they contribute to the organic unity of your speech.

Transitions are like signposts, which tell your audience where you have been, where you are, or where you intend to go. They will most frequently occur upon the completion of a main idea and before you move on to the next one, but you may also need them as connections between subsidiary points or phrases leading to the ideas in single sentences.

Transitions are called "internal summaries" when they link ideas and also review key thoughts. Good internal summaries also point ahead to the next idea to be handled. Internal summaries commonly use such wordings as:

> Since we have already considered that . . . , we should adopt . . .
> In addition to . . . there is another outstanding reason (element, factor, consideration, fact). . . .
> We have seen . . . , yet it remains for us to observe. . . .
> But . . . is only one important viewpoint. Equally as important is. . . .
> Since . . . is so, what can be said of . . . ? (Questions, it may be noted, can often be useful as transitions.)

Where the thought connection to be emphasized is between sub-points, or where the thought relationships are easy to comprehend, a phrase or even a single word such as "so" or "yet"

---

[5] This section is based in part upon an explanation of transitions originally written by Harry P. Kerr, Harvard University. Used by permission.

may be adequate to tie ideas together. Some examples of such phrasings are:

More important than all this is the fact that. . . .
In contrast to. . . .
Looked at from a different angle the problem seems to be. . . .
This last point raises a question: . . . ?
What was the result? Just this. . . .
On the other hand. . . .
When this has been done. . . .
And so you can see that. . . .

Seek variety in transitions. Avoid using only stock phrases or repeating the same few phrases over and over. While you should not be afraid to be obvious in your transitions, you should avoid being too brief. A mark of the unpolished speaker is his tendency to use only "and" or "also" as transitions. He gives the impression of having tacked his ideas together, of having joined them to one another crudely. Yet he is in a better position than the speaker who melts from point to point or vaguely gropes his way from topic to topic. Good transitions (1) show that the speaker is moving from one idea to another, (2) demarcate completed ideas, (3) indicate the relationships between the ideas involved, and (4) remind the speaker of his sequence of thought.

CONCLUSIONS

The final segment of your speech, its conclusion, also performs functions demanded by the audience, the material, the occasion, and yourself. In this segment the audience normally expects (1) a restatement of your core idea or (2) a summing up of main points which clarify or prove your thesis. Both restatement and summary may be needed. Almost any body of material needs a final rounding out that fuses the subject matter with the speaker's intent. To emphasize a detail or simply to fade into silence obscures meaning. Neither audience nor speakers should feel at the end of a speech that they have been left hanging, that the speech ended too abruptly, or that the subject is still up in the air. The audience should know that the speech is finished, and the speaker should feel satisfied that he has accomplished his purpose and produced an intended final impact. This does not mean that the final sentence of a speech ought always to be a restatement or summary. True, recapitulation is the main function of most conclusions, but the last sentences of a speech are often strongest if devised to challenge the audience to further thought or action, or if the closing words operate as a coda to the central theme. The final sentences may echo the beginning sentences or constitute a return to a text or refrain, thus providing a frame for the entire composition. A "thank you" at the very end of a speech may detract from the central idea and an otherwise strong final impression. Indeed, any remarks of appreciation used as last sentences ought to be carefully considered before inclusion since they may destroy the focus of an otherwise effective conclusion.

Introduction, subject sentence, body, transitions, and conclusion will, with rare exceptions, be parts of every speech you will deliver, though they may be cast in different designs from speech to speech. It remains for us to consider the most common structures or designs that speakers employ in arranging materials.

Usable Patterns of Organization[6]

Four conditions largely will determine the most appropriate pattern for a given public speaking situation. As a speaker you ought to consider (1) the particular type and degree of response you seek to elicit from the audience; (2) whether the audience is favorably, unfavorably, or apathetically disposed toward your subject, your central idea, and you as a speaker; (3) how much

---

[6] The descriptions of the cause-effect, problem-solution, withheld proposal, and open proposal patterns in this section are based upon explanations originally written by James A. Wood of the University of Texas, El Paso. Donald E. Williams, University of Florida, prepared the original explanation of the reflective sequence. Used by permission.

knowledge your listeners possess about your subject; (4) how you can best relate your specific purpose to the pertinent interests and desires of your audience.

The standard patterns commonly used in structuring ideas in speeches include: (1) chronological, (2) spatial, (3) topical, (4) ascending and descending orders, (5) causal, (6) problem-solution or disease-remedy, (7) withheld proposal or indirect sequence, (8) open proposal or direct sequence, (9) reflective sequence or pattern of inquiry, (10) Monroe's motivated sequence, and (11) elimination order. Each is explained in some detail below.

Patterns may be thought of as primarily logical or primarily psychological. The chronological, spatial, topical, causal, problem-solution and reflective sequences are structures which may be viewed as primarily logical. Ascending and descending orders, withheld- and open-proposal sequences, elimination order, and Monroe's motivated sequence are methods which may be considered primarily psychological. The reflective sequence and Monroe's sequence are at once logical and psychological in that they adapt material to audiences psychologically by offering it in a problem-solution structure.

We make these distinctions to show you that psychological patterns of audience adaptation may be superimposed upon logical patterns. For example, ascending or descending orders may come into play as you arrange ideas topically or spatially. In like manner, elimination order may be employed in treating causes, effects, or possible solutions. In some instances two psychological orders can be used in handling a particular logical arrangement. For example, ascending and withheld-proposal orders may be used as you develop a topical pattern. Patterning ideas is not an either-or affair; it is a matter of clarifying psychological and logical relationships by adding the meanings of various structural systems to the basic meanings of speech content.

You should also bear in mind that a pattern need not be followed rigidly or in its entirety to be useful as a general scheme for organizing the materials of your speech. It may be used for the organization of the whole speech or for only a particular segment. For example, you might have a chronologically arranged section within the introduction to a speech with an over-all problem-solution arrangement; or, you might have a cause-effect pattern for the problem section of a problem-solution speech. Generally speaking, an introduction will need to be organized independently of the body of a speech and the conclusion is likely to be arranged to reflect the pattern of organization adopted in the body.

CHRONOLOGICAL PATTERN

The chronological pattern is a time order, relating occurrences in the sequence in which they happened or giving directions in the order they are to be followed. The material of a speech will often dictate this kind of ordering. Chronology, an order most useful in recounting events, is almost mandatory in narration. Chronological patterns may be used in all kinds of speeches. They are most often used in connection with informative purposes. This pattern often meets audience demands for comprehensible order and interestingness. A time sequence usually admits of climactic development, of arousing curiosity and creating suspense. Segments of speeches chronologically developed can be found in the narrations of circumstances leading to crime in Clarence Darrow's famous summation at the trial of Loeb and Leopold, or in Daniel Webster's classic speech for the prosecution in the Knapp-White murder case. Examples of entire speeches developed chronologically include many eulogies, speeches of nomination, historical lectures, demonstrations, and instructional discourses.

One weakness of chronological patterning is that such important considerations as cause, effect, desirability, form, cannot easily be emphasized without interrupting the movement-in-time that gives chronology its chief interest value.

SPATIAL PATTERN

The spatial pattern is, as the name implies, a structure based on the relationships of the parts of a whole as they exist in space.

In using such a pattern, you proceed systematically in your description of how something looks or functions. Normally you will describe from left to right, top to bottom, bottom to top, or front to back. Sometimes you will describe by moving from that portion at the center to those on the periphery. For instance, you might describe the control panel in an airplane by pointing first to those centered instruments most often used, then move out toward the surrounding instruments which are less frequently used. You would then be using a pattern of descending importance which happens here to become identical with the pattern of spatial description. In all uses of spatial arrangement you will need to mention each part or aspect according to *plan*; haphazard coverage disturbs understanding of spatial relationships.

Spatial structure is especially useful in speeches of information and in those parts of any speech where it is essential to provide information. A fire extinguisher might be described from top to bottom, a painting from right to left, the floor plan of a house from front to back or story to story. The order in which to proceed when describing spatially will ordinarily be up to you. Your decision on which space portion to take up first ought to hinge on your estimation of how you can provide the greatest clarity for your audience while highlighting the important relationships among parts. If these standards leave you more than one good way of describing spatially, choose the alternative that is easier for you to present.

TOPICAL PATTERN

The topical pattern is really one in which there is no easily identifiable speech structure. The label "topical" is affixed to those organizational schemes which we cannot otherwise account for. Some use the label "classification order" to denote that some kind of orderly categorization accounts for the patterning. Some would say topical patterns are those which naturally arise from the subject matter. Others, among them Walter and Scott, say it is a pattern evolving out of the natural parts of the subject, its aspects, types, or qualities.[7] The word "topical" gives us a clue. If there is pattern, it is arrived at by finding that no standard pattern suitably orders the data, so we turn to invention. We invent a pattern suitable to unique and striking effects. We ask ourselves where the places are to which we go for argument or clarification and we come up with such an answer as: "We often look at social, political, or economic aspects of arguments." Thus we arrive at a *special* classification of materials. It is only one of many such schemes of organizing data. Another might have been: public interests vs. private interests. Thus, we think of the topics we might use, select from them; and they, as we choose to arrange them, become the bases for organizing the ideas in a speech. A topical pattern is an arbitrary grouping of themes pertinent to a particular subject and speech purpose. It is adaptable to any purpose but inquiry. The only demand upon such a pattern is that the audience accept it as reasonable and suitably comprehensive.

In an impromptu speech in Philadelphia, February 22, 1861, Abraham Lincoln adopted a simple but easily understandable topical arrangement treating (1) the principle of unity reflected in the Declaration of Independence and (2) his determination to sustain the Union at all costs. He might as easily have chosen to discuss the (1) economic, (2) social, and (3) political benefits of maintaining the Union. Or he might have discussed the (1) legal and (2) historical justifications for the Union. All these arrangements might be identified as topical.

ASCENDING AND DESCENDING ORDERS

The speaker who uses ascending and descending orders places his patterns, aspects, types, or qualities in sequence according to their increasing or decreasing importance or familiarity. That is to say, he moves from the most to the least important or from the most to the least familiar points or vice versa. He starts with

---

[7] See Otis M. Walter and Robert L. Scott, *Thinking and Speaking* (New York: Macmillan, 1962), p. 61.

the strongest argument and moves to the weakest or starts with the weakest and moves to the strongest. He may start on common ground and move into unfamiliar territory, or he may begin with an unusual aspect or argument and lead the audience to what they already know or to what is already uppermost in their minds. In the case of descending order, for example, a speaker explaining how pulp is processed for the manufacture of paper would take up the most commonly used process, the ground-wood process, and move through his speech to the soda, sulfite, and alkaline processes, which are used less frequently and are less familiar to most people. Similarly, in a speech on recognition of the Communist government of China, the familiar strong argument that the Peking government does in fact exist would precede less familiar and weaker arguments concerning the economic or political benefits of recognition. If you simply reverse the sequence so lesser known methods or weaker ideas come first, you achieve ascending order.

Ascending-descending orders are suitable in speeches to inform, to persuade, or to reinforce. The pattern might also be adapted for use in a speech to entertain. The choice and construction of ascending and descending orders hinge on your judgments of the relative importance of your materials; on your estimate of what will help your listeners to remember and give them a sense of climax; and, sometimes, on whether you have time to develop enough points to make ascent or descent psychologically meaningful.

CAUSAL SEQUENCES

The causal patterns are used in situations where one set of conditions is given as the cause for another set. The speaker may begin with a given set of conditions as the cause and allege that these will produce certain results or effects; or he may take a given set of conditions as the effect and allege that these resulted from certain causes.

In most uses of this pattern the speaker's specific purpose is to urge the elimination of those conditions which function as causes. To achieve this specific purpose, however, he may need to persuade his audience of one or more of these: (1) that the effects are really undesirable to them; (2) that the alleged causes are truly responsible for these effects; and (3) that elimination of these causes will not result in other, undesirable consequences. The first two concerns must either be evident to the audience or the speaker must prove them. The third may sometimes be safely disregarded.

The most common use of this pattern is one in which a speaker points out that certain undesirable conditions (*effects*) now exist and then explains that these are caused by certain other conditions (*causes*). The speaker *may* carry his reasoning through a chain of two or more effect-cause relationships in order to get from the present undesirable effects to the cause which he asks his audience to eliminate. This kind of development might run thus:

I. The nations of the world now spend billions of dollars on armaments. (Present undesirable effect.)

II. This money is spent because the peoples of the world live in perpetual fear of war and aggression. (Establishing first effect-to-cause relationship.)

III. People must live in such fear because there is no international authority strong enough to prevent war. (Second effect-to-cause relationship establishes the real cause of the present undesirable conditions.)

IV. Billions of dollars will be saved by the establishment of a federal world government. (Audience urged to adopt proposal eliminating prime cause and thereby eliminating effect.)

Frequently, the speaker will point out that certain existing conditions will cause undesirable effects in the future and so should be eliminated. The normal sequence is to begin with the present causes and then describe the anticipated future effects. Sometimes a more artistic sequence is to visualize the future effects for the audience first, then link these effects to the present undesirable causes. One might structure his speech thus:

I. The free nations of the world are now drifting toward a third world war which will destroy civilization. (Future, undesirable effects.)

II. This drift is being caused by the free nations' present lax attitude toward Communists' piecemeal aggression and flaunting of international authority. (Present conditions cause future effect.)

III. Therefore, the free nations should force Communist nations to recognize international authority. (Appeal to audience to eliminate present causes in order to avoid future effect.)

Sometimes a speaker draws an analogy between a cause-effect relationship and another similar cause-effect relationship which is already accepted by his audience:

I. At the present time, the free nations of the world are permitting country X to ignore international authority. (Establishing present conditions as cause.)

II. Because the free nations of the world, acting as the League of Nations, did not force Hitler and Mussolini to keep international peace, a world war was necessary to stop fascist aggression. (Referring to past and accepted cause-effect relationship.)

III. Our present lax policy will eventuate in a world war to stop X's aggression. (Drawing parallel undesirable effects from parallel causes.)

IV. Therefore, the free nations should act now to force X's obedience to international authority. (Appeal to audience to eliminate present causes in order to avoid future effects.)

Although causal patterns are generally used to advocate the removal of some condition, they can be used to advocate that certain conditions be encouraged. In this usage the speaker will show how something desirable to his audience (effect) results from other things (causes); therefore, they should set these causes in operation in order to secure the effect. Such a pattern might run:

I. We want permanent peace in the world. (Establishing condition, effect, as desirable to audience.)

II. Permanent peace results from the democratic nations' armed superiority over potential aggressor nations. (Establishing cause for the desirable effect.)

III. Therefore, let us build bigger and better hydrogen bombs and guided missiles. (Appeal for audience to favor conditions designed to cause desirable effects.)

The causal patterns are also often used in informative speeches to describe the relationships of parts of what is being explained, such as the causes of inflation during war or the effects of X-rays on human tissue. On occasion, speeches to reinforce and entertain are cast in this pattern.

Often the biggest difficulty in using causal patterns for either persuasive or informational speeches is making clear that a valid cause-effect relationship actually exists between the two sets of conditions. The demand to be met when these patterns are used is primarily the audience's need to see a clear and logical demonstration that genuine and significant (for them) causal relationships do exist. In turn, to use causal patterns requires that the speaker be capable of cogent thinking and that the materials used in the speech lend themselves to causal development.

PROBLEM-SOLUTION SEQUENCE

The problem-solution pattern is used where the audience faces a problem which you propose to solve. This pattern is also called the "disease-remedy" or the "need-remedy" pattern. Here, the speaker points first to the existence of a problem or evil and then offers a corrective program which must primarily be (1) practicable and (2) desirable. The corrective program must be capable of being put into effect, and it must be capable of eliminating the problem or the evil in question. It must also be one which will not introduce new and worse evils of its own. This is the issue long debated regarding the testing of nuclear weapons. Do the defense benefits obtained outweigh the undesirable effects on human beings?

The specific purpose of a speech in which the problem-solution pattern is used urges the audience to adopt the conditions embodied in the solution portion of the address. This type of organization usually serves best in the following situations.

1. Where the audience is aware that a problem exists and is interested in finding a solution to it, you may advocate one solution as the best of several possible answers. Although you will

generally describe the problem briefly, you will be primarily concerned with showing how your particular solution will solve the problem in the best possible way and how any alleged disadvantages of your solution may be avoided. This latter concern, avoiding new difficulties, will frequently involve you in anticipatory refutation, which means that you will have to dispel arguments against your proposal even though they have not been verbally advanced by anyone.

2. Where the audience is only dimly aware of a problem or need, the problem-solution pattern still serves well. Listeners can be made aware of the problem's exact nature; then, perhaps, the solution will become evident. Here you are primarily concerned with focusing your hearers' vaguely felt needs upon the specific problem you have isolated. You want the audience to see that their interests are vitally affected by the problem. Although you should at least indicate the evident solution, your chief concern is to show that a specific, serious problem does exist. Where your audience is not initially aware of their difficulty, it is unlikely that in a single speech you can do more than establish a precise sense of need; but not even in these circumstances can you disregard the solution section of your sequence altogether. If you do, you will leave the hearers up in the air. You must at least indicate that there are ways of solving the problem.

3. There are situations where the major concerns of both the preceding settings are combined. Sometimes you can carry your audience from awareness of a problem through to a readiness to act on a particular solution.

Now your task is (1) to sharpen awareness of the problem and (2) to show why your solution is the most suitable. Such a speech might be structured thus:

I. A serious problem of juvenile delinquency now exists in the United States. (Referring to felt need.)
   A. This problem not only poses a threat to our personal welfare and property but costs us millions of dollars in taxes for police protection. (Establishing importance of problem to audience.)
   B. Youths seem to have no sense of responsibility for their actions. (Focusing felt need on specific problem.)

II. This problem can be solved by imposing stiffer fines and jail sentences on juvenile criminals. (Statement of solution to specific problem.)

    A. By making youths responsible for the consequences of their actions we will deter them from criminal activities. (Showing *how* proposal will solve the problem.)

    B. The use of special jails will keep juveniles apart from older, hardened criminals. (Meeting objections to proposal.)

Variations on the problem-solution pattern are sometimes used in speeches of information, as when you show how people were faced by a problem and how they solved it. One might report how an early-warning radar system was established to protect the United States. The pattern may be used to inform even if the solution is not yet in effect, provided the answer has been decided and is no longer a question for debate. Problem-solution arrangements may also be adapted to reinforce belief and feeling or, more rarely, to entertain.

From what we have said it can be seen that problem-solution patterns are directly tied to audience demands. The audience must feel or be made to feel that a problem exists or that an evil is present. Often the felt need will originate in you so that you make the initial demand for this pattern. Where this is true, you must make the audience feel that the needed action is justified in terms of their interests. Speech materials also affect your choice of this organizational pattern. They must be capable of being divided into clear-cut problems and solutions. The occasion will determine to some extent those items which you select to depict a problem and to explain a solution. Thus, all forces in the communicative setting are at work in the final determination of how and whether a problem-solution pattern can be evolved.

WITHHELD-PROPOSAL OR INDIRECT SEQUENCE

The withheld-proposal or indirect sequence presents individual cases or instances as the bases for a conclusion about additional members of the same class.

The most important characteristic of the indirect sequence is that when using this pattern you give your audience examples, or some basic assumptions and facts, before you present any generalized inferences or conclusions of your own.

This pattern is especially useful when you speak to a hostile audience. Sometimes it is the only pattern that will enable you to persuade, because it permits you to begin an argument with material your audience knows to be true or with assumptions they accept. A common ground of agreement is established with the audience; when inferences are logically drawn from these accepted materials, the audience must either attack the logic involved or admit that you may be right. This pattern is also effective because it reflects man's normal thinking processes of reasoning from examples and assumptions in order to reach decisions.

Indirectly structured speeches operate generally in one of two basic patterns. In the first a number of examples is given, and a generalization is inferred. The plan might be:

    I. As most of you know, Senator Bergen has accused 77 men of being Communists; he has failed to prove these charges.

    II. According to the Senate record Senator Bergen has used Congressional immunity to avoid answering questions about his recent income-tax returns.

    III. Unquestionable evidence has proved that Senator Bergen has used doctored photographs in slandering his opponents.

    IV. Therefore, we must assume that Senator Bergen is dishonest. (Point of speech given as generalization from preceding examples.)

In using this pattern it is essential that your induction meet the logical tests for validity in generalizations.

In a second type of indirect pattern you first give basic assumptions or premises which are acceptable to your audience; then you give the facts of the specific case about which you are speaking; finally, you apply your basic premises to the specific case.

    I. A government established in a country by popular revolution should be recognized by democratic nations as the legal government of that country. (Statement of basic premise which is acceptable to audience.)

II. The Communist government of China was established by popular revolution against Chiang Kai-shek. (Giving the facts of the specific case.)

III. Therefore, the United States should recognize the Communist government as the legal government of China. (Specific purpose of speech.)

Several specialized, indirect patterns usefully support central ideas. One of these is the applied-criteria pattern in which propositions of fact or value are argued by first setting up criteria or standards and then showing that the alleged fact or value matches them. Another specialized use of indirect presentation develops when what at first appears to be a pattern of inquiry (described below) concludes by showing or strongly implying that only one particular solution solves the problem. The so-called implicative pattern resembles an incomplete, indirect pattern in that description, narration, and exposition are used for persuasive purposes. Word pictures, stories, and explanations hint at conclusions. Arguments presented may or may not be stated in formal fashion. In any case, the method is implicative because the audience is left to draw its own final conclusion or application.

As we have noted, indirect sequences meet demands of hostile audiences and of materials which can be divided into acceptable and known, unacceptable and unknown. To these conditions of audience and material which invite use of this pattern, we may add conditions emanating from the speaker himself. He may be more adept at presenting materials indirectly, in the soft-sell manner, than at approaching his audience frankly and directly. The mood of the occasion may also prompt use of this pattern. So, once again all elements of the public speaking situation may press for adoption of a withheld-proposal sequence. Furthermore, indirect presentation is feasible regardless of the speaker's purpose.

OPEN-PROPOSAL OR DIRECT SEQUENCE

The open-proposal or direct-sequence pattern of organization is in one sense a deductive order and stands in contrast to the indirect sequence. The speaker using this pattern urges the audience to accept a proposition on the grounds that its validity, morality, or practicality necessarily follows from accepted axioms or principles.

The direct sequence is simple to use. Essentially, it consists of telling your audience what you intend to prove or explain and then giving the arguments or clarifications that support your thesis. In many such speeches you will use several different arguments or divisions of clarification supporting your subject sentence, and these can be grouped into categories. A person advocating certain national legislation might develop arguments showing that it is morally right, legal under the constitution, of economic benefit, and practicable. A speaker explaining road building might cover route planning, grading, and surfacing. These categories form the main heads of the body of the speech. Frequently they can be arranged in a sequence giving additional climactic or logical force to the development (the proposal is *desirable*; it is *also practical*; moreover it will have *no significant disadvantages*). The major concern in applying the open-proposal sequence is that the sub-propositions be arranged in the clearest, most natural, and most logical order.

The direct or open-proposal sequence includes, among its variations, the topical arrangements which are so common in speeches of information. It also includes the list-of-advantages pattern for persuasion in which the case for a proposition of policy is structured around a list of benefits arising out of the proposed policy. This latter variation is closely related to problem-solution organization in that each alleged advantage implies or demonstrates a problem and solution.

In general, this sequence is most suitable where listeners are fairly familiar with your subject and where they have favorable or open-minded attitudes toward your proposal or position. The significant advantage of this system of organization is that you can give a number of arguments or categories of clarification efficiently while keeping your audience always informed as to what you are trying to prove or clarify and how you are going about it.

As in the case of indirect sequence, whether one adopts or

avoids the direct-sequence mode of presentation depends on the outlook of the audience, the way subject matter may be reasonably divided, the speaker's skill with direct vs. indirect presentation, and the tone or spirit of the occasion.

REFLECTIVE SEQUENCE OR PATTERN OF INQUIRY

The reflective sequence or pattern of inquiry is a pattern of organization based upon the five steps in reflective thinking outlined by the philosopher, John Dewey—(1) locating and defining a problem, (2) describing and limiting the problem, (3) suggesting possible solutions, (4) evaluating and testing the solutions, and (5) selecting the preferred solution.

To use this pattern requires that the speaker be willing to suspend judgment about a problem. This willingness comes from experience and reflection; life teaches us that snap judgments are often wrong, and that sound opinions must be based on careful consideration of numerous factors. The speech of inquiry and its reflective pattern of organization are for those speakers or auditors who are willing to assemble information and ponder various solutions before they decide.

In a state of mind permeated by doubt the inquirer invites an audience to join him in his quest for the best solution or the best answer to a question. He so develops his speech that his listeners feel the problem is their problem, not his alone. And he does all he can do to give the audience and himself a better basis for coming to a sound decision. This is the function of a speech of inquiry and it is the need served by the reflective sequence of ideas.

Such a speech obviously is both informative and persuasive. But it is persuasion that asks hearers to ponder, to weigh and consider, to explore; it is not persuasion that asks audiences to adopt the opinion of the speaker.

The inquirer both resembles and differs from the informative speaker. The man who gives us information is thoroughly conversant with his subject; his sole aim is to impart his understanding. The inquirer, on the other hand, does not enjoy the same degree of certainty. Instead, he is experiencing a degree of discomfort about his subject, discomfort caused by his inability to settle on a really satisfactory choice among competing solutions or answers. He is certain, however, of some things, for he has studied and thought about the problem that vexes him. (1) He can formulate and clarify the question. (2) He has analyzed the nature of the difficulty and has penetrated beneath its symptoms to its causes, beneath surface phenomena to basic facts. (3) He understands the criteria for a good solution. (4) He knows what solutions are available. His doubt concerns the relative worth of the solutions or the relative validity of the answers. His aim is to impart his information to the audience and to enlist their help in the final determination.

To orient his listeners to his subject, the speaker who adopts the reflective sequence first provides his audience with an understanding of the problem they share. He informs them of its troublesome symptoms and of its underlying causes, carefully distinguishing between symptom and cause. He may also review the problem's historical development, or he may give the details of a controversy that needs to be settled.

He doesn't stop there, however. He next considers the criteria which an acceptable solution or answer must meet. He must satisfy himself that he has formulated the right criteria, since the acceptability of solutions will depend on what standards are chosen. Though he must consider criteria in every case, the speaker does not always find it necessary to present and justify them in the speech. Some are obvious and readily taken for granted: safety on the highways, democracy, speed in settling legal cases. Such standards hardly need formal presentation and require no justification. Sometimes the criteria, though they need be presented, are too complex for explanation apart from discussion of solutions. This might be the case with the aims of a foreign policy, or with the nature of the good life. In such cases criteria will be presented piecemeal as various solutions are discussed. But consideration of criteria is integral to inquiry, so formal presentation of them is frequently advisable.

Having clarified the problem and said what is necessary concerning standards, the speaker using the reflective sequence now turns to the alternative solutions or answers. This is generally the most important element in the speech; hence, he should allow sufficient time for it, restricting the preliminary sections to what is absolutely essential. For each solution the speaker explains and assesses. He explains the solution or answer. He assesses or evaluates the solution or answer thoroughly and fairly in terms of the pertinent criteria, keeping in mind their relative weight or importance.

In concluding his speech the speaker should try to make his audience continue to inquire. Their reflection on the subject should not stop when the speech stops. In fact, inquiry on a larger scale—group inquiry—often begins after a speech of inquiry has been delivered. The speaker, therefore, may well conclude by presenting the salient questions which his listeners should further consider as they continue their search for the best solution. Or he may point out the direction in which he thinks the best answer will be found.

Thus, the speaker who would really inquire may suggest but he will not urge acceptance of a preferred solution. He may omit Dewey's fifth step altogether. All five steps need not be included in every pattern of inquiry. Indeed, some speeches of inquiry go no further than steps two or three. Others omit step one. The pattern, in short, is subject to considerable variation according to the demands of speaker, audience, and occasion.

The speaker himself makes the first demand justifying this pattern of organization in that his state of mind initially determines its use. The readiness of the audience to accept a pattern which does not provide for conclusive settlement of a problem may also be a consideration. Speech materials have less influence on the selection or rejection of this pattern since they at once lend themselves to informing, persuading, or questioning. The occasion is a determinant in that the situation must be one in which men can deliberate. An atmosphere of puzzlement or bewilderment, of careful consideration, will sometimes suggest to you that a pattern of inquiry is your best scheme of organization.

MONROE'S MOTIVATED SEQUENCE

Arnold, Ehninger, and Gerber describe Monroe's Motivated Sequence as follows:

[It is] . . . a comprehensive pattern of organization based upon "the normal process of human thinking," and for this reason assumed to be particularly effective in motivating listeners to respond to the speaker's purpose.

As developed by its principal exponent, Professor Alan H. Monroe . . . , the motivated sequence provides a basic pattern by which all types of speeches may be organized, "needing only to be modified by omitting or lengthening certain parts according to the particular situation." In speeches to actuate, all five steps of the sequence are present. These bear the functional names of Attention, Need, Satisfaction, Visualization, and Action. The first step catches the "attention" of the listeners; the second points to the existence of a problem or "need"; the third advances a proposal that will "satisfy" this need; the fourth "visualizes" the benefits to be derived from adopting the proposal; and the fifth, drawing upon the groundwork thus laid, makes a direct appeal for "action." In speeches to inform, only three steps—Attention, Need, and Satisfaction— are present. The function of the first is again to catch "attention"; the second shows the listeners why they "need" to know the information that is to be presented; and the third "satisfies" this "need" by presenting the information. Speeches to entertain may be either an extended development of the Attention Step or a mock-serious treatment of the speech to inform, convince, or actuate.[8]

This motivated sequence, more than any other, is psychologically planned to lead your audience's thinking naturally and easily from a vague interest in your subject to a definite acceptance of the attitude or action you are advocating. Each step in the sequence is built on the preceding steps. The motivated sequence can be used in a variety of speeches, but it is chiefly useful when you face an audience that has little interest in your subject or

---

[8] Reprinted from *The Speaker's Resource Book* by Carroll C. Arnold, Douglas Ehninger and John C. Gerber. Copyright © 1961, 1966 by Scott, Foresman and Company, Chicago, rev. ed., p. 312.

when you want to arouse a strong and specific response in your audience.

Since this sequence is capable of adaptation to a large number of situations, it is enough to say that all of the elements in the speech situation—the audience, the materials, the speaker himself, and the occasion—are to be considered in successfully executing the particular variation of the pattern appropriate to a given speaking assignment.

ELIMINATION ORDER

"Elimination order" is a pattern of organization wherein several or all possible interpretations of a subject or solution to a problem are considered and all but one are pointed out as undesirable, impractical, or incorrect. This strategy is sometimes called the method of residues because whatever remains is the matter to be accepted by the audience.

The method of elimination is often used as the fourth step of what is otherwise a reflective sequence. This adaptation is especially advantageous when you wish to present an investigation for the purpose of persuading rather than inquiring. At the point of considering solutions you may turn to the elimination of all possible solutions except the one you advocate. The same patterning may be applied during the second half of a problem-solution or need-remedy speech where more than one solution or remedy must be considered. Thus, this pattern may be thought of as a variation which can be adopted within either reflective or problem-solution systems or it may be treated as a scheme of organization applicable to a whole speech.

Influences affecting one's choice of this organizational system arise from the audience and the speaker. Both must be willing to investigate more than one possibility in the given situation. The speech materials, too, must offer for discussion more than one course of action or answer. The occasion also affects your choice: time must be available for full explanation and testing of possibilities, and the atmosphere must favor a several-sided consideration of the subject. Thus, once again, all four elements in the speech situation come into play to determine whether elimination order is a wise choice for disposing your speech materials.

We began this chapter by considering man's special need to find relationships and the public speaker's consequent need to clarify and give evidence of thought progression through his disposition of the ideas he seeks to communicate. Disposition of the content of a speech is, essentially, another form of adaptation to the human propensity to search for structure and unity in all things. Our examination of the normal parts of speeches (introduction, body, and conclusion) and of patterns of organization has been a survey of how speakers have learned to answer the universal demand for organization in spoken discourse.

Most of the time, as we have seen, a reasonable adaptation to the demands of audience, subject, speaker, and occasion will make it necessary that a speech begin by orienting the listener to speaker and subject (introduction). The properly adapted speech will continue with a systematic message that makes listening easier and surer by conforming to a structural pattern familiar to both listener and speaker. It will conclude with some reinforcement of the total experience of the speech.

We have discussed the standard patterns of organization, first, because speech-making is a public art in which relationships must be exhibited in familiar, public terms. The standard patterns of organization are simply the most familiar—the most public— systems our society uses in verbal communication. Second, while not every speech can be effectively structured according to one of the standard patterns we have discussed, all speeches have at least a segment that can be best conveyed according to one of the familiar patterns. These patterns, then, are optional systems among which you will constantly choose. We hope that by understanding what they can accomplish and what they cannot, you will be able to choose wisely. Third, most speeches and most situations in which you will give them will permit you to select from the standard patterns. Clearly, you can adapt to man's need to order his perceptions if you develop the body of a speech in accordance with one of these patterns; if you do not do so, you may achieve a brilliant presentation but you are more likely to achieve obscurity. Fourth and finally, we have discussed patterns of organization in detail because we wished to demonstrate once more that the art of speaking is an art of social adaptation in which the demands of content, speaker, audience, and occasion must always be weighed. This is no less true in the disposition of speech materials than in their invention.

Exercises

WRITTEN

1. a. Choose a subject area, such as urban renewal, current methods in secondary education, or the Democratic party in America today.
   b. Carefully write out three subject sentences for the subject area chosen. One sentence should be devised for a speech of *information*, another for a speech of *persuasion*, and the third for a speech of *inquiry*.
   c. Write out the main heads for each of the three subject sentences you have composed.
2. Write an essay in which you evaluate the following introduction according to the requirements for a good introduction found on pages 218–221.

The Annual February Phenomenon
Three months from today, on another Wednesday evening, the Cornell scene will be a lot different from what it is now. The temperature will be 20 degrees colder; Goldwin Smith Hall will be dark as final exams will have ended; the Library will be closed; and down beneath the Library, past the Baker Towers, the freshman dorm area will be empty. The dorms themselves will not be empty, for every window in the cinder-block cubicles will be brightly lit. We step inside a room to find its pair of freshmen occupants sitting quietly; their cords are shined, button-down collars buttoned down, hi-fi's spinning Shearing. They seem to be waiting for something.

There's a noise from outside the window. We walk over, look out, and see the empty quadrangle of a moment before covered with a writhing sea of tweed and occasional flashes of recognition pins. The February phenomenon known as rushing has once more begun at Cornell University.

We can briefly define rushing as the acquisition of new members by fraternities and the affiliation with fraternities by freshmen. We know that rushing is a lot more than this, for we have all seen it and many of us have been through it from both sides.

Let us consider rushing from the fraternity viewpoint. It often degenerates into a cut-throat, name-calling conversation with the freshman during contact periods. Here the fraternity lacking positive things to say about itself employs such vivid descriptions of other fraternities as: "They're on social pro," or "They're split into cliques." We encounter rushing violations, breaches of the rules written to civilize the Greek jungle. Two of the fraternity men in this audience are members of a house that encountered flagrant rule violations by another house last year. Things such as pickups being made ten minutes before proper time by a house whose date had been broken are common. In this instance the freshman finds himself at Kappa Kappa Do instead of Delta Delta Kappa.

Hash sessions are another part of this February phenomenon. These selection meetings are reminiscent of a cattle sale, and the inaccurate job of selection they do is apparent from the following anecdote, which occurred at one of our more prominent fraternities two years ago. Two members and the rushing chairman created a nonexistent freshman named Fred Wendel. Fred was "contacted," brought over for dinner, and discussed that same evening in hash session. One of the men involved in the ruse spoke for Fred and said what a top man the rushee was. His sentiments were echoed by his partner, and a chorus of "Oh yeah, hot man, bring him back" mysteriously arose. Fred was "brought back," the same hash policy was repeated, but a few more men spoke up for Fred. This nonexistent freshman was unanimously voted a bid to the fraternity the following week. How good are the hash sessions?

The freshman, on the other hand, is a great variable. He may be a bubbling, extroverted individual, or he may be shy and withdrawn. Most freshmen are scared and ignorant when rushing begins; many are more ignorant when it ends. The intensive eight-day period puts them under great pressure, for the quick decision they are forced to make is probably the most important of their college careers. It decides where they are going to live and whom they are going to live with for three and a half years.

The manner in which rushing occurs, the attitudes displayed by the fraternities, and the tremendous pressures exerted so intensely on the freshmen indicate that a re-evaluation with regulation and modification of this February phenomenon is needed at Cornell.[9]

3. Assume that the following sets of main heads have been taken from the "bodies" of outlines for *informative* speeches. Evaluate each set in terms of (a) the wording of the main points, and (b) the overall pattern of organization. Give detailed reasons for your judgments.

a.   I. Every speech should have an introduction, body, and conclusion.
    II. Should the introduction get attention and make the speaker's purpose clear?
  III. A conclusion should summarize and put the entire speech into focus.

b.   I. The social, political, and economic instability of underdeveloped countries is a potential breeding ground for Communism.
    II. We must increase our financial aid and technical assistance to these countries to head off the threat.

c.   I. Cornell University has a long and varied history.
    II. It is often called the "cow college of the Ivy League."
  III. A new library complex provides excellent facilities for research and study.
  IV. There are many fraternities and sororities on campus.
   V. Cornell is truly "an institution where any person can find instruction in any study."
  VI. What about Ithaca weather?
 VII. There is a varied program of extracurricular activities open to the student.
VIII. Many distinguished professors.
  IX. There are many free lectures and other cultural events, including a fine art museum, concerts, plays, and athletic events.

4. Locate the text of a speech in an anthology of speeches, an issue of *Vital Speeches*, or a volume of the Reference Shelf series (H. W. Wilson Co.) devoted to speeches. Read the speech carefully. Identify the overall structure of the speech. Support your labeling of the pattern in a paragraph or two in which

---

[9] This introduction was composed by Ronald Demer for an all-male class in persuasive speaking. Used by permission.

you cite specific portions of the speech which led you to choose the label you did.

ORAL

1. a. In class discussion choose several subject sentences for impromptu speeches. Such sentences as: "The automobile is primarily a vehicle for human transportation"; "Donation of blood to the Red Cross is worthwhile"; "Grades in college should be abolished" will serve well.
   b. Assign each of the subject sentences chosen to three different members of the class, and also assign to each of them *one* of the usable patterns of organization discussed in Chapter 8, e.g., chronological, spatial, problem-solution, causal.
   c. Allow time for each of the three students to prepare a two-to-three-minute impromptu speech using the pattern assigned.
   d. After hearing the speeches, discuss orally the suitability of each pattern to the subject sentence assigned. Also evaluate the speaker's ability to produce a recognizable pattern of organization on short notice.

—❦{ 9 }❧—   *Disposition:*

Outlining

Outlining the speech on paper is essential for careful disposition (ordering) of materials and adequate preparation for extemporaneous and manuscript speaking. Constructing an outline insures a speaker that his ideas are arranged and fully enough supported or amplified. It further insures that he has considered the logical relationships among ideas and the weights and emphases he wishes to accord them.

From outlining the speaker perceives shape and definiteness because of his conscious attention to the existence and proportioning of the parts of the speech. Contours of both the overall and internal structuring emerge to reveal internal builds and climaxes or the lack of them. While outlines are usually skeletal maps of a speech, sometimes they are such complete plans that they are almost manuscripts.

Functions of Outlines

The speaker must decide what kind of outline is best for him. He must decide how far he will go in preparing his thoughts for oral delivery. In classroom situations he may be required to construct *content* or *technical* outlines in order to reveal to a teacher his planned content or strategies. He may be required to submit *full-sentence, phrase,* or *key-word* outlines depending upon the degree of preciseness and refinement the teacher demands as evidence of preliminary planning. In any case, he must outline to keep thoughts clear and sharp.

Beginners find sentence outlines most helpful. Since full sentences express the complete thought to be presented at each point in the speech, their use insures that the speaker has framed each complete thought and understands its juxtaposition and relationship to other complete thoughts. While a thought may stand in the mind of the speaker and be symbolized on paper by a word, indeed by a symbol even simpler than a word such as a cross or a circle, most beginners find themselves handicapped when using shorthand outlines resembling grocery lists. The more experienced the speaker is, the more likely he is to be successful in using abbreviated methods in outlining. However, some of the most famous speakers, Woodrow Wilson and Franklin Roosevelt for example, wrote out every word of their important speeches.

For maximum effectiveness, the speaker's method must be suited to his individual needs. Outlining serves the speaker chiefly; the audience seldom sees the outline. Utility and speaker-adaptation are the marks of a good outline; no rigid set of rules for structuring a speech on paper are possible.

Speakers may resort to various devices to jog their memories. One speaker may underline main heads in his outline in red; another may place asterisks at various points. Still another will draw pictures. Yet another will include notations of the kinds of material he is including: example, story, statistics; he may even mark the vocal variations he wants to produce: loud, soft. No one can say that any of these practices is wrong; for the outline is an instrument, a tool for the speaker. The single exception occurs in the learning situation.

You are asked to submit an outline to your teacher in order to receive helpful, constructive criticism. Your outline, then, is no longer a private paper. It is, instead, a record of preparation to be shared with another interested person who is to make suggestions. This shared paper must be understood by your teacher as well as by you. Since this is so, you, as the writer, must take special care to make ideas and their relationships clear both visually and verbally. You and your critic must both agree upon a system of outlining. You may be asked to employ full sentences, at least to begin with, because one can understand them better than phrases or words. A single word offered in support of another single word may not be comprehensible to your teacher, and it will not indicate whether you have thought through your ideas. For instance, you may know what you will say when you have written the word "Economic" and listed "Cost" and "Profit" as supporting ideas, but your teacher may not see clear-cut connections between these sketchy symbols. He may be led to conclude that at this particular stage of speech preparation your ideas have not been fully enough refined, that they are still in vague or fuzzy condition. You must take special care in preparing your papers so that ideas and their relationships are kept clear.

As a teaching device your instructor may prescribe that you not only construct a "content" outline showing the ideas in your speech but that you add technical labels. He may ask you to indicate your kinds of proof and amplification, sources of attention, or the pattern of structure exemplified. When these labels are added to an outline, you have in reality two outlines. One maps ideas to be uttered; the other maps strategy and tactics. It is common for the inexperienced to mix these two types of mapping. In making outlines you will not give symbols to Introduction, Body, Conclusion, because these are not part of the idea structure of the speech. It is useless to write simply "story" or "statistics" beside a sub-point number without indicating what you intend to say. To identify your tactics or methods enables you to straighten out in your own mind just what it is you are doing as you order ideas and just what kinds of ideas you are ordering. Sometimes your teacher may ask you to use these technical labels in order to test you. But such labels alone will not enable you to tell others what you will say. Alone, they produce an unsatisfactory paper for you to refer to should you decide to deliver a second version of your speech before a second audience. An outline reading as follows would be of little help were you to try to determine what the speaker who made it intended to say.

Introduction

I. Story.—Using novelty, stereotypes, familiarity. Chronological order.
II. Subject sentence.
III. Definitions.
   a. By function.
   b. By classification.

Body

I. Argument.—Open proposal pattern.
   a. Quotation—familiar.
   b. Statistics—visual aids.
II. Argument.—Developed inductively.
   a. Report of Experiment.
   b. Report of Second Experiment.

Conclusion

I. A Summary.

This record of a speech would be of little value to either a critical teacher aiming to evaluate supports or proofs, subject sentences, or attention values, or to a speaker trying to recapture from his personal files what he said six months ago.

Common Practices

No hard and fast rules govern outlining speeches, but universal practices have been found trustworthy. These practices satisfy the requirements of the speaker, the material, the audience, and the occasion. They promote the clarity, the organic unity, and the adaptation so necessary for successful speaking. Recording your plan systematically produces a visual image of the speech which helps you and, indirectly, your audience. Exact and methodical planning insures audience understanding and your own control over your material.

What, then, should you do in constructing an outline which will assist you in remembering what to say when? What should you look for as you check over your outline? Provided you are following commonly accepted practices, you should look for:

A clear indication of the basic divisions of the speech: Introduction, Body (sometimes labeled Discussion or Proof), *and Conclusion.*   Since these labels are not parts of the idea structure of the speech but are technical notations, they will not normally be given symbols. Numerical and alphabetical symbols ought to be reserved as indicators of relationships. Usually the names of the basic divisions of your speech are centered on the page and go unsymbolized. This placement insures that you have an introduction and a conclusion and that you are aware of what constitutes these portions of your speech. In those infrequent instances when no introduction is used, its absence is readily apparent if one forms the practice of formally identifying each division actually to be included.

A consistent system of (a) symbolization and (b) indentation. This aids in clarifying relationships within the speech and in helping you to remember those relationships. The system of symbols you use is up to you; consistency in their use is essential. It matters little whether Roman numerals, capital letters, or Arabic numerals are used to indicate main heads and sub-heads. What matters is that each time a type of symbol occurs it signifies that the ideas thus identified are of approximately the same importance or weight. Uniformity in symbolization will clearly indicate the value you assign to your material and the different symbols assigned will show which ideas are subsidiary to which. Since you will be working out a structure idea by idea, you should place only one symbol before any one idea. This serves as a caution against composing compound sentences containing more than one thought. If you follow the rule: one symbol for *each* idea, you will be reminded to break compound statements in two, giving each of the ideas a separate symbol. You will need to check very carefully in making a phrase outline to see that each symbol stands beside an idea rather than beside a fragment of one or a phrase that represents —for you—several ideas.

Indentation, the physical arrangement of ideas, is a further aid in revealing values assigned and in stirring the memory. If each new idea is indicated by a particular indentation, that fact announces to the speaker that it is time to embark on a new phase of his thought structure. Ideas subsidiary to other ideas should be indented under the subsuming thought. In this way it will be easy to see that support and amplification are subordinate points. Your visual image of your speech will then be a network of ideas with the least important ones indented farthest from the left-hand margin of the page. Though none of the ideas you set down on the page is, ideally, expendable, it will be less of a calamity should an idea given minor weight (one farthest indented) be forgotten.

In outlining inductive patterns, a common practice is to symbolize and indent points and sub-points in the same way you do for deductive patterns, then to place supporting or amplifying sub-points in parentheses. Such practice indicates that the examples, statistics, and definitions, subsumed by a point are to be presented during the speech before the point being amplified or supported.

An outline is not always constructed to indicate the order in which ideas will actually be introduced when the speech is delivered orally. In most cases, speakers follow the sequence of ideas as they appear in their preparatory outlines. It is imperative that they do so when utilizing chronological or ascending or descending order patterns. When using inductive patterns, such as the withheld proposal, speakers will more often depart from idea structures as they appear on paper.

Absence of single sub-points. Wherever one idea is subordinated to another, it indicates a splitting of the subsuming idea for purposes of amplification or support. Usually more than one piece of information is needed to develop a point adequately. Yet, one definition, one example, or one opinion sometimes may suffice to clarify or prove to an acceptable degree. Audience needs may occasionally be met with only one item of amplification. More often, a single subordinate item would be better reinforced if there were other, parallel items. If not, it may very well be combined with the idea to which it appears to be subordinate. An outline containing a multitude of single sub-points should be viewed suspiciously. It is likely that the ideas contained in it have not been developed to the point of audience acceptance and that necessary information and proof have been overlooked. Only when you are absolutely sure that one and only one piece of proof is necessary should a sub-point be allowed to stand alone.

Discreteness of ideas. In outlines, ideas should not be lumped together nor should they overlap. An outline is a structure intended to insure clarity of relationships, which dictates that each idea stand separately within the structure. The need to reveal clearly the relationship of each idea to other ideas is an additional argument for full-sentence outlining. Sentences, if correctly constructed, are expressions of complete thoughts. You must be wary of the compound sentence in outlining since it contains more than one idea, making it impossible to follow the principle of one symbol, one idea. "Ands" and "ors" should rarely appear in the sentences of an outline; they bear special checking when they do appear. Only so can you be sure that relationships are clear.

Appropriate symbolization and placement of subject sentences. Since the core idea (subject sentence, main proposition, central idea, or specific purpose) is the most important idea in the speech, it deserves the highest rank in symbolization. This main proposition or assertion should be unmistakable in your outline. Some teachers and students prefer to label this proposition or assertion "central idea," "main proposition," "subject sentence," or "specific purpose" rather than affixing number or letter symbols, because it is of highest rank in the hierarchy of ideas symbolized in the outline.

In the sample outlines at the end of this chapter and in the diagram on page 255 we have both symbolized and labeled the central idea, indicating that either method is acceptable and that both are common in outlining. No matter which of these practices is followed, the central idea should never appear as a sub-point nor should it be indented beneath any other point. In deductive patterns this central sentence will usually appear near the end of the Introduction or near the beginning of the Body of the speech. Wherever it appears, the central idea should be designated by a symbol or label indicating that it is of most weight or value. Graphically, it should at least be accorded the same rank by indentation as the other most important items in the section. The same is true in symbolizing or labeling and in indenting the central idea when outlining inductive patterns, such as the withheld-proposal sequence. The main idea should be given the symbol and/or label and indentation that will reveal quickly that it is a statement not outranked in importance by any other ideas in the section of the speech in which it appears. Whether the central idea appears in the Introduction, Body or Conclusion, it is the most important idea in that division of your outline.

Clear transitions. Transitions should be uniformly indicated and set off from the rest of the structure. Points of linkage and internal summaries should be clearly indicated. If they are symbolized and indented in the same manner as other parts of the outline, they should be given technical labels such as "Transition" or "Internal Summary." A common practice is to treat these portions of the speech differently from main points or sub-points, omitting symbols, but marking them off by enclosing them in brackets or parentheses. This practice shows that the speaker gave careful attention to how he would move from one point or sub-point to another and to the necessity for repetition and review.

If the above practices are observed, a diagram of an outline may well look like this:

Title

Introduction

```
  I. ............................................................
     A. ........................................................
     B. ........................................................
 II. (Central Idea) ............................................
        (Transition:  ......................................)
```

Body

I. ....

    A. ....

    B. ....

       1. ....

          a. ....

          b. ....

       2. ....

          a. ....

          b. ....

    C. ....

       1. ....

       2. ....

          a. ....

          b. ....

             (1) ....

             (2) ....

       (Transition: ....)

II. ....

    A. ....

       1. ....

          a. ....

          b. ....

          c. ....

       2. ....

       (Transition: ....)

    B. ....

       1. ....

          a. ....

          b. ....

             (1) ....

             (2) ....

             (3) ....

                (a) ....

                (b) ....

          c. ....

          d. ....

             (1) ....

             (2) ....

       2. ....

          a. ....

          b. ....

       (Internal Summary: ....

       ....)

III. ....

   A. ....

      1. ....

         a. ....

         b. ....

      2. ....

   B. ....

      (Transition and/or Internal Summary ....

      ....)

Conclusion

  I. ....

   A. ....

   B. ....

   C. ....

 II. ....

Bibliography
(or Statement of Sources)

....

....

....

....

....

....

Two items appearing in this diagram remain to be considered, title and bibliography or statement of sources.

Titles

The final act in the composition of your speech is ordinarily the selection of a title. Informal situations make titles less necessary than those in which you will be introduced, but formulating a title gives the discourse a finished quality. A title provides a label for use by those reporting your speech or recording the event of which your speech was a part. Titles are normally composed last since that is when you can best cast your eye back over the total composition and decide upon a phrase characterizing it. But sometimes a title will evolve from the very first pieces of data you encounter in the process of invention.

Good titles meet demands made by the audience and the subject matter of the speech. Good titles (1) attract attention by their brevity and provocativeness, and (2) reveal to some degree what the speech is about by emphasizing its theme.

A title must be brief for practical reasons. Sentences rarely serve, and even phrases can be too long. An audience stops listening before the end of a title such as: "The History and Significance of the Indian Tribes in the Western New York Area from the Years 1770 to 1790 with Special Emphasis upon the Youth Between the Ages of 12–18 and Their Role in War Making." A better title would be "The Warring Indian Braves of Western New York During the Late Eighteenth Century." A long title is usually impractical for publicity purposes; a title should be short enough to fit on a poster or into a one- or two-column newspaper head. When a speech has no title or a long and unarresting one, the newspapermen or poster makers often invent one. Reporters did just that when they retitled Franklin D. Roosevelt's "Speech to the Teamsters' Union, September 23, 1944," the "Fala Speech." They also shortened the title of his "Speech at the Dedication of the Outerlink Bridge, Chicago, Illinois, October 5, 1937," to "The Quarantine Speech." The second of these "tag titles" does identify the essential theme of the speech, but the first does not.

Your titles must arouse the curiosity of audiences if they are to hold interest. Images can help since they serve as shorthand symbols which stir up mental pictures. William Jennings Bryan's "Cross of Gold" is a classic example, yet we can think of other lesser-known titles such as "Skeletons All" or "Little Fences and Barriers." Such images in titles not only arouse initial attention but they are remembered long after the speech has been delivered.

These three titles are not completely satisfactory because they do not tell us clearly what the speech is about. They are riddle metaphors but not good ones, for they do not meet the requirement Aristotle wisely noted when he said, ". . . the metaphors by which we give names to nameless things must not be farfetched; rather we must draw them from kindred and similar things; the

kinship must be seen the moment the words are uttered. . . ."[1]
The three titles under consideration are not as poor as other titles:
"A Hope for the Future," "You Ought to Try," "A Happy Solution." These are not only vague and uninteresting but could fit
any number of speeches. These are "umbrella" titles. They cover
everything and nothing. A good title at least hints at the core idea
of the speech. F. Paul McConkey's title, "Roses in the Snow," for
a sermon on the beauties of old age is not only brief and provoca-
tive but relevant. "Idle Worship" as a title for an attack on Madi-
son-Avenue religion, and the title of a eulogy of Henry Ford, "The
Man with the Model-T Dream," are titles that fulfill their functions better than others considered here. Lest these seem too cute,
a danger when we strain too hard for good titles, consider Andrew
Dickson White's title, "The Battlefields of Science" or Nancy
Myers' indictment of television entitled "Moppet Manipulation."

Bibliographies

The educated man is one who knows the sources of his knowledge
and his opinions. He is able to acknowledge how and where he
acquired his ideas and facts, and he often does so voluntarily. In
preparing outlines and manuscripts he annotates ideas and quotations not his own as a natural recognition of other people's
contributions.

You may be asked to include a bibliography or "Statement of
Sources" with your outline. Occasionally acknowledgments of
sources may appear in the outline proper. They should certainly
appear there when the sources are to be mentioned in the speech
itself. More often such acknowledgments will be appended at
the end of the outline as a communication to the instructor or
other reader. Your teacher, as a critic, wants to know what you
actually found useful.

---

[1] From *The Rhetoric of Aristotle* trans. and ed. by Lane Cooper. Copyright, 1932, Lane Cooper, p. 188, Bk III, Ch. 2. Reprinted by permission of
the publisher Appleton–Century–Crofts.

There are many forms for bibliographical entries. The important things are to be complete and consistent. The following forms may be used when you are asked to cite your sources. Note that comment on the scope and value of printed sources is enclosed in square brackets. The notes on other materials are given in informal description.

Observation:

During the week of August 11–17, 1966, I took part in ROTC naval maneuvers and saw the things I describe under Point I of the Introduction.

Interview:

On May 12, 1966, I talked with President J. B. Smith of X Company for about an hour and got the ideas on management's problems which appear in Section III of this outline.

I have drawn at many points on the courses I have taken in business, economics, and oral and written communication.

Articles:

    A. From Periodicals:
    Faulkner, William, "On Fear: The South in Labor," *Harper's Magazine*, CCXII (June, 1956), 29–34.
[Emphasizes the place economic and social fears have in Southern resistance to racial integration in schools. Ideas from this source are incorporated in supporting material for the second main division of my argument.]
    B. From Books:
    Spencer, Herbert, "The Philosophy of Style," in W. T. Brewster, ed., *Representative Essays on the Theory of Style* (New York: Macmillan, 1921), pp. 167–208.
[Ideas on the principles of economy in style which I explain under Point II are taken from this essay.]
    C. From General Reference Books:
    "John Donne," *Encyclopaedia Britannica*, 9th ed. (New York, 1878).[2]
[This account provided me with most of the biographical facts used in my speech.]

---

[2] In citing any *Britannica* since 1932 it is advisable to use the date of printing: "John Donne," *Encyclopaedia Britannica* (1952).

Newspapers:

    A. From signed articles, editorials, and news accounts:
       Folliard, Edward T., "As a Thousand Cheer," *The Washington Post* (September 24, 1944), p. 1.[3]
[Information on audience reaction to Franklin Roosevelt's "Teamsters' Union Speech," September 23, 1944, and some of the details of the speaking occasion were drawn from this article.]
    B. From unsigned articles, editorials, and news accounts:
       "Bushwhacking," *The Washington Post* (September 25, 1944), p. 10.
[This single, critical reaction to Franklin Roosevelt's "Teamsters' Union Speech," September 23, 1944, furnished amplification for Point III, b.]

Pamphlets (where the author or editor is not credited):
    The High School in a Changing World, The American Association of School Administrators (Washington, D.C., 1958).
[This pamphlet provided me with the classification of past trends in high school curricula.]

Sample Outlines

The two outlines which follow will serve to illustrate good outlining procedures. The first is an outline for a speech of information twelve minutes in length. It contains good examples of structure and of outlining mechanics.

Tornado[4]

Introduction

    I. Most of us in the northeast are not particularly worried about tornadoes striking us.
       A. But the fact is a tornado can hit any part of the United States during any season.
          1. (Visual Aid Number 1—Chart showing tornado incidence.)

---

[3] If the article appears in a numbered section of the newspaper, the citation would then read: ". . . (September 24, 1944), sec. 5, p. 1."

[4] Adapted from an outline submitted by Jonathan E. Emerson. Used by permission. The speech was given in 1961.

    2. Nineteen tornadoes were spotted in the middle of the winter over Lake Champlain in New York.

    3. A tornado hit Worcester, Massachusetts in 1953.

B. Since 1953, many large cities have been hit by these storms.

    1. "Twisters in recent years have smashed into Flint; Waco; Cleveland; Chicago; St. Louis; Miami; Vicksburg; Dallas; Fargo; Worcester, Massachusetts; and Columbus, Georgia." (E. D. Fales, Jr., "The Tornado Hunters," *Saturday Evening Post*, May 20, 1961.)

    2. A tornado-warning radar has been set up on top of the RCA Building in New York City.

    3. During 1960, 1,200 tornadoes were spotted, of which 600 touched ground.

        a. This is not an unusual number.

        b. Between 1953 and 1960, there were 5,000 confirmed storms across the country; they killed 1,200 people and injured 13,000. (Fales, *Sat. Eve. Post*)

C. Damage and loss of life can occur in the Northeast.

    1. But our section has no systematic tornado warning system.

    2. Our heavy concentration of cities, industries, and population would make destruction more costly here than in any other section of the country.

    3. Most people in this section are simply unaware of their danger.

II. In all of nature no storm concentrates as much fury in a single area as a tornado.

(Central Idea)

III. For the reasons I just mentioned I want to show you some of the theories on how tornadoes are formed, then describe the specific characteristics of tornadoes, and finally show you how they are predicted and detected.

Body

I. There are several theories about how a tornado originates.

A. There is the lightning theory.

    1. It is offered by Dr. Bernard Vonnegut of Arthur D. Little, Inc., a research firm in Cambridge, Massachusetts.

    2. Vonnegut says: "When lightning occurs it may flash so often in one path that it heats up a 'chimney' in the atmosphere; this 'chimney' sucks up air in a great

swirl, the tornado is started, and opposing electrical charges in the clouds help keep it going."

    B. There is a warm air–cool air theory.
        1. A layer of cool air forms over a layer of warm air.
            a. A hole develops in the cool air.
            b. The warm air rushes through the hole—like water going down a drain.
        2. The resulting swirling funnel contains 600 mph winds.
    C. There is the Venturi Theory that a tornado is caused by the prevailing westerlies.
        1. Westerlies blow across holes in the clouds creating suction which starts tornadoes.
        2. Electrical charges which are a cause of the whirling motion serve to concentrate the tail after the start.
        (Transition: No theory is yet accepted by everyone, but whichever theory you "buy," you can understand why a tornado becomes terrifying to experience.)

II. Eyewitnesses report:
    A. Tornadoes sound like:
        1. The buzzing of a million bees;
        2. The sound of a thousand locomotives.
    B. The storm's tail looks black and vicious.
        1. These tails are reported as from 10 to 400 feet in diameter.
        2. Dirt and debris that have been sucked up give them their color.
        3. A strange blue glow over 100 feet thick is reportedly at the top of some of the tails.
        4. "Blue fire" and the smell of sulfur have been reported around the base.
    C. A Robert Jackson of Hickman Hills, Missouri described his experience:

"I noticed the house next door just kind of raise up on its foundation as if you put a bomb in it. The whole thing just seemed to lift up off the foundation—kinda sideways—kinda raised up and veered off a bit. Then it exploded. It caved in in every direction and wood went everywhere. I saw several cars go off the lot across the highway. The wind is getting rough when it can throw these cars up. I remember seeing one car sailing right along the outside of the funnel—the black, dirty, filthy part of it. There it was, just one car sailing through the air 30 to 40 feet high."

(Transition: Descriptions like Mr. Jackson's are reasons enough to ask what is being done to predict and detect such destructive forces and to warn people of their danger.)

III. The effort to predict tornadoes has yielded some important discoveries about when they are likely to occur, which allows warnings to be issued.

    A. There are several things which must occur before a tornado can develop.

        1. There must be two large air masses.

            a. One must be warm and moist (90° F.).

            b. The other must be dry and cooler (60° F.).

        2. There must be disturbance in the area such as a front of giant electrical storms.

            a. Large thunder clouds are necessary.

                (1) These can be as much as 12 miles high.

                (2) To cause tornadoes they can't be lower than 10,000 feet.

            b. There must be rapid lightning, at least 20 bolts per second.

        3. Low- and high-pressure centers must run together.

            a. (Visual Aid Number 2—chart showing juxtaposition of low- and high-pressure centers.)

            b. A large pressure drop must precede the tornado.

(Transition: When such conditions begin to develop in an area, general tornado warnings can be issued. But if the storms do develop, warning becomes still more difficult.)

    B. It is almost impossible to tell how powerful a particular storm will become or where it will go:

"Tornadoes are fickle. Most travel at a speed of 25 to 40 miles per hour. Still others vary. Some 'live' just a few minutes. But one lasted five hours. It visited destruction on town after town for more than 220 miles. On some terror-filled days, as many as 28 twisters hammer the nation" (*Senior Scholastic*).

    C. The Severe Local Storm Warning Center (known as SELS) was formed in 1958 to warn people of tornadoes, using the kinds of information I have just mentioned.

        1. The SELS Center is described in the May 20 issue of *Saturday Evening Post*.

        2. It has already saved thousands of lives.

(Transition: We have seen how tornadoes originate, what their characteristics are, and what discoveries about them allow in the way of prediction and warning. What can we conclude, then?)

Conclusion

I. Complacency about tornadoes is unjustified in the Northeast.
II. Theories about these storms differ.
III. Information being collected is helping the U.S. Weather Bureau predict and warn about these storms through the Severe Local Storm Warning Center.
IV. "We go from mystery to mystery. The more we learn, the more impossible it seems that tornadoes can really exist. By all the rules, Nature can't possibly put so much violence in a dot. And yet, there you are." (Clayton F. Van Thullenar, research chief and top administrator, SELS.)

Bibliography

1. Anonymous, "Best Pictured Tornado; Dallas," *Life*, XLII (April 15, 1957), 48–49.
   [Material here, including pictures, enabled me to describe vividly tornadoes under Point II of the body.]
2. Anonymous, "Definite Weather Pattern Needed for Tornadoes," *Science News Letter*, LXXIII (June 21, 1958), 392.
   [Sub-point A under Point III of the body was derived largely from this helpful account.]
3. Anonymous, "Hope for Tornado Control," *Science News Letter*, LXXI, (April 20, 1957), 246.
   [Supplementary material, in the end not very valuable, on Point III, C of the body was found here.]
4. Anonymous, "New Warning System for Tornadoes," *Look*, XXIII (October 13, 1959), 60 ff.
   [Information on the Severe Local Storm Warning Center was supplemented by material found in this article.]
5. Anonymous, "Scientist Has Method for Detecting Tornadoes," *Science News Letter*, LXXI (June 8, 1957), 360.
   [This was an extremely interesting article on a particular person's idea as to how tornadoes might be predicted. It would have been included under Point III, C of the body but my time limit prohibited me from including it.]
6. Anonymous, "Seeing Them Coming: Doppler Radar," *Newsweek*, LI (May 5, 1958), 79.

[This article provided information on the radar system mentioned in my introduction.]

7. Anonymous, "Tiros I Photographs Tornado-Producing Cloud," *Science News Letter*, LXXVIII (August 6, 1960), 88. [Interesting and clarifying photographs but not really very helpful in the construction of my speech.]

8. Anonymous, "Tornadoes: How, Why, When, and Where," *Senior Scholastic*, LXXIV (February 27, 1959), 35. [This article was helpful in the development of Point II of the body of my speech.]

9. Armagnac, A. P., "Tornadoes: Giant Electrical Machines," *Popular Science*, CLXXVI (April, 1960), 100–102 ff. [Armagnac aided me in the construction of the explanation under sub-point A of Point III of the body.]

10. Fales, E. D., Jr., "The Tornado Hunters," *Saturday Evening Post*, CCXXIV (May 20, 1961), 24–25. [Fales was most helpful to me in providing the figures on incidence and life damage of tornadoes used in my introduction.]

11. Lear, J., "How Stormy Weather is Born," *Saturday Review*, XLII (July 4, 1959), 31–36. [This account contained particularly good material on how a tornado originates.]

The second outline illustrates suitable procedures for a persuasive speech. It is based on a student's outline for a six-minute speech, but we have added persuasive materials to strengthen the original plan.

You Should Consider Public Service as a Career

Introduction

I. Just now we are collegians living in our own, secure little world.
   A. But graduation will come.
   B. The question won't be "a job"; it will be "What kind of job?"
II. The able college graduate isn't a "seeker"; he's sought after.
   A. You and I will not need to stumble into a line of work, for most college graduates with good records have several job opportunities to choose among.
   B. Every spring representatives of business, government, and education are sent to our camps to recruit our graduates.

III. No matter what your major, you have an opportunity to choose the kind of employer for whom to work.
  A. Today educational organizations employ everyone from lawyers and business administrators to teachers and engineers.
  B. Industries do the same.
  C. What you and I are likely to forget is that government at all levels offers the same range of employment opportunities.
IV. It is particularly unfortunate that public service, that is, civil service, is so much overlooked by college students choosing careers.
  A. My boss this summer told me that his job in government was the most challenging he ever had.
  B. Dr. Marvin Stern, ex-Deputy Director of Defense, called his civil service work, "The most stimulating and rewarding" of his career; he had also worked in a high paying industry.
     (Central Idea and Transition: I want to show you that there are very good reasons for considering a career in the civil service. I shall not lean on the "crutch" of patriotism because the reasons have to do with your own self-interest.)

Body

I. Civil service offers opportunities in a wide variety of fields, as I have already hinted.
  A. Engineers and dietitians, psychologists and tax collectors, auditors and physical and speech therapists, communications experts and mathematicians are all found in the job classifications of the civil service systems.
  B. The *Occupational Outlook Handbook,* published annually by the U.S. Department of Labor, shows government as a possible employer for the great majority of the hundreds of occupations discussed there.
II. The usual worry about government employment is that it doesn't pay enough.
  A. This worry is not altogether justified.
     1. (Visual Aid Number One—salary comparison chart for selected professional groups.)
     2. At the beginning levels, where most of us will start, the situation is better than you might suppose: ". . . in many of the lower-paying federal jobs, salary scales

267

... were higher than in private industry." (*U.S. News and World Report*, October 15, 1962.) Five years later, this is even more true.

3. In higher-level jobs, industry does outbid civil service in dollars and cents, but this is also changing.
   a. The federal government's pay-raise bill of 1962 made many civil service jobs competitive with industry in salary.
   b. The Department of Labor predicts that between 1960 and 1975 the number of federal employees will increase by 50 per cent; to get these people government will have to be even more competitive.
4. If you compare government salaries with salaries of "middle management" in industry or with top salaries in education, government comes off very well.
   a. (Visual Aid Number Two—comparison of bureau chiefs and under secretaries with industrial district managers and vice presidents.)
   b. Architects typically earn from $5,000–$30,000 a year; home economists from $5,000–$17,000; social workers from $4,800–$8,000. In each case government salaries run almost to the tops of those figures. (*Occupational Outlook Handbook*, 1964.)

B. We mislead ourselves by contrasting what a defense secretary made as a top executive in a major industry with what he gets in government; we ought to compare *representative* salaries for *comparable* jobs.

III. Where civil service positions have big advantages is in stability, in security of employment.

A. Government service operates on a merit system.
   1. You are hired, classified, and advanced on ability to do a job.
   2. There are clear standards for higher ranking positions —you can prepare yourself to win advancement.
   3. Thanks to improvements made over the last 50 years, jobs are not created and wiped out politically or because a bureau chief changes. Industry can't say as much.

B. At higher levels of civil service financial security compensates for lower salary levels.
   1. According to a survey of "Requirements for Ideal Job or Career," more than 61 per cent of over 4,500 college students interviewed counted "a stable, secure future" as "highly important" in choosing a career.

(Morris Rosenberg, *Occupations and Values*, 1957, p. 12.)

2. Here's part of the promise industry attaches to its higher pay scale: "A dozen executives and 20 or 30 other members of _____'s corporate staff are moving from Hamilton and elsewhere to New York, and as they align themselves with their counterparts . . . , the infighting that is normal to the situation is almost certain to begin. . . . [The chief officers of the newly merged companies] could not even settle upon a new name for the company, much less which of the two should become chief executive." (*Forbes*, March 15, 1967, p. 49.)

3. Government service isn't without unsettling changes; but once he has earned his rating, no civil service careerist gets thrown into the street because the company reorganized.

IV. Civil service offers fringe benefits over-matching those in education and equal to all but the very best in industry.

A. Under present tax levels fringe benefits are more important than cash income once a normal living standard is reached.

B. There are government training programs for specialized fields like tax collection, investigation, food and drug inspection, etc.

    1. Just as a summer employee I received on-the-job training in computer programming.

    2. Just as in business, these training programs are financed by your employer.

C. Government grants generous leave benefits.

    1. A minimum of thirteen leave days and a maximum of twenty-six days are granted per year.

    2. In addition there are eight paid holidays.

    3. Thirteen days of sick leave are granted annually, and these may be accumulated indefinitely.

    4. Men in the Reserves or National Guard receive up to fifteen days of paid military leave annually.

D. There are excellent group insurance, health- and death-benefit programs.

E. Incentive awards can range as high as $25,000.

F. The civil service retirement plan provides greater benefits than most private plans.

    1. The employee gives 6.5 per cent of his salary toward retirement.

    2. Government matches that sum so the employee retires on 13 per cent of his cumulative earnings.

    3. There is a real possibility that retirement benefits will be tied to the Consumer Price Index as the military retirement program was late in 1966.

V. Finally, don't suppose you have to live in Washington, D.C.

    A. "There are about eight federal workers outside the Washington area for every one in it." (*U.S. News and World Report*, October 15, 1962.) And the "outside" figure is still rising.

    B. Governmental service actually offers opportunities for all kinds of work all over the United States and in many foreign lands.

        1. The forest-resources expert in Colorado is as much a public service careerist as the clerk in Washington.

        2. So is the cultural attaché in Montevideo, Uruguay.

        3. And do you call this monotony? (Case of girl with M.A. in speech who began in Personnel Section of Department of Commerce and in three years had moved through positions as speech-writer and researcher to co-ordinator of domestic and international transportation for the staff of her division in 1967.)

Conclusion

I. This morning I have tried to give you hard-headed reasons for considering a career in civil service.

II. Though I've talked about federal civil service, there are similar opportunities in many states and cities.

III. The variety of opportunities is very wide, the pay is fair to excellent, there is the great advantage of stability and security in your job, fringe benefits are generally very good, and the idea that all civil service jobs are tedious and without challenge is simply not true.

IV. Don't let first impressions fool you.

    A. Of course there's red tape, and the Application for Federal Employment—Form 57—is enough to discourage anybody who doesn't think beyond first impressions. Visual Aid Number Three—unroll application.)

    B. What I've tried to show is that behind this unattractive doorway lie first-rate opportunities to do the things you've prepared yourself to do, under really attractive circumstances.

Statement of Sources

1. Anonymous, "Help Wanted in Washington," *Saturday Evening Post*, CCXXV (June 2, 1962).
2. Anonymous, "If Government Workers Get a Pay Raise . . . ," *U.S. News and World Report*, LIII (October 15, 1962).
3. Anonymous, "The Merger that Wasn't Made in Heaven," *Forbes*, XCIX (March 15, 1967).
4. "After College . . . What?" edited by the United States Civil Service Commission, 1961.
5. *Federal Employees' 1963 Almanac*, edited by Joseph Young (Washington: Federal Employees' News Digest, 1962).
6. *Occupational Outlook Handbook, 1963–1964*, Bulletin 1375 (Washington: U.S. Department of Labor, 1964).
7. Rosenberg, Morris, *Occupations and Values* (New York: The Free Press, Inc., 1957).
8. *Working for the U.S.A.*, edited by the U.S. Civil Service Commission (Washington: U.S. Civil Service Commission, 1962).

An outline is the basic tool by which extemporaneous speakers fix the design of their speeches as compositions, test the reasonableness of that design, represent to themselves and others the relationships among their thoughts, and fix their speech plans in their own minds. A completed outline is a visual representation of how speech materials are going to be disposed or handled in the speech to come. Both the making of an outline and review of it are invaluable aids to what ancient writers on rhetoric had in mind when they used the Latin term, *memoria*—the speaker's ultimate command of his material, his plan, and his own thinking processes in the moments of delivery. These things being the justifications for making outlines, the only legitimate justifications for any formal procedures in outlining must be that they are practically helpful. It is on just such a practical basis that we have tried to weigh the merits of outlining procedures in Chapter 9.

The mechanics of outlining are good or bad in proportion to how well they serve your needs and the needs of any constructive critic. Six common practices in outlining are invariably helpful:

1. Clear identification of the basic divisions of the speech: Introduction, Body, and Conclusion.

2. Use of consistent systems of symbolization and indentation to signal the relative importance of the relationships among ideas.

3. Recognition that the appearance of single sub-points in an outline is likely to indicate that a relationship has not been clearly thought out.

4. Firm adherence to the rule of discreteness in outlining; one thought per symbol; one symbol per thought.

5. Clear and unmistakable identification of the central idea or subject sentence.

6. Clear and unmistakable identification, in uniform fashion, of important transitions and internal summaries.

The sample outlines we have provided for your study and analysis conform to these practices in most details. They illustrate the general principles of disposition we have discussed in Chapter 8.

Exercises

WRITTEN

1. Arrange the eleven statements below as an outline for the body of a speech. There is no title, introduction, or conclusion. Select the subject sentence and give it proper place and status in your outline.

    In Mississippi there is one doctor for every 1500 inhabitants.

    One and a half million man-years of work are lost annually in the U.S. because of illness.

    There is an uneven distribution of doctors in the country.

    Thirteen hundred counties have no hospital facilities.

    There is need for a change in the present system of medical service.

    In New York State there is one doctor for every 487 inhabitants.

    The nation sustains large losses from preventable illness.

    Medical services are not available to all parts of our population.

Thirty thousand cancer victims could be saved each year through more surgery and radium treatment.

Hospital services are unevenly distributed in the country. The majority of our best equipped hospitals are located in large cities.

2. Make a list of suggestions for improvement of the outline entitled "You Should Consider Public Service as a Career" (See pp. 266–271).

3. In a sentence or two evaluate each of the following speech titles:
   a. "What You Must Do"
   b. "Acres of Diamonds"
   c. "Billy the Kid—Juvenile Delinquent?"
   d. "A Case for Socialized Medicine in the United States Today with Special Emphasis upon the Role of the General Practitioner in the Rural Areas"
   e. "Goya"
   f. "From Trees to Paper"
   g. "Suburbia: A New Way of Life"
   h. "Some Evidences of the Pedagogical Philosophy and Techniques of Quintilian as They Are Found in Modern Speech Education"
   i. "The Sleeping Dragon"
   j. "The Eternal Verities"

ORAL

1. Outline a speech by one of your classmates as you listen to him deliver it. Arrange for a conference during which you compare the outline you composed with the outline he used. Look for similarities and differences between the outlines and discuss why these occurred as they did.

2. Compose an outline for a six-minute speech of information or persuasion. Observe the suggestions made in this chapter and in Chapter 8.

---❧{ 10 }❧---   *Style*

Among all other lessons this should first be learned, that wee never
affect any straunge inkehorne termes, but to speake as is commonly
received: neither seeking to be over fine, nor yet living over-carelesse
using our speeche as most men doe, and ordering our wittes as the
fewest have done.

THOMAS WILSON, *Arte of Rhetorique*[1]

Man's expression of inner self probably emerges more clearly in
his style than in any other aspect of his speech-making. The ways
in which a speaker symbolizes thought reveal his capacities to discriminate among meanings, to conceive ideas clearly, to represent
them precisely. His style leads us to generalizations concerning
human behavior. Styles reflect men's adjustments to their times.
The relatively unguarded expression found in speaking sharply
mirrors habits of thinking. Thus examination of style provides
information for conclusions about men's accommodations to society and in turn about society itself. Words, figures of speech, and
images alone and in combination reflect the minds of men so well
that the study of spoken style is eminently humane.

    Speeches consist of ideas converted into words. *Acoustic* words

---

[1] Thomas Wilson, *Arte of Rhetorique* (London, 1585), p. 162.

274

are essential for all *oral* communication and expression. Whenever we say anything *orally* acoustic symbols stimulate the audience, and stand for our ideas. We encode our thoughts and express our emotions. We depend upon the listener to decode the message and to arrive at intended meanings and feelings. Ideas may be located and organized with skill and great care, as we have shown in the preceding chapters; but the work of speaking is not finished until the ideas are couched in the language of speech, voiced, and given further meaning through bodily action.

The words we choose as symbols of our ideas, their capacity to stir up meanings in our listeners' minds, and the influence of their combination and structuring are inseparable from the ideas themselves. For instance, one may say, "I think I'll go to bed and go to sleep." Or, "Methinks I will betake me to my nocturnal couch and lie in the arms of Morpheus." Or, "I guess I'll hit the sack and konk out." Though basically similar in idea, none of these three sentences expresses exactly the same meaning. Since the primary concern in public speaking is to arouse exact meaning, success depends very much upon the speaker's ability to choose and combine language symbols for aural reception. If we are to be practical we must be concerned with the creation of "style" in public speaking.

What Is Style?

Style in speaking is that part of the art which emerges from choices and combinations in language, their grammatical construction, and their psychological impact. Style, this third canon of rhetoric, stands for some of the most complex and personal of all the processes involved in speech-making. We become concerned with these processes once we have selected ideas and arranged them in the logical and psychological sequences we deem most effective. Some language decisions are made during stages of invention and disposition; but whole speeches almost never exist, even in the mind, until after the problems of language have been faced directly. Our purpose in this chapter is to discuss the nature of style and the role it plays in oral composition.

We must make it clear that we shall be using the term "style" in a limited sense. Style may be thought of as pervading all of the finished speech including the way it is uttered. Gestures and facial expression many operate as symbols to stir up thought so that style in delivery is worthy of consideration. Here, however, we shall consider style only as it relates to the process of speech composition, the conversion of ideas into words. We shall explore the role language plays as the vehicle of thought. The selection of words, and their combination and structuring into thought units are special topics for reflection in this chapter.

In the field of rhetoric, including composition and grammar, the English word "style" has referred historically and etymologically to manner of writing. The word was taken from the old French "style" which was derived from the Latin *stilus*. The spelling with the "y" is due partly to the French influence and partly to confusion of *stilus* with a Greek word *stylos* meaning "pillar." In classical Latin the term *stilus* came to have a meaning similar to the later English word. *Stilus* was a term applied by early Romans to a number of different writing instruments. These instruments, usually of metal or bone, had a sharp point on one end for writing on wax tablets and a blunted surface on the other for erasing. *Stilus*, later applied metaphorically, came to mean the distinctive characteristics of a man's handwriting. It was then extended to mean composition and subsequently to connote good expression in speech and writing.[2]

Between 1650 and 1750, this word "style" displaced the Latin word *elocutio* as the name of the third canon of rhetoric. *Elocutio*, as the term had been used, embraced the proper choice of words and their collocation. As *elocutio* ceased to mean style it displaced another Latin term, *pronuntiatio*. Thus, *elocutio* came to mean the study of delivery. Completing the changes in the language of rhetorical theory, *pronuntiatio* ceased to mean the study of voice

---

[2] This discussion is based upon the *Oxford English Dictionary*, Smith's *English-Latin Dictionary*, and Liddell and Scott, *A Greek-English Lexicon*.

and bodily action in delivery, and by 1850, *pronuntiatio* or "pronunciation" meant simply the study of the correct phonation of English words.[3]

As a consequence of these shifts in meaning, the history of the word "style," in its modern sense, began in English rhetorical textbooks in mid-fifteenth century. By 1720, Jonathan Swift was declaring, "Proper words in proper places make the true definition of a style."[4]

Subsequent definitions give us insight into the nature of style in rhetorical composition as we conceive it today. Before we devise a definition of our own it will be well to look at some of the definitions arrived at by those who have given the matter serious thought.

Perhaps one of the most famous definitions of style is that of Comte de Buffon, who in his speech to the French Academy in 1753 said, *"le style est de l'homme même"* or "style is the man himself" and: "Style is simply the order and movement one gives to one's thoughts. If these are connected closely, and rigorously compressed the style will be firm, nervous and concise. If they are allowed to follow one another loosely and merely at the lead of diction, however choice this be, the style will be diffuse, nerveless and languid."[5] These definitions introduce the ideas that style is individualistic, depending to a great extent on the total personality, and that it is in essence "movement" of idea.

Fifty years after Buffon, Hugh Blair in his book *Lectures on Rhetoric and Belles Lettres* emphasized ideas and thinking in a definition of style, saying that style ". . . is the peculiar manner in which a man expresses his conceptions by means of language. . . . Style has always some reference to an author's manner of think-

---

[3] These shifts in meaning are discussed in detail in Frederick W. Haberman, "The Elocutionary Movement in England 1750–1850" (unpublished Ph.D. thesis, Cornell University, 1947).

[4] Jonathan Swift, "A Letter to a Young Clergyman," 1719/20, in *The Works of Jonathan Swift*, ed. by Walter Scott (Edinburgh, 1814), VII, 337.

[5] Buffon, "Discours sur le Style," in *The Art of the Writer: Essays, Excerpts, and Translations*, ed. by Lane Cooper (Ithaca: Cornell University Press, 1952), pp. 153–154, 148. Copyright, 1952, Cornell University. Used by permission of Cornell University Press.

ing. It is a picture of ideas which arise in his mind, and of the manner in which they rise there."[6]

Coleridge, in 1818, contended that style is not translatable, saying that words cannot be changed without changing meaning. He insisted, "Style is, of course, nothing else but the art of conveying the meaning appropriately and with perspicuity, whatever that meaning may be, and one criterion of style is that it shall not be translatable without injury to the meaning."[7]

In 1886, John F. Genung highlighted dignity and distinction as ends of style when he said: "By style is meant, in general, manner of expressing thought in language; and more particularly, of giving such skillful expression as invests the idea with fitting dignity and distinction."[8]

The attempts to define this most complicated and elusive part of rhetoric do not stop with the nineteenth century. Thonssen and Baird, in 1948, broadened the scope of style in public speaking when they declared, "The expression which he [the speaker] then gives to his ideas, together with *whatever rhetorical devices he uses to enhance effectiveness,* may be called his style."[9] The "rhetorical devices," of course, might range from word choice to intonation and gesture.

Finally, Porter G. Perrin defines style by distinguishing it from grammar:

> But whatever *style* may mean to critics and philosophers, for a student or writer, it is most helpfully taken in a more concrete sense, to mean a speaker's or writer's use of language, the sources of the reader's or listener's impressions of his manner of thought and expression. The connotation of *style* is of the effectiveness of the expression (rather than of description of usage or questions of correctness). In contrast to grammar, the

---

[6] Hugh Blair, *Lectures on Rhetoric and Belles Lettres* (London, 1783), pp. 101–102.

[7] Samuel Taylor Coleridge, "On Style (1818)," in *The Art of the Writer,* p. 180.

[8] John F. Genung, *Practical Elements of Rhetoric* (Boston: Ginn, 1892), p. 13.

[9] Lester A. Thonssen and A. Craig Baird, *Speech Criticism* (New York: Ronald, 1948), p. 429. (Italics ours.)

typical structure of the language, style refers especially to the words and expressions in which the speaker or writer has a choice among the resources his language offers. An analysis of a writer's style takes into account the qualities of words, phrases, idioms, sentences, and arrangement of material.[10]

Keeping in mind these definitions and what we have already said about style and its inseparable linkage to ideas, we would assert that style, as applied to the rhetoric of oral discourse, may be defined as *the personal manner of utterance or expression giving ideas impact and movement.*

In this definition we have emphasized impact, movement and personal manner. Much of our concern in the remainder of this chapter will be with developing a personal style. As a consequence, before proceeding it would be well to consider commonly held misconceptions about style which might prevent or hinder this kind of development.

Misconceptions About Style

A prevalent misconception about style is that it is decoration. This attitude stems from such dicta as Lord Chesterfield's: "Style is the dress of thoughts." From this viewpoint style is thought of as clothing or covering, as something you *put on* ideas or *do to* ideas. Ideas are looked upon as windows to be trimmed; composition becomes something from which you occasionally step back to see if the baubles and tinsel applied give a beauteous effect.

This concept of style as exornation, as superimposed beautification, is often associated with an equally erroneous conception that style is something to be exhibited. Speakers who try to dazzle their audiences with clever wordings or impress them with long or archaic words or quaint expressions misconceive the function of style and its relationship to idea, audience, and occasion.

---

[10] Porter G. Perrin, *Writer's Guide and Index to English*, rev. ed. (Chicago: Scott, Foresman, 1950), pp. 773–774.

We cannot accept these two conceptions of style. We believe that wordings are part of the meaning, that if truly effective they are inherent in, or *at one with* the thought. Rather than worry about what to do with the idea or how to exhibit it, we believe that one should think clearly in the first place so that the chosen words say accurately and clearly what one is thinking. We would agree with George Henry Lewes:

> We see at once the mistake directly we understand that a genuine style is the living body of thought, not a costume that can be put on and off; it is the expression of the writer's mind; it is not less the incarnation of his thoughts in verbal symbols than a picture is the painter's incarnation of his thoughts in symbols of form and colour. A man may, if it please him, dress his thoughts in the tawdry splendour of a masquerade. But this is no more Literature than the masquerade is Life.[11]

What Lewes says of writing and literature applies as well to public address.

Characteristics of Style

A traditional way of looking at good style is to consider its characteristics or traits. These traits combine in varying proportions to create the speaker's personal, distinctive style and the variations within it. You will enhance your speaking considerably if you accept these qualities as those your own style, however personal, ought to possess.

ACCURACY

All style has a degree of accuracy; the thought is expressed with either precision or fuzziness. As a speaker your accuracy depends upon your ability to choose the words which best express your thoughts to your listening audience. Your vocabulary will

---

[11] George Henry Lewes, "The Principle of Beauty," in *Representative Essays on the Theory of Style*, ed. by William T. Brewster (New York: Macmillan, 1921), p. 217.

determine your degree of precision as well as your audience's understanding of that store of symbols.

In addition, you should attend to grammatical accuracy in fashioning your symbols into meaningful clusters. Slips in grammar affect the audience's image of you as a person and of your ability to express yourself. Good grammar is assumed by the audience. As Cicero said:

> . . . nobody ever admired an orator for correct grammar, they only laugh at him if his grammar is bad, and not only think him no orator but not even a human being; no one ever sang the praises of a speaker whose style succeeded in making his meaning intelligible to his audience, but only despised one deficient in capacity to do so.[12]

So a second attention should be to the accuracy of grammar.

A third concern in achieving accuracy calls for a consideration of what is correct on the specific occasion. Here, correctness and accuracy blend with propriety, a virtue of good style. Producing correct tone or feeling for the particular occasion will only result from judicious selection of words with due attention to level of difficulty and kind. Formal, stately occasions call for more formal language than informal classroom situations. The level of abstraction and the technicality of wordings can be accurate or correct only if the audience understands what is said and the occasion justifies the way it is said. The most convivial gathering of astronauts would allow levels of technicality and precision that would prove bafflingly imprecise and incorrect to a high school class in general science.

Accuracy, determined by speaker, audience, the idea to be expressed, and the occasion is of primary concern to any speaker.

CLARITY

Once you are sure that you are correct in symbolizing and blending your idea, your next concern becomes clarity. Aristotle,

---

[12] *De Oratore*, trans. by H. A. Rackham (Cambridge, Mass.: Harvard University Press, 1948), pp. 41–42, Bk III, Ch. 14.

at the beginning of his discussion of style in *The Rhetoric,* said: "We may therefore . . . regard it as settled that a good style is, first of all, clear. The proof is that language which does not convey a clear meaning fails to perform the very function of language."[13] So you must ask yourself, "How clearly have I expressed the idea? How completely does the audience understand me?"

Aristotle went on to say: "Clearness is secured through the use of name-words [nouns and adjectives] and, verbs, that are current terms. . . ."[14] Concrete rather than abstract words will help; so will good transitions and simple, familiar sentence structures. The more directly you say what you have to say, the more likely you are to be clear.

Once again, clarity is a matter of degree. The more obscure the expression of idea, the more inefficient the communication. How far you go in amplification, in detailing your explanations and arguments according to what you know about your audience's requirements, will determine how clear you will be. Your care in choosing words will also determine your degree of clarity.

You must remember that unless you are clear you will be misunderstood, and that if you are misunderstood you cannot hope to achieve your purpose. It is easy to mistake clearness for accuracy. An accurate and grammatically correct symbolization of idea may still prove unclear to an audience. Listeners may simply not understand symbolization that is accurate on a level of comprehension too high for them. On the other hand, clarity of expression does not necessarily guarantee accurate symbolization of ideas. Misinformation may be transmitted clearly. Ideally, a speaker is both clear and accurate in expression, but it does not always follow that accurate ideas are clearly worded or conversely that clear wording and clear structuring of symbols guarantee accurate transmission.

The primary demanding element for clarity is, as we have already indicated, the audience. The idea itself is next in the

---

[13] From *The Rhetoric of Aristotle,* trans. and ed. by Lane Cooper, p. 185, Bk III, Ch. 2. Reprinted by permission of the publisher Appleton–Century–Crofts.

[14] *Ibid.*

hierarchy. Ideas cry out for clear treatment. The occasion may exert some pressure for clarity if it is of a special nature. The speaker demands least, since his ideas are clear to him even though they may not be clear to anyone else. There is the rub! Your clarity, for yourself, will tempt you to disregard your listeners' clarity, the opportunities your subject offers you, and special aspects of your occasion.

PROPRIETY

Propriety, or appropriateness, is also characteristic of a good speech style. Style for good public speaking, unlike that for an essay or a novel, is meant for a particular audience in a particular place at a particular time. Particularity and close adjustment are the goals of oral style, not universality or adaptation to respondents in all places at all times.

One's style must, of course, be appropriate to the subject matter treated. "The style again," as Aristotle declared, "should not be mean nor above the dignity of the subject, but appropriate. . . ."[15] To describe a commonplace operation, such as changing a tire, in flowery, poetic language would be ridiculous. Such menial subjects are not good ones for stylistic experimentation. To depict a sunset in plain vernacular is to rob the subject of meaning and inherent emotional quality. To say "the sky was kind of red, sort of like a tomato or a radish," would be as inappropriate as to say of a tire, "the shiny black vulcanized rubber besmirched by dust and grime, ought to be carefully loosened from the band which girdles the wheel."

Style must also be suited to the particular audience. You would hardly use the same vocabulary level or informality in phrasing for speeches before a group of college alumni and before a group of boy scouts or persons lacking in formal education. The word symbols used for these groups would vary as would the amount of elaboration necessary for clarity and interest. Yet, in

---

[15] *Ibid.*

adapting to the particular audience, you must be careful to be always yourself. You must not sell yourself or your listeners short. A college graduate who tries to sound like a farmer at a Grange meeting, a juvenile delinquent at a boys' reformatory, and a college professor in the classroom is play-acting. He becomes ridiculous. So in tailoring your style to the audience, do not forget that it must also be tailored to yourself. Your style, as Buffon noted, is you, yourself. It is a very personal thing—your manner of expression. Consciously straining too hard or trying too strenuously to adapt to the audience or striving for a special kind of speaking style, as some beginning students do, usually results in a style which smells of the lamp or sounds like a caricature of someone else.

If style must be appropriate to the subject matter, the audience, and the speaker himself, it must still be appropriate to the particular occasion. To use the same style in a corporate business meeting as you would use for informal remarks at a fraternity meeting would be to court disaster. On certain occasions it is traditional to be dignified and formal and to strive for niceties of expression. On other occasions it is more appropriate to be relaxed, informal, and to indulge, with taste, in slang and colloquialisms. In composing your speech take into account the setting, its physical aspects and emotional tone, if your style is to be appropriate to the occasion as well as to subject, audience, and self.

ECONOMY

Most of us when speaking use too many words. We spend words unwisely, using several where one would do. We clutter thoughts so that even when we do not obscure, we irritate with unnecessary circumlocution. Economy is an attribute of desirable style.

By economy in language we mean the right choice of words, in right amount and best order for instantaneous intelligibility. We mean economy of the listener's attention.

Herbert Spencer in his essay, "The Philosophy of Style,"

emphasized the importance of economizing the "mental energies" and "mental sensibilities" of auditors or readers. "To so present ideas that they may be apprehended with the least possible mental effort, is the desideratum towards which most of the rules . . . point," he said.[16] Spencer claimed language is a hindrance to thought even though it's a necessary instrument. He held that economy of the respondent's attention is the secret of effect and depends upon the right choice and collocation of words, the best arrangement of clauses to clarify the ranks of principal and subordinate propositions, the judicious use of figures of speech, and the rhythmic sequence of syllables. Spencer summarized his "principle of economy" thus:

> A reader or listener has at each moment but a limited amount of mental power available. To recognize and interpret the symbols presented to him, requires a part of this power; to arrange and combine the images suggested requires a further part; and only that part which remains can be used for realizing the thought conveyed. Hence, the more time and attention it takes to receive and understand each sentence, the less time and attention can be given to the contained idea; and the less vividly will that idea be conceived.[17]

Extreme brevity is characteristic of passionate language, but the fewest number of words for proper expression is not always the smallest number possible. Economy of attention is economy only if the idea is fully clear and understandable. At times, economy in style means not brevity or frugality in wording but the necessary amplification. The proper amount of wordage needed in developing an idea, either in clarifying or in proving, will produce the most concise statement possible. And speakers must remember that listeners cannot review or reexamine unless speakers provide the necessary words.

Speaking the simplest way without downgrading your vocabulary is proper economy. If you see to it that you have excised superfluous introductory lead-ins to sentences or that you have

---

[16] *The Philosophy of Style*, p. 11.
[17] *Ibid.*

avoided unnecessary adjectives and adverbs and unnecessarily inverted word orders, you will be concise and promote clarity.

FORCE

A good speaking style has drive, urgency, and excitement. It compels the listener to pay attention as it propels ideas forward. We often equate force with intensity, but we must remember that force or intensity in style is often greatest when language is quiet rather than blatant.

Economy and preciseness produce force. Spencer supplies the link when he says, ". . . other things equal, the force of all verbal forms and arrangements is great in proportion as the time and mental effort they demand from the recipient is small."[18] Shortness, terseness, and the resulting abruptness all produce force in style. Even short words help, for as Spencer elaborates:

> . . . the shortness of Saxon words becomes a reason for their greater force. One qualification, however, must not be overlooked. A word which itself embodies the most important part of the idea to be conveyed, especially when the idea is an emotional one, may often with advantage be a polysyllabic word. Thus it seems more forcible to say, "It is *magnificent,*" than "It is *grand.*" The word *vast* is not so powerful a one as *stupendous. . . . nasty* is not so effective as . . . *disgusting.*[19]

Spencer was probably wrong in thinking Saxon words have special forcefulness, but he was right in believing that, in general, the quick blows of short words yield force in style.

We can see the connection between force and preciseness if we note the greater strength of images and shapes which are definite in outline over those which are ragged or vague. Solidly massed units are stronger than scattered ones. An argument has more force when it has perceivable form. Conversely, a point is weakened by asides, irrelevant excursions, or supporting material

---

[18] *Ibid.,* p. 33.
[19] *Ibid.,* pp. 13–14.

which carries us too far from the centrality of the idea. The single well-defined bullet hits home harder than a scattering of buckshot. So it is with spoken statements.

Force is required in all elements in a speech situation. Sometimes the best adaptation to the audience requires strong statements. Sometimes the ideas demand forcefulness if they are to be given proper significance. Sometimes the speaker's physical mien dictates that he speak strongly, with real verve and vigor. Finally, some occasions demand a powerful, direct approach.

STRIKING QUALITY

The characteristic of good style which we choose to call "striking quality" comprises heightened effect and sublimity. Writers have called this characteristic "interestingness," "impressiveness," "ornateness," "vividness," or "beauty."

We reject the term "beauty" with reference to rhetorical composition, because speech making is a utilitarian art. Its primary function is never to be beautiful. Beauty is relative and dependent on individual tastes. Striking quality is easier to measure and detect. A speech admired for the sole reason that it aroused the imagination as a poem might would be suspect as rhetoric. Similarly suspect would be one whose main virtue was that it was euphonious. Some words are beautiful, others are ugly in sound. Some mental images produced by words are lovely, others are repulsive. The revolting as well as the attractive can draw our attention and subsequently have an effect. Beauty has place as a constituent of striking quality, but it is not the only element in the quality. The unknown writer called "Longinus" said in *On the Sublime*:

> . . . the choice of proper and striking words wonderfully attracts and enthralls the hearer, and that such a choice is the leading ambition of all orators and writers, since it is the direct agency which ensures the presence in writings, as upon the fairest statues, of the perfection of grandeur, beauty, mellowness, dig-

nity, force, power, and any other high qualities there may be, and breathes into dead things a kind of living voice. All this it is, I say, needless to mention, for beautiful words are in very truth the peculiar light of thought.[20]

Ruskin, in discussing beauty of style in fine art, enumerated as its qualities: infinity, unity (with variety), repose (even in motion), symmetry, purity, and moderation. He added that the last quality girdles and safeguards all the rest, and "in this respect is the most essential of all."[21] In a chapter on the "Greatness of Style" Ruskin named as the requisites of style: love of beauty, wise choice of noble subject, sincerity, and invention produced by imagination.[22]

Ruskin's emphasis on moderation in the use of the striking is in key with the theories of both "Longinus" and Buffon. "Longinus" points out, ". . . stately language is not to be used everywhere, since to invest petty affairs with great and high-sounding names would seem just like putting a full-sized tragic mask upon an infant boy."[23] Buffon echoed him: "Nothing is more inimical to this warmth [the luminosity of style] than the desire to be everywhere striking."[24]

Striking quality in speeches comes from the ability of the speaker to combine words in euphonious combinations, his ability to give poetic turns to wordings yet keep them prose, and his ability to paint word pictures which stir the listener's emotions. The further the speaker moves toward uniqueness of expression, the more striking we are apt to think his speaking. "Hence," as Aristotle advises, "it is well to give the ordinary idiom an air of

---

[20] Longinus, "On the Sublime," trans. by W. Rhys Roberts, in J. H. Smith and E. W. Parks, *The Great Critics*, 3rd ed. (New York: W. W. Norton, 1951), pp. 95–96.

[21] John Ruskin, *The True and the Beautiful* (New York: Wiley and Halsted, 1859), p. 4.

[22] See John Ruskin, *Ruskin's Works* (Boston: Estes and Lauriat, 1897), XXII, pp. 46–70.

[23] Smith and Parks, *The Great Critics*, p. 96.

[24] Cooper, *The Art of the Writer*, p. 151.

remoteness; the hearers are struck by what is out of the way, and like what strikes them."[25]

Perhaps this liking for the remote is the explanation of why striking quality in style attracts individual listeners. If so, we are led back to the speech material and the audience as the primary constituents of speaking situations that demand something striking in acceptable style. The speaker's individual desire to be aesthetically pleasing is another force demanding that utterance be striking. He may be fond of imagery, pleasing sound combinations, and attractive rhetorical figures. As long as his fondness does not produce exhibitionism as a goal, it is all to the good.

The occasion may require style of striking quality. For example, there are occasions where it is difficult to find new ideas to match the circumstances. The presentation or acceptance of an award or situations calling for welcomes or farewells may pose such problems to a speaker. He must say something, but it has all been said many times. So he must find a unique or striking way to word his familiar message. By his listeners' standards, originality may consist chiefly in producing striking variations on familiar themes.

LIVELINESS

Force, economy, and striking quality contribute to liveliness in oral communication. If the mission of rhetoric is to endow ideas with movement and its goal is, as C. S. Baldwin said, "the energizing of knowledge and the humanizing of truth," then there is no more important stylistic quality in oral discourse than liveliness. "Propulsion" or movement must be accepted as aspects of this liveliness. If speeches are to reach climaxes of reason and emotion, there must be both energy and the kind of movement

---

[25] From *The Rhetoric of Aristotle*, trans. and ed. by Lane Cooper, p. 185, Bk III, Ch. 2. Reprinted by permission of the publisher, Appleton–Century–Crofts.

that carries the idea forward and propels it toward its most influential form. This effect comprises energy, movement and some degree of suspense.

Aristotle recognizes the necessity for suspense when he says that listeners ". . . like words that set an event before their eyes; for they must see the thing occurring now, not hear of it in the future, the speaker must aim at these three points: Metaphor, Antithesis, Actuality."[26] He thereafter advises that we make our verbal pictures move—that we make them motion pictures rather than still photographs. Not still-life images but "objects invested with life, and thereby an effect of activity" is the goal.[27] The successful stylist to Aristotle is one who ". . . makes everything live and move; and movement is activity."[28]

In discussing "actuality" Aristotle says,

> We have said that liveliness is secured by the use of the proportional metaphor, and by putting things directly before the eyes of the audience. But we still have to explain what is meant by setting things "before the eyes," and how this is to be effected. What I mean is, using expressions that show things in a state of activity.[29]

Liveliness, then, comes from animation, conflict, suspense, actuality (or realism), specificity, and proximity. It comes from the use of present tense and active voice. It comes from economy in wording, from simple rather than complex structuring, from vividness in imagery, and from any other resource of language that sets moving images before the minds of listeners.

Relate events in a "you are there" rather than an "I was there" fashion. Take your audience with you as you re-live the suspenseful moment when your boat capsized or your car crashed. Let the audience feel the tape breaking across your chest at the finish line of a race, the touch of your friend's hand at the moment of goodbye, the pull of your muscles as they lift a rock or kick a football.

---

[26] *Ibid.*, p. 207, Bk III, Ch. 10.
[27] *Ibid.*, p. 211, Bk III, Ch. 11.
[28] *Ibid.*, p. 212, Bk III, Ch. 11.
[29] *Ibid.*, p. 211, Bk III, Ch. 11.

Use lively imagery. Make your images cumulate and build. Let your appeals to sight, touch, taste, hearing, and smell, to thermal and kinesthetic sensitivity, so combine that the images rising in the mind are experienced. Consider a sentence like: "I smell the pines in the crisp morning air and hear the crunch of snow beneath me as I plod up the path with weary muscles crying out at every step." In this single sentence four kinds of sensory appeal combine to bring the experience to reality. Experiment with animation, actuality, and imagery and you will find that your speeches have movement. They will run to their goals rather than limp to their conclusions.

The demands for liveliness come above all from the audience. Hearers want to be moved, to respond empathically, to be excited by ideas. Then, at times, they want to be lulled. Bouncing, vigorous, hard-muscled style must be used in moderation as must striking qualities. A racing style may be out of place at eight o'clock in the morning, for occasions also determine the appropriate degree of liveliness. The solemnity of a commencement or a worship service may call for gentle pace rather than for vigorous movement. Whatever the occasion, you will speak strongly if you appeal to experience, to active exercise of mind and body. Remember that liveliness through metaphor, antithesis, realism, and progressive movement of ideas is possible with or without high excitement. Remember also that some speech materials lend themselves better to lively discourse than others. Narratives are especially susceptible to animated treatments while inquiries often demand a diligent search for the means to liveliness.

To say that liveliness is the most important of all qualities of good oral style is no exaggeration; it is a forthright summary of all we have just said. Accuracy, clarity, propriety, economy, force, and striking quality are virtues of good oral style, but they are constituents of the ultimate virtue of discourse that influences —liveliness. You must realize that the characteristics of good style are interrelated and that while one or another of the characteristics of good style may seem to dominate a passage of discourse and subsequently to cause another, the ultimate aim in composition is to achieve movement of idea. Economy may engender force or striking quality. Propriety may produce clarity or economy. But in the end the demand for progression of ideas places liveliness at the top of the list. The time-bound, audience-bound, occasion-bound speaker cannot disregard this hierarchy of stylistic values peculiar to his art. It is fitting then that we turn next to the peculiarities of oral discourse as contrasted with written composition.

Oral and Written Style

At first glance it may seem obvious that there must be some differences between oral and written style. Both deal with words, sentences, and language in general. Yet, written style often has oral elements, and many fine writers tell us to give our writing the quality of conversation. If we do so, our writing can enhance our speaking and vice versa.

James A. Winans once said, "A speech is not an essay on its hind legs." He meant that the essay is not oral even though it may be rhetorical. And the chances are that your essays, themes, and term papers, if read aloud, would lack some of the traits your writing for speaking ought to have.

Little research and scholarly experimentation has been done on the differences between oral and written style.[30] Such research provides us with general points of departure rather than decisive pronouncements. But the generalizations are worth testing by experience. These general differences in the two kinds of style, we are quick to add, are differences not of kind but of degree.

---

[30] See Gladys L. Borchers, "An Approach to the Problem of Oral Style," *The Quarterly Journal of Speech*, XXII (1936), 114–117; Gordon Thomas, "Effect of Oral Style on Intelligibility of Speech," *Speech Monographs*, XXIII (1956), 46–54; Joseph A. De Vito, "Comprehension Factors in Oral and Written Discourse of Skilled Communicators," *Speech Monographs*, XXXII (1965), 124–128; James W. Gibson, Charles R. Gruner, Robert J. Kibler, and Francis J. Kelly, "A Quantitative Examination of Differences and Similarities in Written and Spoken Messages," *Speech Monographs*, XXXIII (1966), 444–451. The latter study includes a valuable survey of contemporary studies of oral and written style.

Drawing upon the research just mentioned and upon our personal observations, we arrive at the following hypotheses which we invite you to test in your speech making. In contrast to written prose style, oral style uses:

1. More personal pronouns.
2. More variety in kinds of sentences.
3. More variety in sentence lengths.
4. More simple sentences.
5. More sentence fragments.
6. Many more rhetorical questions.
7. More repetition of words, phrases, and sentences.
8. More monosyllabic than polysyllabic words.
9. More contractions.
10. More interjections.
11. More indigenous language.
12. More connotative than denotative words.
13. More euphony.
14. More figurative language.
15. More direct quotation.
16. More familiar words.

Aristotle recognized these differences when he said:

> . . . each kind of rhetoric has its own appropriate style. The style of written prose is not that of controversial speaking. . . . A knowledge of both the written and spoken style is required. . . . The written . . . style is more finished; the controversial is far better adapted to dramatic delivery. . . . On comparison, speeches of the literary men sound thin in the actual contests; while those of the orators sound well but look crude when you hold them in your hands—and the reason is that their place is in a contest.[31]

We urge students, when working on speech manuscripts, not to worry whether the speech looks well on paper. Any manuscript

---

[31] From *The Rhetoric of Aristotle*, trans. and ed. by Lane Cooper, p. 217, Bk III, Ch. 12. Reprinted by permission of the publisher Appleton–Century–Crofts.

ought to be neat and readable in the mechanical sense; the important point is that if one brings only the standards of writing for the eye to bear upon writing intended for the ear, he will be applying irrelevant criteria and he will fail to apply important criteria. For example, the principles of paragraphing have limited relevance to the composition that will be heard. Outstanding speakers exhibit widely varying practices for marking off major and minor ideas on the manuscript page. Whatever is done, the convenience of the speaker, not the general reader, must be served.

The same is true of sentences. Speaking appropriately uses many more sentence fragments than formal writing. Every novelist who is expert in writing dialogue and every good playwright knows this well. So, to apply formal standards of sentence construction and sentence completeness in evaluating the manuscript for a speech would be to force the communication into forms it need not and does not normally fit. Consider the fragment we quoted from Franklin D. Roosevelt's address, "The Philosophy of Social Justice Through Social Action" (pp. 151–152).[32] Using the best available records, L. LeRoy Cowperthwaite's best judgment of what Mr. Roosevelt actually said in Detroit yields the passage quoted again below. Notice how little the language resembles what we ordinarily call polished writing *for the eye*. Notice the broken sentence structures. Doubtless they were rendered smoothly meaningful by pause and vocal inflection. Notice the reinforcement gained by repetition of the words "crippled children"—reinforcement that writing for the eye might achieve in less obvious ways. Plainly, this is a very carefully established sample of the *oral* style of one of the most successful political speakers in the history of the United States. This is the way he *talked*:

> Take another form of poverty in the old days. Not so long ago, you and I know, there were families in attics—in every part of the Nation—in country districts and in city districts— hundreds and thousands of crippled children who could get no adequate care, crippled children who were lost to the com-

---

[32] The text of President Roosevelt's speech printed here is based on an official stenographic report, his own manuscript, and a recording.

munity and who were a burden on the community. And so we have, in these past twenty or thirty years, gradually provided means for restoring crippled children to useful citizenship; and it has all been a factor in going after and solving one of the causes of poverty and disease.

Our point is not that good communication composed for the ear must look exactly like this on the page. The page of a speech manuscript should, however, display the variety of language forms and the myriad of reinforcing and emphasizing devices that listeners require in order to keep control over thoughts that are being developed *acoustically.*

Impaled on paper, some sentences of a speech will look strange, and many constructions will depart from the standard patterns of good visual communication. Other differences will reflect the fifteen qualities listed above. Usually, the page ought to exhibit fewer "howevers," "thuses," and "therefores" than an essay might; it ought to contain such words and phrases as "but," "and so," or "the result of high cost is." These last are simply the connectives of normal conversation.

Speeches ought to contain few indefinite pronouns. "This" and "that" are ambiguous words for a listener. They always require him to remember some noun used earlier. It is often too hard to recall that the "this" now heard actually means the "cathedral" heard five or ten seconds previously.

Whether one is writing or speaking, he will convey his meaning more forcefully and usually more clearly if he uses verbs in the active voice. There is more efficient meaning and more action in "The dog bit the man" than in "The man was bitten by the dog." "It is believed by most observers that a decision will be made by the President on Thursday" is bad writing and stupid speaking. Listening is neither easy nor a highly efficient way of absorbing information. Good oral style should compensate for these limitations by its directness; one of the easiest, most obvious compensations is to use active verbs as much as possible, in the present tense where that is appropriate. There are times when the detachment produced by the use of passive voice is desirable, but ordinarily active voice serves best.

Scientific evidence does not justify an unqualified declaration that if you incorporate in your speaking such qualities as the sixteen we have enumerated and if you keep your talk in the active voice as much as possible, you will achieve a successful oral style. The bases of good style in speaking are largely the same as the bases for good style in writing, but oral style needs to be adapted to the special circumstances under which speaking takes place. Crucially important is that speaking is heard, not read. This is why oral style must be conversational, personal, and responsive to the thought processes of listeners. We believe that if you try to inject the qualities we have been discussing into your spoken language, you will begin to increase your conversational quality and rid your speaking of the written or essay-like sound that disturbs and hampers efficient listening.

The Development of a Style

You have your own particular manner of utterance or expression, your own speech style—good or bad. Consider the members of your class in public speaking. You will notice that some of them stand out from the rest in style. One may have a more poetic style than the others—use more imagery, savor his words more. Another may be rough-hewn in style—terser, plainer, or more homespun in his wordings. Still another may be abstract, use colloquialisms or slang, or be exceedingly precise in technical explanations. Why these styles impress you as distinctive may be difficult for you to determine, but each speaker habitually uses a particular kind of language or a specific set of stylistic devices such as imagery or rhetorical questions. Each consciously or unconsciously endows his speeches with particular characteristics of style; the style of each has hallmarks, and yours does, too.

You and your classmates have different styles in part because you work differently. When you revise and reword, you modify and change ideas in order to say what you mean. Sometimes you backtrack to a prior wording when you find that it more specifically expressed intended meaning. If you speak impromptu or extemporaneously, however, you will have no opportunity for such polishing. You must express yourself as accurately as possible the first time. In the extemporaneous mode you may, of course, try out wordings as you work from your outline during oral rehearsal, but you usually do not freeze wording in quite the way you would when memorizing or working from a manuscript. At every point in composition you make choices which give your style the qualities that distinguish it as yours. In all cases, you must remember that while readers may flip back through a book to re-read thoughts, listeners can never re-listen to that portion of your speech which was not clear to them upon first hearing.

In your work in public speaking you will seek to improve your style. You already have a style of some sort. You have a vocabulary at some stage of development and special habits of expression peculiar to you. Your background, prior education, and methods of writing have exerted influence on your style. Some of your habits of expression are good ones which need emphasis. Others are faults to be eradicated.

Your task is to improve your style, to use words so that what you say will be increasingly correct, clear, appropriate, economical, forceful, striking, and moving for your audience. You must start by surveying your present speech style and work from there. It takes a long time to change a style; you cannot expect a new one to emerge overnight, but you will be surprised at how you can modify your style through conscious attention and experimentation.

Your aim ought to be to nurture variety within your distinctive style. An inflexible style will not meet the demands of enough different speech situations. As Herbert Spencer once said, "To have a specific style is to be poor in speech."[33] Distinctive styles in speech are unavoidable but the same style for all occasions would be ineffective. The many adjustments necessary to the given speaking situation preclude the use of any one style in all cases.

---

[33] Herbert Spencer, *The Philosophy of Style* (New York: D. Appleton, 1920), p. 47.

The style of a chemistry or mathematics lecture would hardly be suitable for a popular lecture on the advancement of science. An inspirational sermon would be poorly couched in the jargon of a salesman. Since adaptation is the key to all good public speaking, variety in style is essential if you are to reach the crest of development in your speech making.

There is no fixed style of speaking for each speech purpose. Aristotle intimates that style varies with different kinds of speeches, that controversial style differs from others, that ceremonial speaking is more literary than courtroom address.[34] Blair also matches styles with various speech types and assigns special stylistic characteristics to occasional, legislative, courtroom, and pulpit speaking.[35] He says, for example, that courtroom speaking requires more orderliness, conciseness in narration, purity, and plainness than pulpit speaking. The classification of speeches which both Aristotle and Blair employ is based not upon speech purpose but upon situation. These authors observe that certain relationships among speaker, audience, and occasion call for certain manners of address. Not purpose but situation governs the characteristics of style.

Some persons, for example, say that informative speaking is distinguished by language of fact and explanation, the diction of definition, example, comparison and less figurative vocabulary. We believe that such a broad generalization is unsatisfactory because the situation for informing rather than the purpose determines what is appropriate in the given case. This is why there is no section in this book in which style is matched to speaking purposes. All the characteristics of style are present in every speech in some degree. No one characteristic is exclusively associated with any one purpose. The demands governing style are more fluid and flexible than those governing invention and organization. Seek a personal, distinctive style within which many variations may be

---

[34] From *The Rhetoric of Aristotle* trans. and ed. by Lane Cooper. Copyright, 1932, Lane Cooper, p. 219, Bk III, Ch. 12. Reprinted by permission of the publisher Appleton–Century–Crofts.

[35] See Hugh Blair, *Lectures on Rhetoric and Belles Lettres* (Philadelphia: Hayes & Zell, 1860), Lectures XXV, XXVII, XXVIII, XXIX, pp. 261–264, 284b–292, 298b–305, 312b–322.

made, arising from adaptations to the requirements of idea, audience, occasion, and your own needs. What is it that you are to adapt? The resources imbedded in language itself.

Language Related to Style

The qualities of language in any speech are in part determined by the speaker's understanding of the resources offered by the meanings of words and the ways in which words may be combined. Words are neither fixed in meaning nor do they combine in only a few ways. Every language is more or less flexible. Spoken language is generally more flexible than written because there are opportunities to add meanings through voice quality, inflection, and action. Thus, if you are to develop variety in your present command of language you must know the wealth of variations available to you in spoken English. Then, learn to use them more extensively.

CONNOTATION AND DENOTATION

All *oral* communication involves the use of an oral language. Words are symbols for meanings since they stand for ideas. No word has exactly the same meaning for any two individuals. Words are black marks on paper or combinations of sounds which travel through air. We endow them with meaning. The meaning assigned depends upon the human being who perceives the words, and our backgrounds make us interpret word symbols in particular and sometimes peculiar ways. Parental authority, environment, and learning experiences all combine to determine exactly what a word will mean to us. When we do not know how to interpret a word, we turn to a dictionary or a glossary or some other person for the meaning. Even then we find that the meanings we gather do not always suffice.

Words always have at least two kinds of meaning: denotative or connotative. Some words denote much and connote relatively little—for most people. Denotative words are thought to be more logical, objective, impersonal, and extensional. They refer explicitly to objects and actions outside the mind which are verifiable through observation. Purely denotative words require few further words of explanation. A fairly denotative statement would be, "President Jones called the meeting to order. Secretary Smith read the minutes of the last meeting."

Connotative words are those which, for most people, have important emotive, subjective, personal, and intensional meanings. Their meanings are turned toward the self, are private, suggestive, and depend upon the individual's emotions. Such words as "mother," "homecoming," "democracy," "Communist," and "lover" are rich in connotation. They arouse emotional responses, create images in the mind, and evoke the established attitudes of the listener. These words can be explained—rendered precise or "public"—only through the use of other words.

Many words, of course, are both connotative and denotative because their objective meanings touch off very personal reactions. The word "house" can in many cases be considered denotative, as in a sentence reading, "There were twenty houses in the three-hundred block of Elm Avenue." This same word in other contexts may call to mind a particular house or a particular experience with a house and thus becomes strongly connotative.

In distinguishing between the two kinds of meaning, Professor S. I. Hayakawa is helpful:

> . . . the extensional meaning is something that cannot be expressed in words, because it is what the words stand for. An easy way to remember this is to put your hand over your mouth and point when asked to give the extensional meaning.
> The intensional meaning of a word or expression, on the other hand, is that which is suggested (connoted) inside one's head. Roughly speaking, whenever we express the meaning of words by uttering more words, we are giving intensional meaning, or connotations. To remember this, put your hand over your eyes and let the words spin around in your head.[36]

---

[36] S. I. Hayakawa, *Language in Action* (New York: Harcourt, Brace, 1946), p. 47.

WORD CHOICE

Our discussion of connotation and denotation has shown that our systems of language are imperfect. Semantics, the science of word meanings, deals with some of these imperfections. It is enough to say here that confusion in word meanings poses many problems for the public speaker. It is almost too much for him to hope that he will stir up the exact meanings he intends, since almost any symbol may mean one thing to him but quite another to his listeners. He is constantly making choices and revisions in order to maintain practical control over his intended meanings.

A word choice is a mistake, of course, if it implants a distorted message in the mind of a listener. As the illustration at the beginning of this chapter suggests, word choices *can* and *do* change meanings. Mental pictures are altered and modified by changes in wording. To say, "I saw a *red* wagon" prompts a different image from "I saw a *pink* wagon" or "I saw a *fuchsia* wagon" or "I saw a *vermilion* wagon" or ". . . a *Chinese red* wagon" or ". . . a *Coca-Cola red* wagon." The manufacturers of nail polish could extend the list of reds *ad infinitum*. Similarly, to say, "The child skipped *gaily* down the street" is different from saying the child skipped "merrily" or "joyously" or "boisterously," or even "happily." But a change of adjective or adverb is secondary to a change of noun or verb. Substitute "lad" or "youth" or "teen-ager" or even "girl" or "boy" for *child,* and the meaning changes instantly. Or substitute "shuffled" or "skated" or "strolled" for *skipped* and the mental picture is again modified drastically. To stir up an intended meaning, just any word will not do even though it conforms to all grammatical conventions.

At times the wrong choice of word, a malapropism, can make meaning ludicrous or spoil the mood created by a speaker, undoing several minutes' work. We think of the student who said that a speaker's body was "stagnant" when he meant "static," and of the student who spoke of "illiciting" rather than "eliciting" audience responses. We also think of the student speaker who, in describing a thief's actions during a robbery, coined a new word when he declared that the thief "slurked" around the corner. Whether the intended meaning was "slunk around" or "lurked at" or "sneaked around" was found out only by questioning the speaker. When he was questioned something fundamental came out: the idea, the image, was not exactly clear in the speaker's own mind. His coined word was in fact a way of evading clear, denotative meaning. From these examples, we gain two basic propositions about word choice: (1) First, determine your own exact meaning. (2) Once your meaning is clearly known, the next problem is to select the accepted terms that conform most closely to the meaning in your own mind.

WORD CHANGES

We must also note that language is in a state of flux, that the meanings of words change with time and locality. The general meanings of a given time or society cannot be relied upon in every circumstance. Wordings are often peculiar to geographical areas. In one region of the United States you may purchase "hot dogs and pop," in another "frankfurts and soda," and in yet another "wienies and tonic." Verbal expressions are also often fads or sayings used by particular in-groups at particular times. On college campuses, slang terms are markedly susceptible to change. Vivid phrasings and wordings continually replace one another. The jargon of professional groups also changes with time. Anthropologists, philosophers, semanticists, educationists often use specialized vocabularies which exclude outsiders, and these vocabularies are continually modified. Some words are added, some are replaced, and others are dropped. Words and expressions become tired and worn out. Certain expressions become clichés: "black as pitch," "blue as the sky." It is rare for a vocabulary of any society or person not to shift. It grows, it shrinks, and the word shadings change.

Shifts in man's way of symbolizing meaning present a major problem to the public speaker. In deference to his audiences he must often speak their particular language at their particular time and according to their judgment of what is appropriate to the occasion. He may rely basically on that language which would convey his meaning clearly throughout *most* of the culture to which his hearers belong. He will err often if he does not study the particular language usages of the time and place in which he will speak. Let him also remember that here are opportunities as well as cautions.

FIGURES OF SPEECH

Figures of speech are forms of expression which serve to intensify meanings. They make their points indirectly by stating things vividly in terms of something else. They are not literally meant or interpreted. They enhance ideas by making them more graphic and appealing. Like all comparisons, contrasts, and exemplifications, figures of speech are especially useful in translating the unknown into terms of the known.

Some thirty identifiable figures of speech are commonly used in written and spoken discourse. It is not as important to know their names as it is to recognize them as resources. Among those most often used in speech-making are the following, illustrated with excerpts from speeches.

Simile is a stated comparison between things which are essentially dissimilar except for the particular qualities alluded to in the simile. Such comparisons contain the words "like" or "as." For example, "There are voices hot, like scorching blasts from a furnace . . . and others cold as if they came from frozen hearts" (Peter Marshall, "Letters in the Sand")[37] or "In all things that are purely social we can be as separate as fingers, yet one as the hand in all things essential to mutual progress" (Booker T. Washington, "Atlanta Exposition Address").[38]

---

[37] In Catherine Marshall, *A Man Called Peter* (New York: McGraw-Hill, 1951), p. 322.

[38] In W. M. Parrish and Marie Hochmuth, eds., *American Speeches* (New York: Longmans, Green, 1954), p. 464.

Metaphor is an implied comparison between two essentially dissimilar things. Linking words such as "like" or "as" are omitted. For example, "Said the old priest, 'A diamond is a congealed drop of sunlight' " (Russell Conwell, "Acres of Diamonds").[39]

Antithesis (an-'tith-ə-səs) is the parallel construction of words, phrases, or sentences which contain opposed or sharply contrasting ideas. The fact that the antithetical ideas are expressed in similar language gives the hearer a sense of balance. For example: "Let us never negotiate out of fear. But let us never fear to negotiate" (John F. Kennedy, "Inaugural Address").[40] When no opposition of ideas is involved in parallel language structures the terms "balanced construction" or "parallel construction" are usually used to identify the figure.

Onomatopoeia (ˌän-ə-ˌmat-ə-'pē-(y)ə) is word choice in which sound suggests the meaning of the word. For example, "The wind whispers them, the birds whistle them, the corn, barley and bulrushes hoarsely rustle them . . ." (Ralph Waldo Emerson, "The Memory of Burns").[41]

Alliteration is repetition of the initial sounds in words or in stressed syllables within words. For example, "*P*roperty can be *p*aid for; the lives of *p*eaceful and innocent *p*eople cannot" (Woodrow Wilson, "War Message").[42]

Personification is endowment of objects, animals, or ideas with human attributes. For example, "Today learning no longer hides in the convent or slumbers in the palace. No! she comes out into every-day life, joins hands with the multitude and cushions the peasant" (Wendell Phillips, "The Lost Arts").[43]

---

[39] In Ashley H. Thorndike, ed., *Modern Eloquence* (New York: Modern Eloquence Corp., 1923), VIII, p. 139.

[40] In Carroll C. Arnold, Douglas Ehninger, and John C. Gerber, eds., *The Speaker's Resource Book*, rev. ed., (Chicago: Scott, Foresman, 1966), p. 226.

[41] In Lewis Copeland and Lawrence Lamm, eds., *The World's Great Speeches*, 2nd rev. ed. (New York: Dover Publications, 1958), p. 654.

[42] In Carl G. Brandt and Edward M. Shafter, Jr., eds., *Selected American Speeches on Basic Issues (1850–1950)* (Boston: Houghton Mifflin, 1960), p. 303.

[43] In Thomas B. Reed, ed., *Modern Eloquence* (New York: The University Society, 1900), VI, p. 845.

Synecdoche (sə-'nek-də-(ˌ)kē) is the substitution of parts for wholes or of wholes for parts of things. For example, "We tie all countries close together, put each doorstep on a universal ocean, but how are we to direct these accomplishments to improve the basic qualities of life?" (Charles A. Lindbergh, "The Future Character of Man").[44]

Hyperbole (hī-'pər-bə·lē) is exaggeration or overstatement for the purpose of emphasing without deceiving. For example, "He whispers in a shout, and converses, in ordinary, confidential moments, in a shriek." (Robert Burdette, "The Rise and Fall of the Mustache").[45]

Irony implies something different from, usually the opposite of, what is stated. Sarcasm is a form of irony. For example, ". . . as I have spent several months in the [Sandwich] Islands, several years ago, I feel competent to shed any amount of light on the matter" (Mark Twain, "On the Sandwich Islands").[46]

Metonymy (mə-'tän-ə-mē) is substituting the name of some closely associated thing for the real name of what is referred to. For example, "Then Texas responded to the bugle calls of liberty, and the march of the flag went on!" (Albert J. Beveridge, "The March of the Flag").[47]

Climax is the arrangement of words, phrases, or sentences in series according to increasing value or strength of impact. For example, "Therefore, in this campaign, the question is larger than a party question. It is an American question. It is a world question" (Albert J. Beveridge, "The March of the Flag").[48]

Repetition is the reiteration of the same words or phrases or sentences in order to reinforce ideas. For example, "We must imagine greatly, dare greatly and act greatly" (Adlai E. Stevenson, "The People's Natural Resources").[49]

---

[44] In *Vital Speeches*, XX (March 1, 1954), p. 294.

[45] In Ashley H. Thorndike, ed., *Modern Eloquence*, VIII, p. 108.

[46] *Ibid.*, p. 131.

[47] In F. C. Hicks, ed., *Famous Speeches by Eminent American Statesmen* (St. Paul, Minn.: West Publishing, 1929), p. 197.

[48] *Ibid.*, p. 189.

[49] In Adlai E. Stevenson, *Major Campaign Speeches of Adlai E. Stevenson*, 1952 (New York: Random House, 1953), p. 90.

A *pun* is substitution of one word for another having different meaning but similar sound. For example: "And so I say it is not capital you want. It is not copper cents, but common sense" (Russell Conwell, "Acres of Diamonds").[50]

There are several lesser known figures of speech which deserve attention here because they are used by speakers more often than by writers.

Aposiopesis (ˌap-ə-ˌsī-ə-'pē-səs) is the practice of breaking off utterance of one thought without finishing it, in order to express another, due presumably to the emotional state of the speaker. The cause of self-interruption might be anger, sorrow, fear, or some other strong feeling. Many sentence fragments will fall in this category. For example: "Only yesterday, it seems to him, the little baby girl, bringing the first music of baby prattle into his home; then a little girl in short dresses, with school-girl troubles and school-girl pleasures; then an older little girl, out of school and into society, but a little girl to pa still. And then—. But somehow, this is as far as pa can get; for he sees, in the flight of this, the first, the following flight of other fledglings; and he thinks how silent and desolate the old nest will be when they have all mated and flown away." (Robert Burdette, "The Rise and Fall of the Mustache.")[51]

Apophasis (ˌap-ə-'fā-səs) is the ostensible omission or concealment, through denial, of what the speaker has really in fact declared. For example: "I am not pleading so much for these boys as I am for the infinite number of others to follow, those who perhaps cannot be as well defended as these have been, those who may be down in the storm, and the tempest, without aid. It is of them I am thinking, and for them I am begging of this court not to turn backward toward the barbarous and cruel past." (Clarence Darrow, "The Plea of Clarence Darrow.")[52]

Epanorthosis (ˌepə-ˌnȯ(r)'thōsəs) is the retraction or cancelling of what the speaker has already stated. For example:

---

[50] In Ashley Thorndike, ed., *Modern Eloquence*, VIII, p. 151.

[51] *Ibid.*, p. 128.

[52] In Maureen McKernan, *The Amazing Crime and Trial of Leopold and Loeb* (New York: The New American Library, 1957), p. 192.

In olden times it used to be popular to call the Sandwich Islanders cannibals. But they were never cannibals. That is amply proven. There was one there once, but he was a foreign savage, who stopped there a while and did quite a business while he stayed. He was a useful citizen, but had strong political prejudices, and used to save up a good appetite for just before election, so that he could thin out the Democratic vote. (Laughter.) But he got tired of that, and undertook to eat an old whaling captain for a change. That was too much for him. He had the crime on his conscience, and the whaler on his stomach, and the two things killed him. (Laughter.) He died. I don't tell this on account of its value as an historical fact (Laughter), but only on account of the moral it conveys. I don't know that I know what moral it conveys, still I know there must be a moral in it somewhere. I have told it forty or fifty times and never got a moral out of it yet. (Laughter.) But all things come to those who wait. (Mark Twain, "On the Sandwich Islands.")[53]

The catalogue of figures of speech could be continued, for there are other ways of bending language to the service of special or emphatic meanings. Those we have identified are those you are most likely to use—those you have probably been using in conversation and formal speaking simply because you have heard others use them.

Each of the figures we have identified above is common in English usage. If your thought is well adapted to your speech situation, you need not fear that the language device itself will draw attention away from your idea. These figures of speech are relatively familiar to most competent users of English, but they are still not standard or everyday usages. Each startles the listener mildly when it occurs in speech and so momentarily rivets attention on what is being said in that instant.

A competent public speaker needs to know there are special ways in which he can give exceptional emphasis to his thoughts. The speaker who does not know and understand at least the sixteen usages we have discussed as figures of speech simply does not know fully his art or its possibilities. He is as inept as a landscape

[53] In Ashley H. Thorndike, ed., *Modern Eloquence*, VIII, pp. 135–136.

contractor who knows everything about his business except the conditions under which plants thrive or die. Study carefully the figures of speech we have identified. Look for them in speeches you hear and read. Learn to distinguish between functionally useful and ostentatiously distracting usages of these figures. In composing your own speeches, review how figures might help where special touches of emphasis or vividness are needed if your listeners are to grasp your full meaning.

Improving Your Style

What sort of program for long-range improvement should you follow? To manage your speech well, try to:

1. *Become language conscious.* Become sensitive to good and bad uses of words. Discover your faults in grammar and those points of style where you seem to be most limited. Ferret out such weaknesses as want of vividness, poor syntax, malapropism, use of clichés. Listen carefully. Read widely. At times read aloud to test the "orality" of your prose.

2. *Increase your speaking vocabulary.* Try consciously to extend the number of words and phrasings at your command. Do not go out of your way to master unusual words and unique phrases; learn the meanings of language you normally encounter but do not understand. You are after the most accurate and most appropriate words. Keep a dictionary handy and refer to it whenever you see or hear unfamiliar words. *Roget's Thesaurus* will also help, but look up its synonyms in the dictionary to fix precise meanings in your mind.

3. *Write.* By expressing yourself on paper you will learn to make conscious word choices. Writing will improve your vocabulary and the accuracy with which you use words. Aim for the best written expression when writing for the eye and the best oral expression when writing for the ear.

4. *Rewrite.* Once you've written it, put your speech aside; but come back to it, and rewrite it. The best speech makers who

work from manuscript often put their speeches through several drafts. Franklin Roosevelt, master of the craft as he was, put some of his speeches through as many as twelve drafts before he was satisfied. Benjamin Disraeli wrote, rehearsed alone and before friendly critics, and rewrote again—in order to speak extemporaneously! In rewriting, smooth out wordings, correct unclear constructions, tinker with phrasings, rearrange language and ideas. By polishing your utterance on paper you will make it more precise and vivid, whether you are to speak from manuscript or extemporaneously.

5. *Study published and live speeches.* Note what makes for success and failure in style. Take cues from the good models. Avoid the faults of bad ones. Imitate the style of others, but for practice and exercise only. Do not study the style of great speakers to copy them; study them to incorporate their best attributes in a distinctive style suited particularly to you.

6. *Speak in public.* Take advantage of opportunities to refine your expression of ideas in both conversation and public address. Speak as often as possible. The more you speak, especially in the extemporaneous and impromptu modes, the better you will become at finding ways to finish phrases and statements effectively no matter how you started them. The more experience you have with thinking on your feet and symbolizing your ideas as they develop in your mind, the more fluent and attractive your style will become.

Style is that part of the art of public speaking which emerges from our choices and combinations of language. Its grammatical aspects and its psychological impact have been the subjects of investigation in the preceding pages. "The personal manner of utterance which gives movement and impact to ideas" is not decoration to be exhibited but that facet of speech making derived from reasonable and imaginative management of words.

Wording and thinking are inseparable processes wherever communication deserves its name; hence, style in speaking must always be viewed as one more means to winning a particular response under particular circumstances. The origins of the word, *style*, and the meanings assigned to it through history remind us that what we call oral style cannot be separated from the whole act of speaking, except for purposes of discussion. Style, good or indifferent or bad, is present in all speaking; and it colors listeners' perceptions of the speaking. But there is no universally suitable style for the individual speaker or for any of his customary purposes: informing, inquiring, reinforcing, persuading, and entertaining. We have therefore contended that each speaker must understand the resources of language for effective expression of ideas and to develop through practice and experience that style best suited to his needs and talents.

It is not easy to determine exactly how language usage affects those who listen or to prescribe the processes by which stylistic excellence is to be acquired. What speakers must come to appreciate is that words have denotative and connotative meanings, that figures of speech offer resources for achieving special degrees of clarity and force and that a good dictionary is invaluable. Sensitive judgments concerning the demands of subject, audience, occasion, and self must guide the speaker toward those choices that yield the stylistic virtues of accuracy, clarity, propriety, economy, force, striking quality, and—above all—liveliness.

The resources of language are so diverse and the powers of language so subtle no one has ever yet understood either fully. But college students, statesmen, ministers, lawyers, teachers, and hundreds of others have consistently demonstrated that, given some understanding of language, thoughtfulness, readiness to adapt, and intelligently planned and evaluated practice can yield what we have defined as style: *The personal manner of utterance which gives movement and impact to ideas.*

Exercises

WRITTEN

1. Select the definition of style which you consider to be best from the standpoint of public speaking. Write an essay in which you defend your choice.

2. Choose a speech from *Vital Speeches* or from an anthology of public addresses. Study it carefully. Write an essay in which you (a) identify the stylistic devices the speaker has employed in his use of language as support for his ideas; and (b) point out particular word choices marked by clarity, propriety, and economy.

3. Rewrite the following sentences for oral delivery:
    a. Therefore, it is evident that before you can provide an elucidation of the operational functions of the system for the propagation and dissemination of information you would be required to make a thorough investigation of the public relations branch of the corporation.
    b. If one had one's preference, one would be likely to hold a preference for one's own photographic equipment with which to photograph one's own favorite subjects.
    c. Easily seen is the fact that the playing field is surrounded by a large metal fence over which the ball often passes when a home run is made.
    d. Even although I had been selected to represent my college, had planned my itinerary to the meeting, which incidentally was held sixty miles from the college itself, had packed my clothing for the journey, which I did the night before, had reserved my seat in the airplane, which was a jet and was flight 107, and had persuaded my close friend, whose name was Mark Smith, to convey me to the airport, I was still in fear that the weather would prevent my going to the convention at all.
    e. "Like I said," she said, "Jane's cheeks looked as red as roses, however, I discovered that the effect was all due to the application by her of cosmetic in large quantity."

4. Rewrite the following paragraph in such a way as to give it the motion-picture quality discussed in the section of this chapter devoted to liveliness.

My most embarrassing experience was when I was a boy. It was the result of my getting into a place I had no business being. I had crawled under our old back porch and had found some paint cans. I had pried off the tops with a stick. Then I had put my hands into one can after another. First I put them into a can of green paint. Then I put them into a can of red paint, and then into a can of yellow. The color which resulted was an ugly brown. When I finally finished, my clean clothes had paint dribbled all over them. I was a mess. What was embarrassing though was that I couldn't get the paint off. After a licking by my mother, a bottle of turpentine was given to me, and I tried to get the paint off with that. I rubbed and rubbed with a cloth, but there was so much paint it just wouldn't come off. I was embarrassed for a whole week because it was summertime, and I looked as if I were wearing a pair of brown gloves. I guess I felt most foolish when my piano teacher came to give me my lesson, and I had to explain why my hands were as they were. I also felt very foolish on Sunday. I was sure that everybody was looking at my hands when I was up there singing in the choir.

    5. a. Identify the kinds of imagery used in the following passage taken from a speech by a college student.

The quiet rural atmosphere had been effectively shattered. Chickens and feathers flew fast and furiously from both sides of the road. Cattle, only a moment before peacefully pastured, ran in aimless directions. Farmers' horses became frightened and reared into the air. A low-slung sports car, flashing and brilliant yellow in the afternoon sunlight, thundered through the rural village, a beautiful blonde movie queen at the wheel. An aroused policeman hauled the straw-haired beauty over to the side of the road, arrested her, and brought her before a justice of the peace who fined her five dollars. The indignant beauty thrust a 10 dollar bill into his hand and stalked out of the courtroom. "Just a minute," shouted the judge, "your change." "Keep it," she hurled back as she hopped into the auto, "I'm going out of here a hell of a lot faster than I came in."[54]

        b. Identify the figures of speech used in the above passage.
        c. List the kinds of imagery *not* used.
        d. Write a paragraph commenting upon the strengths and weaknesses in the rhetorical style of the passage.

---

[54] From the manuscript of a speech entitled "Seven Years of Silent Excitement," by Nelson T. Joyner, Jr. Used by permission.

ORAL

1. Compose and deliver a two-minute narrative in which you use (a) at least three different figures of speech and (b) at least three different kinds of imagery.

2. Take a speech you delivered during a prior session of your class. Drawing upon what you now know about style, re-do the speech or a portion of it and deliver it again. Discuss the effects of the deliberate stylistic changes with your listeners.

The utterance of a message in the presence of other people is an intimately revealing act. When we speak to others we lay open for inspection our minds, knowledge, integrity, social grace, and even our muscular coordination. For most persons this is a worrisome business. Many cast about for rules of physical action. They hope to discover in prescriptions the means of seeming knowledgeable, poised, and self-controlled. This is one reason no facet of public speech has been more discussed than delivery.

Theorists have explored the mechanics, the patterns, and the potentialities of vocal and gestural expression with astonishing patience and detail. Natural gestural communication has been charted and reduced to rule. Vocal patterns have been analyzed and recorded in complicated notational systems so that what is natural might be imitated precisely. This has been carried to extremes so men and women might speak their meanings clearly and conventionally. The assurance with which such efforts have been carried out is suggested by the following statement written less than a hundred years ago:

> By the study and work of Delsarte a science has been created, every fleeting sign of emotion has been fixed, and may be reproduced at will; and this for the instruction of the artist who may never have observed them in another, nor himself felt the impressions that give rise to them.[1]

---

[1] Angelique Arnaud, "Arnaud on Delsarte," in *Delsarte System of Oratory* (New York: Edward S. Werner, 1887), p. 246.

Such energetic attempts as the Delsartians' exemplify man's desire to guard against the uncertainties of speech. We take risks of losing face when we speak. Physical and vocal activity furnish cues by which other people form judgments of our worth and self-control. The crucial question for those who practice the art of public speaking is: Can the risks of speaking be minimized by adopting rules of delivery? This is the question men and women of Western culture have been disputing since the days of Gorgias and probably before. Yet every speaker must settle it for himself —by choice or by default. Before trying to establish your own answer, you ought to know something about answers others have made to the question.

Schools of Delivery

THE IMITATIVE SCHOOL

In his book, *The Province of Expression*, S. S. Curry said that what is probably the oldest method for developing delivery can be labeled the "imitative." He added: "Many in every age have practiced this method; but the teachers who have practically followed it while not theoretically believing in it are numerous. . . . Those who believe in this method quote from Aristotle and contend that art is founded upon imitation, or at least must begin in imitation."[2]

Those committed to imitative action argue that the only way to get at a subjective art like delivery is by imitation. They contend that all art requires example. For them, the teacher serves as a model whom his students ought to imitate. The "touchstone technique" is the key to learning. The art of delivery is supposedly so subtle that analysis of it is impossible; therefore, copying becomes the best method of improving delivery. Little attention is

---

[2] S. S. Curry, *The Province of Expression* (Boston: Expression Co., 1927), p. 301. Professor Curry discussed "imitative," "mechanical," and "impulsive" schools of delivery.

paid to action of the mind during speaking or to the adaptation of the speaker's delivery to a particular audience. Direct study of the elements of delivery, movement, and voice are often bypassed. Such a method, as Curry insisted, appears to violate the laws of nature which remind us that all expression comes from within, that everything in nature is original. Imitative delivery takes no account of the fact that individual temperaments differ, audiences differ, occasions differ.

THE MECHANICAL SCHOOL

The mechanical or elocutionary view of delivery begins with analysis of the vocal and visual elements of presentation. It is rooted in careful study of vocal modulation, inflection and stress, posture, facial expression, and gesture. From such empirical study, rules are derived for the correct or "natural" expression of thought and emotion.

Early elocutionists often argued as to whether they presented "natural" or "mechanical" approaches to delivery. The fact was, as Professor Haberman has pointed out: "Implicit in the minds of the elocutionists was the sense of a mechanical order in nature. Thus their rules and their systems, of which they were so vain, were claimed to represent the order that is found in nature; they were 'nature still, but nature methodized.' "[3]

One of the founders of the mechanistic approach was Thomas Sheridan, dramatic coach and father of Richard Brinsley Sheridan, the British orator and dramatist. The elder Sheridan wrote several works on elocution, the most important of which was his *Lectures on Elocution*, published first in London in 1762. Others besides Sheridan attempted to furnish rules and mechanical guidance for delivery. Joshua Steele's *Prosodia Rationalis*,[4] with its system of

---

[3] Frederick W. Haberman, "John Thelwall: His Life, His School, and His Theory of Elocution," *The Quarterly Journal of Speech*, XXXIII (Oct., 1947), p. 294.

[4] *Prosodia Rationalis: or An Essay Towards Establishing the Melody and Measure of Speech, to Be Expressed and Perpetuated by Peculiar Symbols* (London, 1779).

musical notation for the speaking voice, and Gilbert Austin's *Chironomia*,[5] with its painstaking descriptions and prescriptions for achieving correct posture, gesture, and movement, are typical of the mechanistic scholars. One of the books to carry the mechanical method of studying delivery nearest to perfection was Dr. James Rush's *Philosophy of the Human Voice*, published in 1828. Every passion, Rush thought, had a particular stress. He divided stress into categories with such labels as "radical," "medium," "intermittent," and "compound." He further held that such qualities of voice as stress and inflection could be regulated by rule. Like Steele, he believed that the proper natural passions could be represented by printed notations such as those found in musical scores. Though books such as those just mentioned are rare today, there are still some contemporary works which recommend careful annotation of scripts to remind the reader of intended vocal and bodily manipulations.

Those who have approached the study of delivery through mechanical methods have sought to improve upon nature by providing rules whereby "natural" or ideal delivery may be attained. Nothing is left to chance or inspiration. All elements of the performance are prescribed; how a thing is to be said must be decided before any utterance takes place.

Impromptu and extemporaneous modes of delivery are poor vehicles for achieving perfection under such a system. The mind of the speaker using any mechanical method usually dwells upon the manner of speaking more than upon what is being said. Correctives based upon rules are prescribed for particular imperfections, and the danger is that picayune details receive a disproportionate amount of attention. Even though a mechanical approach to delivery may emphasize the importance of thorough, scientific knowledge about the natural behaviors of the voice and body during speaking, it makes no allowance for adaptation at the moment of utterance, and it produces inflexibility if adhered to completely. It is a method alien to audience-centered performance.

---

[5] *Chironomia or a Treatise on Rhetorical Delivery* (London, 1806).

Curry attributed the popularity of mechanical delivery to human nature.[6] Men like to think all that is needed to produce good speech are a few rules for vocal and visual action. They want to ignore the action of mind, for criticisms of one's ideas are taken more personally than criticisms of one's techniques in transmitting them. The mechanical or elocutionary system appeals particularly to those who are certain that the substance of what they say is above reproach. It also appeals to those who search for a scientific base for their conduct during delivery. Its difficulty is that it emphasizes the external aspects of speaking above the creative processes that are the justifications for speaking at all.

THE IMPULSIVE SCHOOL

At the opposite pole from the speaker who follows a mechanical method is the speaker who allows impulse to govern his communication. The impulsive school of delivery is traced erroneously to the writings of Richard Whately.[7] From Whately's criticisms of mechanical delivery and from other sources, certain teachers derived an anti-elocutionist viewpoint which has persisted in some quarters to the present day. Those who hold this extension of Whately's position contend that it is best to leave delivery to impulse. They advocate no system at all. Total naturalness is their goal. They overlook the fact that art demands skill and control as well as spontaneous inspiration. They also overlook the unconventional habits and abnormal conditions which ought to be corrected by training. They advocate allowing the feelings one has at the moment, whether relevant or not, to hold sway. They would say that when the feeling predominates, delivery becomes what it was meant to be—natural.

---

[6] S. S. Curry, *The Province of Expression*, pp. 324–325.

[7] See his *Elements of Rhetoric*, of which there are a number of printings published in England and the United States.

THE THINK-THE-THOUGHT SCHOOL

As we have indicated, the impulsive approach to delivery does not rest on a true interpretation of Whately. Whately insisted that a speaker ought to concentrate upon what he is saying. It is evident from his writings that he did not advocate impulsive delivery. He did say:

> The practical rule then to be adopted, in conformity with the principles here maintained, is, not only to pay no studied attention to the Voice, but studiously to *withdraw* the thoughts from it, and to dwell as intently as possible on the Sense; trusting to nature to suggest spontaneously the proper emphases and tones.
>
> *   *   *   *   *
>
> He who not only understands fully what he is reading [aloud], but is earnestly occupying his mind with the matter of it, will be likely to read as if he understood it, and thus to make others understand it; and in like manner, with a view to the *impressiveness* of the delivery, he who not only feels it, but is exclusively absorbed with that feeling, will be likely to read as if he felt it, and to communicate the impression to his hearers. But this cannot be the case if he is occupied with the thought of what their opinion will be of his reading, and, how his voice ought to be regulated;—if, in short, he is thinking of *himself*, and, of course, in the same degree, abstracting his attention from that which ought to occupy it exclusively.[8]

At another point Whately said,

> When however I protest against all artificial systems of Elocution, and all *direct* attention to Delivery, *at the time*, it must not be supposed that a *general* inattention to that point is recommended; or that the most perfect Elocution is to be attained by never thinking at all on the subject; though it may safely be affirmed that even this negative plan would succeed far better than a studied modulation.[9]

---

[8] Richard Whately, *Elements of Rhetoric*, Douglas Ehninger, ed. (Carbondale, Ill.: Southern Illinois University Press, 1963), pp. 352–353.

[9] *Ibid.*, pp. 346–347.

It is apparent that Whately really recommended thinking the thought, occupying the mind with ideas rather than with worry about prescribed behaviors in delivery.

We see, then, that Whately put ideas at the center of his theory of delivery, yet he did not recommend that the use of body and voice be ignored. There are some extremists who would go farther. They would say that all you need to do is to think the thought; delivery will then take care of itself. They are a bit like the followers of the impulsive school who admonish, "Feel the feeling." We would say neither thinking the thought nor feeling and reacting will alone generate good delivery. One may do either with his back to the audience, while mumbling into his beard, or while focusing his gaze on the rafters.

Delivery as Adaptation

The approach to delivery which we advocate is a modification of Whately's theory reinforced by the teachings of James A. Winans. We hold that to think the thought is not enough, though it is primary. We propose that you ought to achieve both a keen sense of communication and a vivid realization of your idea at the moment of utterance, and, moreover, be able to control all the channels of action—mental, physical, and vocal—to support and reinforce ideas. We say there are no hard and fast rules for delivery. Delivery must be adapted to all the demanding elements in the speech situation: the material, the audience, the occasion, and the speaker himself. None of these elements is ever frozen or absolutely set; they make fluctuating demands. Even so, there are certain principles which may be followed to achieve effective, adaptive delivery.

GENERAL PRINCIPLES

Good delivery helps the listener to concentrate upon what is being said; it does not attract attention to itself. If this is adopted as a governing premise, we can further say that in reaching this objective:

1. *Remember that you are not speaking to perform or to exhibit yourself.* Delivery should be viewed as a means to an end, not as an end in itself. During public speaking the message is the most important thing to be exhibited. Your mission should never be to show off your body, your grace, or your clothing. It must be to communicate ideas.

2. *Realize fully the content of your words as you utter them.* To create or re-create ideas vividly at the moment they are being uttered means that you reactivate a subject and ideas to support it, that you regenerate the enthusiasm that led you to speak in the first place. This enthusiasm must last from the first moments of preparation through the last syllable of your speech. You must be in control of assimilated ideas so that they are at your bidding. You must have become so intimately acquainted with them as you structured, worded, and orally rehearsed them that no matter what happens during the actual presentation of your speech, you will be master of your speech, your feelings toward its substance, and your audience's response to it. Professor Winans, who formulated this precept, put your needs well when he said:

> . . . there should be full and sharp realization of content. And this includes more than bare meaning; the implications and emotional content must also be realized. The reference here is not merely to those striking emotions commonly recognized as such, but also to those attitudes and significances constantly present in lively discourse: the greater or less importance of this or that statement, the fact that this is an assertion and this a concession (with an implied "granted" or "to be sure"), this is a matter of course while this has an element of surprise, and so on through all possible changes.[10]

The ideas you work with must be in your grasp so that you can support them through your own behavior, vigorously and forcefully. The ideas you have painstakingly worked over must

---

[10] From *Speechmaking* by James A. Winans. Copyright, 1938, D. Appleton-Century Company, Inc., p. 25. Reprinted by permission of Appleton–Century–Crofts.

come alive. They must flow. You must be running over with them, yet in control of them and your thoughts about them. You must be able to lose yourself in your speech and still maintain control of your experience.

No matter how well you know your materials, you ought to give the impression of meeting the ideas for the first time. You ought not be serving up limp remnants from creative experience. What was alive as you prepared and as you rehearsed orally must come to life again in the actual speech situation. Overrehearsal, loss of enthusiasm, repetition to the point of being "sick of the whole thing" will promote mechanical, boring, dull delivery. The process of speaking, you must remember, is one of creation and re-creation.

3. *Cultivate a keen sense of communication.* This second step which we borrow also from Professor Winans is closely allied to the first. Thinking of public speaking as dialogue rather than as soliloquy will help achieve this keen sense. Talk *with* the audience, not *at* them. Dwell on ideas until you are sure of the response for which you work. Try to feel on the platform what you experience during verbal exchanges with your friends over the dinner table, on the athletic field, or in bull sessions. We experience this sense of sharing minds daily; trying to recapture the same sense in public speaking makes for lively delivery. By assuming a false, tense, artificial mood we rob public speaking of the urgency and eagerness it ought to have. As Professor Winans said:

> We should make sure in our efforts to bring this communicative tone into our delivery that it springs from mental attitudes; for it, . . . should [not] be assumed as a trick of delivery. The attempt to assume it is likely to result in an over familiar confidential or wheedling tone which is most objectionable.[11]

4. *Be direct.* People are seldom evasive when they are in earnest. Look the audience in the eye. If you look elsewhere, so will your audience. If you look at your audience, they will look back at you. Looking at a spot on the back wall will not produce

---

[11] *Ibid.,* p. 28.

directness. You will give the impression that you are in a trance. A dead-fish stare while you call up ideas and wordings will not do. Neither will darting your eyes from person to person in the audience or addressing one side of the audience to the exclusion of the other. In the first instance eye contact will be so fleeting that it will be no contact at all. In the second, a whole segment of the audience will think that you have ignored them.

Your eyes are decidedly expressive parts of your face. Haven't they been called "the windows of the soul"? Eyes and mouth, more than other parts of your body, reveal your emotions. And it is your feeling for content that delivery must convey. So you should face front and direct your eyes to your listeners. Try looking at a segment of the audience or at one or two people in a particular area of the room as you develop an idea. When you have finished with that idea, and as you start the next one, direct your gaze to another part of the audience. As you move to subsequent ideas, refocus each time. Then you will talk with your audience, not at them or past them.

Directness is fundamentally a matter of direct eye contact. Attain this much and the probabilities are that you will also be tolerably direct mentally, vocally, and physically.

5. *Punctuate and support your ideas with your body and your voice.* Channel your physical resources to reinforce your message. Let your bodily actions and your vocal intonations operate as means to the end of warm, emphatic communication. In speech-making, facial expressions, gestures, pitch changes, variations in vocal rate and volume, pauses, shifts in posture, and walking take the place of the commas, italics, exclamation points, and question marks in written communication. Intelligibility and clarification often depend greatly upon support and emphasis from your physique. Learn to use *yourself* often and with control. Some special considerations in this connection are discussed below under the heading "Bodily Action" (pp. 325–329).

6. *Remember that your delivery generates emotional and physical responses.* What you do with your body and your voice will stimulate your audience to respond in like manner. Later in this chapter, we shall discuss these empathic responses more fully.

As a guiding principle, however, we observe here that you ought to be aware that what your listeners see and hear will cause them to have physical and emotional reactions. If you are nervous and fidgety, your audience will become so. If you sound as if your throat hurts, theirs will hurt. If the audience detects that you are tense and rigid, they will experience the same physical states. If you are confident or indecisive, smiling or depressed, tough or soft in manner, the listeners will feel so too. Your auditors will respond to what they perceive; therefore, it is up to you to control what they take in. Your manner will determine the experiences they will have. These experiences may be pleasant or unpleasant, relaxed or tense, casual or formal according to your behavior. Once you have made your decisions in invention, disposition, and language choice, you are responsible for making the audience aware of them by the visual and vocal cues you provide for them.

7. *Focus the attention of the audience.* Realize that your task is to control your audience and that in doing so you must direct their attention to whatever heightens your meaning, be it an image created with words or a visual aid. It is not enough merely to gain attention at the outset of a speech; you must maintain it by constantly directing attention to the stimuli playing the most important roles in stirring up meanings. You are remiss if you allow audience attention to wander. You are also remiss if you do not replace an irrelevant stimulus with a relevant one. Displace distracting stimuli—a flapping window shade, a smell from the laboratory down the hall, your listener's fatigue—with strong stimuli bearing upon your message. Bodily movement and vocal variation are always available to you for this purpose. Control of attention through these means is normally as necessary as control achieved by selection of material, structure, and style.

8. *All aspects of your delivery should promote conversational quality.* We noted differences between conversation and public speaking in Chapter 1 (pp. 11–13). We observed there that public speaking contrasts with conversation in that we speak more loudly, are relatively uninterrupted, focus attention more sharply, are more systematically prepared, and have less opportunity to perceive the responses of our auditors. But effective public speak-

ing has important characteristics of good conversation: directness, spontaneity, animation, and emphasis. It is therefore conversational *quality*, not conversational *style*, that ought to be sought for the most effective delivery. Reproduced conversation will not satisfy. Speeches ought to be so delivered that they sound like conversation enlarged—more dignified, more eloquent, and more forceful than conversation itself. Alertness, the working of mind and body in lively response to the meanings of ideas and audience reactions, is necessary to speech-making. Even the strong emphasis and sudden outbursts that characterize good conversation ought to characterize your public speaking.

Public speaking is not exhibitionism; it is sensitive re-creation of ideas by a speaker whose whole being directs, punctuates, stimulates, and focuses meaning—after the manner of a conversationalist now aware of his enlarged responsibilities.

BODILY ACTION

We implied earlier that the chief instruments of delivery are physical actions involving the face, limbs, and torso and expressive use of the voice. The broad principles we have just outlined apply to any aspect of delivery, but bodily communication deserves some special consideration.

Any speaker must understand that his actions are of two kinds: overt and covert. Overt action is open to inspection, easily perceived by the audience. Covert action is covered or concealed. An audience may sense concealed action in the organism of a speaker even though the action cannot be seen. For example, the contractions of hidden muscles of the throat or leg are actions audiences may sense through perceiving the speaker's tension but without being able to locate the activity itself. Both overt and covert action take place during speaking and the speaker is aware of both.

Strong feeling often turns covert action into overt action. A spectator at a football game may so strongly wish his team to score that he actually crouches, reproducing the thrust he wants a ball

325

carrier to prepare for. On the other hand, the spectator may not go all the way in his response; he may perform the action only partially. For fear of audience censure, he may inhibit his actions allowing only muscular contractions well hidden beneath his skin or clothing. Less dramatic but similar behaviors occur constantly on the public speaking platform. It is not unusual to see speakers sufficiently moved by indignation or determination to bring a clenched fist into sight from behind the lectern and to hear the rap of hidden knuckles as he utters his strongest words.

All action, then, is covert or overt. And whether evident or concealed, all these actions associated with speaking express something. The practical questions about them concern whether they express relevant meaning and whether they do it conventionally. In order to talk clearly about whether given actions serve their practical ends it is first useful to have a few common terms by which to refer to specific kinds of bodily action.

Descriptions of action. It is common practice to refer to categories of action when describing or evaluating movement. "Eye contact" is the phrase used to denote the focusing of the eyes upon the audience. "Posture" or "stance" usually refers to the position of the whole body. "Movement" is the label ordinarily used to indicate walking or movement of the entire body. "Gesture" is the word used to indicate movement of the hands and arms. "Facial expression" is self-explanatory, as are "head action" and "shoulder action."

Adjectival labels are also applied to aspects of these actions. Postures are often characterized as "parade rest," "limp rag," "skating," "whipped dog," "the Colossus of Rhodes." "On the balls of the feet" is a phrase used to describe good posture.

Gestures are labeled in three ways. One set of terms indicates their functions: emphatic, descriptive, and suggestive. Other terms indicate the position of the hand at the time of gesture: palm up, palm down, clenched fist, and index finger. Still another set is based upon inherent qualities of gesture: habitualized, natural, nervous.

Good gestures. These are characterized by vitality, proper coordination, good timing, integration with other bodily movements, habitualization, appropriateness, and the ability to hold some energy in reserve. Good gestures employ broad strokes in large situations and subtle movements in small ones, and usually just precede the ideas they reinforce.

Principles of Good Bodily Action. The question students ask are: "How shall I walk?" "How shall I stand?" "How shall I move?" "What shall I do with my hands?" "How can I register feeling in my face?" We accept no prescriptions. Mechanical planning and execution, which prescription implies, do violence to the individualized nature of the public speech. However, generalized hypotheses can be made about the successful use of action.

1. Action should be in key with audience temperament and should prompt the reactions sought.
2. Action should be appropriate to the occasion.
3. Action should reinforce, enhance, emphasize, and convey meanings.
4. Action should never detract from what the speaker is saying.
5. Action should refine the focus of attention.
6. Action should provide for the speaker's comfort by being easy and unlabored.
7. Action should reveal total concentration of the organism upon the expression and communication of the message.

The Demands for Action. The audience demands stimuli to direct attention and increase understanding. They demand animation. The audience drowses if the speaker's body is asleep, if movement and gesture are vague, unchanging, or monotonous. A speaker who is eager to express himself will reveal his attitudes by bodily tonus and expression and his audience will respond in kind.

Further audience requirements for action derive from the ages of listeners. A group of kindergarten children listening to a talk on Africa may wish the speaker to be the elephant he describes. The five-year-old demands much action, for his attention span is short and his comprehension level, comparatively speaking, is low. His imaginative level is high, so he responds with great delight when the speaker is literal and offers representational action in amplification of ideas. On the other hand, if you were to address a gathering at a home for the aged, you would disturb your audience if you used a great deal of action or action that was especially fast. Unless your aim were humorous effect, you would not dare assume your hearers had never seen an elephant. The postures and gestures that gave joy to the child by seeming to represent the trunk of the animal are absurd in the sight of the mature. The younger the audience, the more plentiful and suggestive action may be. The older the audience, the more likely it will be that reserved and subtle action is meaningful and fitting.

The message, too, exerts pressure for bodily action. Since the listener's eye reads only the speaker's body and its surroundings during a speech, it receives whatever signals the speaker chooses to make in order to clarify his message. As we have noted, action is part of the punctuation of a speech. It is evident to the sensitive listener that an index finger shaken in the right way or brought down forcibly upon a table is in reality an exclamation point, just as a spread palm in horizontal motion may serve the same function as underlining. So it is that material often requires bodily action for proper emphasis. Often, too, action serves to clarify. A step or two in a new direction during a transition breaks and refocuses audience attention as a speaker moves from point to point. Other action is directly suggested by material, especially material involving literal description. For example, the easiest way to suggest spherical or square shapes is by gestures. During demonstrations of techniques necessary in military, gymnastic, or dance instruction, action is not just inherent in the material, action *is* the material, a part of the message to be conveyed.

The occasion may also govern action, as in religious ritual. Quick, jerky movement in a softly lit, sedate, ceremonial setting would normally be as inappropriate as would lazy, languid movement at a political rally. Even the time of day exerts influence upon action. When it is late and the audience is tired, speakers do well to increase the flow and variety of their movement. Action must suit the setting and the time of day.

The action of the mind and the action of the body seek coordination. Action reduces the speaker's tension even as it conveys his attitudes and feelings to listener-viewers. The speaker who lacks confidence will feel better when he moves. Unhappily, such movement can take the form of fidgeting. Excess energy, engendered by defense mechanisms when the speaker feels danger, needs to be controlled. But if the speaker will direct his action toward reinforcing his message, it will be appropriate to his speech, to his audience, to the occasion, and he will gain relief.

VOICE

Those who define speech broadly argue that a shrug of the shoulders or a crook of the finger is "speech," but it is impossible to conceive of public speech consisting of gestures alone. All public speaking requires vocal ability.

Management of the voice, then, ought to be a serious concern of every public speaker. He must be able to control his voice and use it flexibly. Yet, a sound course in public speaking cannot be a course in voice training. To take time for vocal exercise in a public speaking class is usually inadvisable unless all members of the class possess identical weaknesses in vocal habits. Voice improvement is most wisely achieved by individual work on poor habits or by a separate course of study. Poor vocal habits ought to be remedied by private exercise and practice. Public, group exercises consume valuable time which ought to be devoted to speech-making.

Minimum skill in vocal performance for public speaking means that you must (1) be heard, (2) be understood clearly, and (3) be free from annoying vocal habits and distortions. Most of us can fulfill these minimal requirements. Some do not meet the requirements simply because they have acquired poor habits in the formation of particular sounds—a "p" sounds like a "b" or an "l" like a "w." Others' voices rasp or squeak, so that the quality distracts from what is being said.

All of us can improve the vocal aspects of our performance. Most of us are endowed with adequate physical equipment for acceptable voice production. We make sounds which are usually heard and understood. We may be sloppy and inaccurate or lack distinctness, but every day we convert ideas into sounds which convey meaning. But it is still universally true that anyone, no matter how pleasant his voice and clear his diction, can make it pleasanter. Even the Laurence Oliviers and Maurice Evanses, after years of experience, continue to exercise their vocal mechanisms to improve intelligibility and quality.

Ideally, good voice attracts no attention because of peculiarities identifying it with a particular class of persons or a particular locality. But we are not here providing a manual for those who wish to eliminate regional dialects, upgrade substandard speech, improve voice and diction through drill and exercise, or correct defects. Therapy to remove defects or to improve manipulative skill is a highly individual matter to be undertaken in addition to, and many times before, work in speech composition. Here, we intend only to explain how normal vocal behavior relates to public speaking.

We have already indicated, that voice, like action, must be under the speaker's control. You must think what you are saying and you should not be affected or "speak with your mind on your larynx," but you ought also to pay attention to understandability and vocal flexibility. To attain clearness and variety a good public speaker needs to be generally acquainted with the process of producing meaningful sounds and with the variables of vocal expression: articulation, volume, rate, pitch, and quality. He can then refine his habitual control over these natural resources.

Voice production. Speech is an "overlaid function" of the speech organs because each of them has some other primary purpose such as breathing or swallowing. Inspiration takes place as air is taken into the lungs through the nose and/or mouth, passed through the pharynx (throat), the larynx (voice box, vocal folds, or Adam's apple), the trachea (windpipe), the bronchi, and bronchial tubes. As air fills the lungs, they expand; the chest walls within which they are contained move outward and upward to create the partial vacuum that causes this lung expansion. The scaleni, intercostal, and elevator muscles which control the actions of the ribs come into play in this raising of the ribs and consequent expansion of the rib cage. During this action, the front wall of the abdomen also expands as the diaphragm—the muscular floor of the chest and the roof of the abdomen—moves downward compressing the visceral organs. When the rib muscles and the diaphragm relax, the latter moving upward in a recoiling action, the size of the chest cavity is again reduced and the air forced out of the lungs and through the trachea. As this exhalation takes place, the air passes through the larynx and between the vocal folds which vibrate to produce sound as the air passes through the glottis (the opening between the vocal folds). The length and thickness of the vocal folds and their state of tension are responsible for the pitch of the voice produced.

The voiced and unvoiced sounds produced during exhalation are given character and quality as they are resonated from the surfaces of the pharynx, mouth, and nasal cavities. The sounds are reflected from these surfaces and reinforced by them. Finally, certain sounds are turned into consonants by the articulators: the tongue, the teeth, the lips, and the soft palate which controls the passage of air between the mouth and nose. These sounds combine to form words, and the cycle is complete.

From this simplified description we see that the production of voice is a motor process involving breathing; a phonation process involving the vibration of the vocal folds; a resonation process involving the reinforcing surfaces of the mouth, throat, and nose; and an articulation process involving the formation and codification of specific sound symbols.

The cycle we have described repeats itself over and over again as we speak, and what happens at the various stages in the cycle is responsible for the distinctive attributes of the voice. The physical adjustments and modifications which take place during speech and the general physical condition of the speaker are responsible for the individuality of each human voice. It has been argued that our voices are as distinctive as our fingerprints. Certainly we know we can readily identify one another by voice alone, that by the sound of the voice we know who is at the bottom of the stairs or around the corner.

Articulation. The most effective public speakers attain a high degree of clear, distinct, sound formation. They articulate sounds well. They are not content to slur over words, to drop off word endings, to run together sounds which ought to be kept separate, even though such slovenly practices do not always lead to misunderstanding. They aim for distinctness. Where the elision of sounds is called for, they naturally blend the sounds skillfully. They carefully guard against mistakes in articulation which result from addition, omission, or substitution of sounds. That is to say, they do not add sounds as in "athalete" for "athlete," "exscaped" for "escaped," "acrost" for "across." Nor do they omit sounds by saying "reglar" for "regular," or " 'nuff" for "enough." Nor do they substitute one sound for another by saying "hypmotism" for "hypnotism," "cartoon" for "carton," "ya" for "you," or "fella" for "fellow." They pronounce words in accordance with the conventions acceptable to their particular audiences. Generally speaking their authorities are dictionaries, community leaders, or experts in the field in which a given word is commonly used. They attack words with definiteness and end words crisply unless the word is supposed to die away gradually. They are attentive to "-ing," "-tion," and "-nd" word endings. They aspire to neat, businesslike utterance that is relaxed and unlabored. Through such considerations as we have enumerated, they aspire to meet the demands of their audiences and their content for clear, controlled, understandable utterance. Meanwhile, they seek to create a personality image which pleases their audiences and themselves. And lest all this seem idealistic, let it be said that no speaker loses influence by conforming to the *best* standards of content, audience, and occasion. He does lose standing if he falls short of these demands.

Volume. The effective public speaker keeps himself in good physical condition and sees to it that he is sufficiently rested to produce appropriate volume or force. Appropriate volume is the degree of loudness which meets the needs of the audience and the physical setting for the speech. Without straining, an audience ought to hear every word a speaker says, no matter what the size of the place in which he speaks. Speech must be easily heard. Where loud, strong utterance is required, the speaker ought to be able to produce it, but where the situation calls for soft or soothing utterance the speaker must be equal to that necessity.

Force is described in some textbooks as explosive, effusive, and expulsive. Explosive force is loudness characterized by violent changes in volume. Effusive force is gentle, sustained, and flowing. Expulsive force is somewhere in between and is marked by abruptness of initiation of the sounds.

Beginning speakers are often unskilled in assessing the demands of audience and occasion for vocal force. Some beginners speak in tiny, whispery, subdued voices which cannot be heard beyond the fifth row, because they are unable to judge how forcefully sounds must be produced in order to reach the rear of the room. Just as often, the beginning speaker speaks with too much volume. He unnerves his audience with too much force because he erroneously thinks that all speeches ought to be delivered loudly. He is like those people who think they must shout into the telephone in order to be heard at the other end of the wire. Too often this speaker mistakes force or loudness for intensity. He thinks that to be intense he must increase volume. Much intensity is, of course, of a very quiet sort and achieves its influence by its very want of force.

To make proper adjustments to situational demands for volume requires experience and practice. Where a student speaker repeatedly misjudges, a hearing test is in order. It may be that he does not hear himself accurately and as a result is using more or less force than needed.

Rate. Optimum effectiveness in public speaking requires a rate of speaking suited to the abilities of the audience to comprehend and to the emotional coloring or mood to be conveyed. Beginners tend to race through their speeches, stumbling over words, slurring them and blurring articulation. The audience cannot then keep up. The speaker passes from one symbol to another so rapidly that his listeners grasp them erratically. Ultimately, listeners may come to feel they are running a losing race and so give up. The remedy is disciplined self-control on the speaker's part. If he paces utterance to meaning, his listeners will have no cause to complain.

Where ideas are not under control, are not at the speaker's beck and call, rate may become inappropriately slow, lagging behind the audience's abilities to comprehend. Again, the result is irritation. The audience wishes the speaker would "get on with it."

Where rate is either too fast or too slow the speaker has disregarded his audience and his own meaning. Usually he is speaking at his listeners rather than thinking out his material with them. The cause of slowness may be poor preparation. Perhaps he is finding his ideas for the first time in slow, disjointed wordings while his audience waits impatiently. The cause of undue rapidity may be want of the keen sense of communication we have already discussed. Meaningfulness, self-discipline, and consideration for the audience are the only serviceable roads to improvement.

Ineffectual pausing and phrasing are characteristic of poorly managed rate. The too-rapid speaker does not take time to group words into meaningful thought units; nor does he stop frequently enough for the audience to catch up with him and absorb his ideas. The too-slow speaker breaks ideas within thought groups so that meaning is distorted or lost; his pauses are simply stops during which he collects his thoughts. He hesitates, often filling the resulting silence with "uhs" and "ers." His disfluency destroys meaning and effectiveness.

The skilled speaker controls rate as he observes audience cues which signal that listeners are or are not absorbing his message. If he sees frowns or puzzled looks, he may slow down, at the same time modifying content by repeating what he has already said or by adding new ideas to make his point clearer and more acceptable. If he sees his listeners staring vacantly or assuming lolling, indifferent bodily postures, he may speed up or slow down in order to produce variety and thus recapture attention. If he sees knowing smiles or heads nodding in agreement and understanding, he may speed up since he has been given a "go" signal which says that what he is saying is readily understood and he need not belabor it. Speed ought to match the rate of comprehension.

The content of the speech often demands variations in rate and certain quantities (meaning elongation of particular sounds, usually vowels). A blow-by-blow description of a boxing match would sound ludicrous if delivered at largo pace and with elongated vowel sounds. Similarly, to describe a quiet, calm, romantic canoe ride with rapid rate, sounds of short duration, and abrupt, staccato rhythms would neither reinforce meanings nor create appropriate mood. Just as rate ought to match comprehension, it ought to suit the material's emotional tone.

If rate is correlated with reception, meaning, and mood, it will be varied. To speak at the same rate throughout a public speech is monotonous and invites listeners to turn its attention elsewhere if it does not lull them to sleep.

Pitch. Flexibility in pitch is a further attribute of the skilled speaker; lack of variety in pitch is as hampering as lack of variety in volume or rate. Monotone in pitch, volume, and rate can destroy the meaning of even the best ideas and the attentiveness of the most willing listeners.

Each of us has a pitch level which is natural and normal. Hanley and Thurman say, "Research findings for superior young adult male and female speakers are that their average (habitual) pitch levels are C_3 and $G\#_3$ respectively . . . or one octave and two musical notes, respectively below middle C."[12] These authors and other authorities recommend that no one institute a program

---

[12] Theodore D. Hanley and Wayne L. Thurman, *Developing Vocal Skills* (New York: Holt, Rinehart and Winston, 1962), p. 144. By permission of Holt, Rinehart and Winston, Inc.

for relocating his habitual pitch without prior medical consultation. They further add:

> Pitch (frequency) is a function of balances among length, tension and mass in the vibration of a taut string, which your vocal cords resemble to a considerable degree. In your vocal mechanism these balances or this adjustment has been arrived at over a span of years. Your average level changed from infancy to childhood to young adulthood, where you now stand. In the absence of better information, we believe, it should be assumed that your physiological maturation has been as normal in the larynx as it has been in your upper arm, or ankle, or any other anatomical locus. If this is true, if you have normal cords which vibrate under normal tension, then the frequency at which they vibrate most often is the best, the one at which you can produce sounds longest, with least effort. Temporary movements away from that frequency are good, for obvious reasons. But an ill-considered shift of any magnitude away from that habitual level can result in vocal strain and other more serious effects. . . .[13]

Some speakers unintentionally adopt pitches too high or too low. This is especially true at the beginnings of speeches and at points where tenseness and nervousness impair ability to vary pitch levels. From any such artificial basic pitch it is difficult to inflect upward or downward for emphasis or meaning. Thus a speaker who does not take such steps to reduce tension as were discussed in Chapter 3 will find himself adopting pitch levels that do not allow reasonable expression of meaning.

Changes in pitch are effected by raising or lowering the key of the voice either gradually or abruptly between or within words. Gradual changes in pitch are referred to as "slides," since we actually slide from one key to another. Abrupt changes are called "steps." The way in which we modify pitch oftentimes determines what we mean and the degree of emphasis we place upon an idea. Through inflection it is possible to convey meaning opposed to the meanings of one's words. "Oh no" can convey a variety of meanings depending upon the way it is inflected. "Oh, no" inflected upward by means of a step may convey disbelief. "Oh,

---

[13] *Ibid.*, p. 145.

no" inflected downward by means of a slide may indicate inde-
cision. "Oh no" inflected downward by means of a slide may
indicate dismay or may mean "yes."

The demands for pitch changes come most often from the
material in the speech. If public speech is to have conversational
quality, inflection and stress must resemble the inflections and
stresses of lively conversation. In ordinary conversation we do not
think much about pitch inflections, stresses, or changes of key;
we automatically make changes consonant with meanings. But, as
Whately emphasized, if public speakers do not respond to their
materials as they would under normal circumstances, their pitch
patterns are likely to belie their words. You are most likely to
adopt the steps, slides, and stresses that communicate comfortably
and clearly if you concentrate on your meanings and on your
listeners' need to understand them. If your habitual pitch and
stress patterns do not serve you well in impromptu and extemporaneous speaking, we suggest that you seek the help of a speech
specialist who can competently analyze your speech patterns and
devise a special program of retraining. The public speaking platform is not a suitable place to think about your pitch and stress
patterns; there, the task is to *use* the conventional patterns you
have elsewhere learned to command.

In addition to variety in pitch, an audience demands the
comfortable empathic responses which result from appropriateness in inflection. If an audience perceives from inflections that
you are not thinking what you are saying or that you lack enthusiasm or are falsely enthusiastic, if they see that you are uncomfortable and therefore unable to move freely within a pitch range,
you cannot expect them to respond appreciatively or comfortably
to your message.

Your own need for flexibility in pitch arises from your need
to avoid feelings of strain. Also, you listen to your own voice as
you speak and are stimulated or bored by what you hear.

The occasion or setting must be considered in establishing
pitch controls. Pitch helps to establish mood. High pitch can
create impressions of tension and excitement; low tones can help
to convey solemnity or calmness. Pitch and the power to project

adequate sound are related. To fill a large hall or to speak above competing noises one must adopt his most comfortable and efficient pitch range so that all resources of a relatively relaxed vocal mechanism are at his disposal in overcoming the difficulties imposed by the setting.

Quality. Quality is produced by changes in the shapes and sizes of the resonators: pharynx, mouth, nasal passages. No uniformly accepted set of labels exists for describing vocal qualities, but labels have been attached to various types of voices.

In criticizing the vocal aspects of a speech it is common practice to say that a speaker's voice is breathy, nasal, denasal, pectoral, oral, guttural, metallic, strident, or orotund. These terms are really attempts to say something about what is happening along the path of the breath stream which produces sound. To say a voice is *nasal* means that an unusual amount of the breath stream emanates from the nose strongly reinforced by resonance in the nasal passages. To speak of a voice as *denasal* means that there is little nasal resonance on the "m," "n," and "ng" sounds due to some closure of the nasal passages. What we have called nasal is sometimes spoken of as positive nasality; denasal quality is sometimes called negative nasality.

To say a voice is *pectoral* is to imply that the sound seems to be reinforced in the chest or pectoral regions. It is doubtful that chest resonance really occurs, but some voices sound that way. To refer to a voice as *oral* is to indicate that vocal placement seems forward in the mouth so that sound seems reflected off the teeth and gum ridges. *Guttural* voices are those that seem especially reinforced low in the back of the throat. *Metallic* or *strident* voices sound as though they are heavily supported by strained and tense surfaces, presumably those within the mouth including the hard palate (roof of mouth). *Orotund* voices are those thought pleasant because they seem reinforced by a suitable balance of relaxed surfaces, which suggests that the cavities involved must be rounded. The truth is that none of these descriptive terms accurately describes acoustic phenonema in any precise way, but the terms do describe our psychological reactions to what we hear. They enable us to talk meaningfully about these perceptions, and they remind us how ready listeners are to make judgments on the basis of vocal quality.

Breathy and *aspirate* describe voices produced by inadequate control over the breath stream. When more breath is released than is used in vibrating the vocal folds efficiently, the result is a whispery sound, usually of inadequate volume. Often the reason for this phenomenon is that the vocal folds are not firmly approximated; the air passing between them causes *some* vibration but also some sheer escape noise comparable to the sound of whispering.

The ways a speaker tenses the muscles involved in voice production and resonation and his general physical condition determine his vocal quality to a large extent. Tensed muscles are likely to produce *metallic* quality; too much relaxation is likely to produce unconventionally *nasal* sounds. A person in excellent physical and nervous condition is likely to manipulate his resonators so as to produce satisfactory vocal quality. A person in full control of all his muscles is likely to produce full, resonated tones. An invalid or aged person who lacks control over his general musculature has poor control of his speech.

Qualities suitable for public speaking cannot be assumed at will, but elimination of what Hanley and Thurman call "negative tonal characteristics" is possible through special training and through self-analysis and discipline. The effort sometimes needed to achieve agreeable vocal quality has its rewards. The conditions that quality depends upon contribute to your general well-being. The empathic effects of good vocal quality support effective communication. Strained voices produce comparable strains in listeners and, of course, no "negative tonal characteristic" can produce affirmative aesthetic experience.

Knowing how voices are produced, how vocal sound is articulated, and what effects flow from various attributes of voice and utterance is a necessary basis for exercising that self-control all effective public speaking requires. The public platform is no place to perform vocal or articulatory experiments; it is a place for revealing the precision of muscle and quality control that comes from private experimentation and reflection. You ought to experiment with your vocal resources, as with your bodily resources. Only so will you establish the habits and acquire the versatility essential to understanding and favorable, empathic responses on the part of listeners.

EMPATHY

As we have already implied, the bodily action and vocal quality of a public speaker are visual and acoustic stimuli that subtly affect listeners. We have several times referred to a part of these effects as *empathic*. Our entire discussion of delivery can be put in proper perspective by considering the general concept, *empathy*.

Empathy is defined as, "The ascription of our emotional feelings to the external object which serves as their visual and auditory stimulus."[14] The German word for empathy, *einfühlung*, provides a clue to the distinctions which must be made between sympathy and empathy. Sympathy is a feeling an observer experiences *toward* a speaker, a feeling he has *for* him. Empathy is a "feeling in with" the speaker. The psychologist, Woodworth, said, "As sympathy means 'feeling with,' empathy means 'feeling into,' and the idea is that the observer projects himself into the object observed and gets some of the satisfaction from watching an object that he would get from being that object."[15] Shaffer, Gillmer, and Schoen add, "These empathic actions, postures or expressions are not deliberate mimicry and the persons displaying them are usually unaware of what they are doing. As non-voluntary acts, therefore, they are explained in the same manner as suggestion."[16]

The implications for you as a public speaker are apparent.

---

[14] *Funk & Wagnalls New Standard Dictionary of the American Language* (New York: Funk & Wagnalls, 1960), p. 813.

[15] Robert S. Woodworth, *Psychology, A Study of Mental Life* (New York: Holt, 1921), p. 491.

[16] Laurance F. Shaffer, B. Von Haller Gillmer and Max Schoen, *Psychology* (New York: Harper and Brothers, 1940), p. 195.

You must so act and sound that the audience receives the sensations (or suggestions) you wish them to have. They must perceive you in ways that make them want to take part in what is going on, to participate with you in your speech.

Most of us have had the experience of watching a speaker teeter on the edge of the platform so that his balance seemed precarious. We have heard speakers whose rates and bodily actions were so slow that we wanted to push them along. We have listened to speakers so gravel-voiced that we came away with sore throats. As we literally "take in" speakers, we sometimes do so so strongly that we ourselves make movements in imitation of them. In all such cases we manifest empathy. Some other examples of empathy at work can be seen in people at the theatre who cry with the tragic hero, people at a track meet who lift their bodies as the high jumper clears the bar, or people at a circus who shift as they watch a tightrope walker balancing above the crowd.

There are more subtle empathic reactions. They include our responses to an architecturally unbalanced building, our muscular tonicity in reaction to chamber music, our empathic reactions to sculpture or paintings. It is not necessary to go deeply into the theories of empathy advanced by Theodor Lipps, Vernon Lee (Violet Paget), or Karl Groos. The theories of empathy as a largely mental-psychological activity, a kinesthetic motor response, or awareness and inner-mimicry are interesting and bear inspection. But no matter what theory one accepts, the fact remains that empathy is inevitable during normal perception and therefore inevitable in response to public speeches.

The public speaking situation is one in which normal perception is continually taking place. Visual and auditory cues, as much as language, draw responses from audiences. Undesirable empathic responses are taking place when members of an audience squirm, close their eyes, look out the window, or yawn. When a listener nods his head in agreement with you, smiles when you smile, laughs with you, leans forward in his seat when you lean forward, you may be sure that he is "feeling in" with you. To be an able speaker you must become sensitive to audience reactions and learn to elicit, identify, and react to them, and your delivery is your most direct means of assuring that your listener not only listens, but participates in your speech and reacts to your content as you mean him to react. The primary reason for developing conventional expressive vocal and bodily action is to assure that relevant rather than irrelevant empathic responses will be generated by your delivery.

All aspects of bodily and vocal expression in public speaking must help listeners concentrate upon what the speaker means. Empathy is the mark of listeners' deep and full concentration upon the speech. If the thought and behavior on which they concentrate reinforce the speaker's purpose, the impact of content and delivery nears the ideal. But this coordination of matter, manner, and listeners' perceptions is less often the product of the inspired moment than of moments carefully prepared for by planning and rehearsal.[17] Effective delivery and compelling empathy are hardest to achieve when speeches are delivered from manuscript or when portions of material within extemporaneous speeches must be read. We turn next, therefore, to the topic of reading for public speaking.

Reading for Public Speaking

THE SPEAKER BECOMES READER

Public speakers become public readers when they read an entire speech from manuscript, when they memorize a speech and read it from memory, or when they read quotations, prose or poetry, as parts of a speech. In each circumstance the method of delivery changes the role of the speaker. We pointed out in Chapter 1 (pp. 13–15) that the person who reads aloud becomes an interpreter—one who stands between the author of the material

---

[17] For extended discussion of extemporaneous speaking and rehearsal for this mode of delivery see Chapter 3, pp. 59–61; 65–67.

and the audience. When he presents his work from memory, a speaker similarly stands between the author he was and the speaker he is. Since the position of the reader is intermediate, the primary demands upon him come from the material. Elements in the particular occasion and the conventions of the audience force but minor modifications in his behavior. His personal skill affects his communication, but the material to be read chiefly determines what ought to be done.

If we put aside private reasons such as personal convenience or uncertainty, there remain but two good reasons for reading to an audience: (1) to bring something new and unusual to the fore or (2) to give listeners meanings which they would not get from reading the material by themselves either silently or orally.

Reading a speech or a portion of it involves stirring up meanings in those who listen. By uttering the sounds signified by black marks on a white page, you take responsibility for translating the marks into meaning. You must endow the printed words with the meanings their composer, or you, if you happen to be the author, intended them to have. Where you were the composer, you presumably know what the words mean; the problem becomes one of revitalizing your own ideas. If someone else composed what you choose to read, you must understand what the author meant before you can give the meaning to others. Whether you undertake to revitalize your own ideas, or to bring to life what another author meant, you have analytical work to do before you read.

Most students read badly because they are not aware of what work is involved in getting and giving meaning. This is sufficient reason for discouraging beginners from reading their speeches. Most beginners read even short quotations so poorly they distort meaning and rob the material of its sense. Perhaps one college student in ten reads prose meaningfully aloud. We cannot treat oral interpretation here fully, but we can offer basic suggestions to public speakers who must sometimes read. Since a public speaker's reading is primarily for utilitarian rather than aesthetic purposes, the observations that follow focus on reading to convey practical meaning, leaving out of consideration the equally legitimate object of reading to create aesthetic pleasure.

GENERAL PRINCIPLES

The following suggestions are arranged in the approximate order in which you are likely to confront the problems discussed.

Discover author's purpose and method.   To determine an author's purpose and method, sift the material for clues. Is the communication essentially utilitarian? Aesthetic? Or does the author's intent fall somewhere between? At the utilitarian end of this imaginary continuum might stand a technical report or the minutes of a business meeting. At the aesthetic end you would expect to find love lyrics. Any author's purpose in composing will lie somewhere along the line between these types. Consider the different communicative purposes that distinguish a news report, an editorial, a personal essay, a fictional narrative, a scene from a play, a ballad, a sonnet.

When an author's purpose is practical, as the news reporter's and editorialist's purposes usually are, he may explain how a thing can be done, why it should be done, or how to get people to do it. He may simply describe. Or he may explain through abstract proof. But some editorialists, many essayists, and most narrators also try to bring meaning to readers by giving significant form to selected portions of human experience. Most authors have the same purposes you have: to inform, persuade, reinforce, inquire, or entertain. You must discover *which* purpose dominates in each passage. You must ascertain the writer's central idea, the theme of his work. This tells you what tone or mood to adopt in your general delivery. It also gives you a framework for further analysis of the material.

Discover the complete meaning.   One of the chief causes of poor reading is failure to obtain complete meaning from the material. To discover the purpose is not enough. You should learn what the material says and what the author's philosophy or attitude is. In so doing you may have to turn to other materials and read about the author or read critical essays written about the material.

Getting the full meaning entails knowing the meaning of all

the words. You must know their dictionary meanings and their denotative and connotative meanings. You will also have to study the contexts of these words before you can interpret them precisely as *this* author meant them. You should realize that the associations and the responses words touch off are important. Make sure, then, that you are aware of the referents intended by your author. Examining language carefully, a task you may find glorious or laborious, will be essential to grasp the material, to reconstruct suggested meanings, and to respond emotionally to the ideas.

To achieve complete meaning you will sometimes have to study the setting for the material. The historical period depicted or to which the piece belongs will be as much a matter for concern as its objective meaning. You may have to answer for yourself such questions as: "Who is saying this?" "Why is he saying it?" "Who is the intended listener?" Whether the words were spoken at Gettysburg National Cemetery or in the give-and-take of a Lincoln-Douglas debate will affect the manner in which you read them.

Knowing the author's mood is a related requirement for attaining complete meaning. Mood is the author's expression of attitude. You, as the middleman, must reflect feelings in harmony with the author's and for that reason, unless you are an experienced and accomplished reader, sight reading can be dangerous. The establishment of mood is especially important to effective presentation of materials with aesthetic purposes. You cannot quote poems and stories effectively unless you understand and are able to transmit mood. Even your reading of utilitarian material is enhanced if you can adopt the manner that reflects your author's attitude toward the subject about which he wrote.

Sometimes paraphrasing a passage or writing a précis will aid you in assimilating its full meaning. You must undertake whatever research, peripheral reading, or repetition is needed to discover complete meaning. Only if you understand the whole can you understand how to read a work or any of its parts.

Discover the structure and unity of the selection. Every well written composition has perceivable structure and unity. Some planned development of ideas dominates the work. If you know what lines of thought or feeling contribute most to the structural pattern and the unity of the material, you have important hints about what to emphasize in reading. If you quote at length, you have need to examine the form the author has chosen as his medium of expression. News story, prose narrative, ballad, sonnet, and dramatic scene have distinctive structural patterns. For example, the most important facts or meanings are usually found near the start of a news story, but near the end of a dramatic scene. What is worth quoting, what is representative of the author's meaning, and what must be emphasized if an entire selection is read are all revealed by attention to the structure and unity of the work.

Discovering structure also means examining grammatical constructions so you can clearly see minor relationships. It means paying close attention to transitional portions of the work. Whether they are minor or major structural features, your purpose is basically to discover what relational patterns you must express by manner of utterance.

Cultivate a sensitivity to rhythm. Some of the subtlest shadings of meaning achieved through language are conveyed by changes in rhythm, changes in the beat or measure of sounds. This is especially true of poetry, but it is also important in some prose. If you choose to quote Daniel Webster, Winston Churchill, Adlai Stevenson, or John F. Kennedy, you will seldom convey the full meaning of the passage if you do not express the rhythmic patterns so characteristic of these speakers' prose. Only by preserving rhythm, or by breaking it, can the meanings of some authors be realized. It is seldom necessary to break prose rhythms but it is frequently necessary to do so with poetry. You should be careful not to let meter dominate your utterance to such a degree that you destroy meaning. The extreme example of this fault is the small child's sing-song recitation of poetry. In all written and spoken forms rhythm conveys significant meaning; therefore, your capacity to "hear" these meanings and reproduce them will often determine what you should and should not try to quote.

Cultivate imaginative capacities.   A further requisite for good reading is imagination, the power to see what others cannot in a particular circumstance or combination of words or emotional undertone. Develop your ability to perceive authors' unique achievements, their use of special patterns of expression, new relationships between ideas, and new word pictures. The more aesthetic the author's purpose the more valuable imagination is in interpreting his material.

Imagination comes from experience and from temporarily divorcing yourself from reality. It comes, in part, from a capacity to dream. Let your mind range as you work over material to be read. Visualize the possibilities. Create several versions of possible meaning in your mind, then choose the best one for your final interpretation.

Using your imagination is especially important if you plan to quote extensively from fictional and poetic materials. Without the imaginative component, the reading of such writing is lack-luster, pedestrian. The interpretation of fantasy requires imaginative abilities of the highest degree.

Cultivate ability to group and pause.   Grouping or phrasing is the art of breaking a text up into ideas or speech units. A word is a grammatical unit; the idea is the speech unit. According to W. M. Parrish:

> When we are creating thought as we go along, as in conversation, we generally make the grouping clear to our hearers, that is, make our ideas distinct. In reading from the printed page, our eyes must be trained to run quickly along the succession of words and organize them into proper groups before the voice attempts to utter them. If the voice fails to communicate this grouping to one's hearers, it fails to communicate meaning, for meaning lies in the grouping. . . . If we fail to do so, we throw upon our hearers the burden of sorting our words apart, a task as difficult as sorting out the words from an unspaced sentence in print.[18]

---

[18] Wayland Maxfield Parrish, *Reading Aloud*, 4th ed. (New York: The Ronald Press Co., 1966), p. 21. Copyright 1966 The Ronald Press Company. Used by permission of the publisher.

In reading poetry the inexperienced tend to group mechanically at the end of each line, a practice to be avoided. You must learn to group by thought. Realistic grouping is no less necessary in quoting prose, though the problems are less complex.

You should be aware that there are two types of punctuation, oral and written. Oral punctuation makes meanings clear to an auditor by noticeable changes in voice or action, as written punctuation makes similar meanings clear to a reader. The two kinds of punctuation do not always coincide. There are many times when you will want to ignore the written punctuation altogether. Pausing at every comma, semicolon, or period does not always enhance meaning. It may confuse. One who reads aloud must determine which written punctuation assists him in grouping audible thought and which does not. Punctuation in oral reading and in public speaking, as we have already noted, is achieved by changes in volume, rate, or pitch, and by gestures and other bodily movements which make groups of words stand out clearly and so convey meaning incisively.

A pause is a psycho-physiological event. Proper pausing does more than any other one thing to make reading natural and realistic. "There is never any need to pause for breath alone, as the pauses for thought are so many that the lungs may always be full, a necessary condition for good voice support. . . . We must learn to fill the think tank and the lung tank, automatically and simultaneously."[19] A pause is not mere silence. It is not a dead stop. In a true pause silence is pregnant with meaning. When the voice stops for a true pause, thought continues to manifest itself. The reader sees ahead and gains command of the next idea; the listener digests what has been said and becomes curious about what is to come. Pauses help both the oral reader and the listener to apprehend clearly the relationships between the words and phrases.

Professor Parrish gives two very good reasons why young readers do not pause. He says:

---

[19] S. H. Clark and M. M. Babcock, *Interpretation of the Printed Page* (Englewood Cliffs, N.J.: Prentice-Hall, 1940), p. 5.

First, they lack confidence. The excitement of reading before others causes a nervous acceleration of what is normally too rapid a rate of utterance. Under such circumstances, the cessation of vocal activity for a fraction of a second seems an ominous silence full of dreadful possibilities. The reader feels that his audience will begin to wonder whether he has not broken down. . . .

A second reason why young readers seldom pause is just that they do not *deliberate*. They skim. Their minds do not *dwell* upon the ideas to be communicated. So surely as the mind begins to dwell upon the words being expressed there will be a focusing on separate word-groups (how else *can* one think?), and these word-groups will generally be separated from each other by pauses.[20]

We add, parenthetically, that Parrish's observations are true of speakers as well as readers.

Cultivate ability to subordinate ideas. You must realize that in oral reading and in speaking ideas are not all of the same value. Some ideas are subordinate to others. They support and amplify. In your analysis of material to be quoted you must notice these relationships. We have discussed the relations of structural analysis to this discovery. You must learn to *convey* relationships of degree by voice, gesture, and movement, to emphasize the most important ideas and de-emphasize the less important ones. Some readers read every word in the same way, with the same rate, pitch, and volume, even the same gesture. Their reading is boring. It lacks the variety of enlarged conversation and so fails to clarify the meaning inherent in the material. Thinking the thought, feeling the meaning, and releasing voice and body to reinforce these experiences offer the best means of expressing discovered relationships.

Cultivate ability to maintain visual directness. The ability to preserve visual directness is an even greater problem when reading to an audience than when speaking to them. Speakers who bury their noses in books or who gaze at papers on the lectern break the flow of communication and destroy the sense of live-

---

[20] Parrish, *Reading Aloud*, p. 36. Copyright 1966 The Ronald Press Co. Used by permission of the publisher.

liness which ought to prevail during public speaking. As Henneke says,

> The reader has a special eye problem. He must look at his manuscript and still maintain eye contact with his audience. His best answer is a compromise. His eyes should follow the manuscript until he is certain of what he is going to say. Then he may look at his audience until he has completed saying that phrase or group of phrases.[21]

In this way readers may read without wholly destroying the intimate speaker-audience relationship that gives speech its special social meaning.

We would add that preservation of visual contact with an audience during reading is a skill attained only through much practice. To take in a group of words, then to lift the eyes and focus upon the audience as these words are uttered requires that you remember what the eye first took in long enough to deliver it meaningfully and without interruption. The process demands a high degree of physical coordination plus memory and self-control. Some beginning students who find it difficult to achieve all this resort to memorizing quotations. Others who do not memorize familiarize themselves thoroughly with all quotations or excerpts before speaking. If they proceed wisely in this task they find they are following precisely the steps of analysis and practice we are recommending on this and the immediately preceding pages.

In short, visual directness—or its absence—usually reveals whether the reader has thoroughly or haphazardly prepared to read.

Cultivate the "illusion of the first time." Flexibility and variety are essential for all good speaking or reading. In extemporaneous speaking one thinks anew and responds afresh to ideas sifted though never fixed by preparation, but in reading from

---

[21] Ben Graf Henneke, *Reading Aloud Effectively* (New York: Rinehart, 1954), p. 143.

memory or the printed page it is fixed content and form that must be recaptured. The speaker's stimulus is never quite static, unless he overprepared; the oral reader's stimulus is inevitably static. It is precisely that thing to which he responded again and again during preparation. Only response to content and form is variable for the reader. Thus, the illusion of fresh experience with content is much harder to convey when reading than when speaking.

It is not limitations of vocal and bodily equipment that constrain most oral readers; it is inability to recapture whole meanings and to respond with full powers of intellect and imagination while under the stresses of public communication. There is no easy remedy. As is true with other arts, so it is here: given understanding of how to study material and of the resources of delivery, only practice, evaluation, and more practice can produce the controlled but lively responses to static stimuli that superior reading requires. Here the reader resembles the musician. The "illusion of the first time" to which audiences enthusiastically respond is largely the result of experience and painstaking practice. But for the speaker who reads only brief passages in the midst of extemporaneous speaking there is this encouraging fact: careful analysis, modest experiments with the resources of delivery, plus less than formidable amounts of practice can produce meaningful readings of utilitarian prose and uncomplicated kinds of poetry.

In this chapter we have examined delivery as a means to an end rather than as an end in itself. The schools of delivery that have held influence in modern times are, if nothing else, reminders of the fascination men have always had for the part of speechmaking that is most personal and most intimately revealing. For our day, and on the basis of man's experience with the various schools of delivery, it seems sensible to approach personal presentation of speeches by first recognizing that constructively communicative physical behavior arises as controlled but free response to thought and feeling fully experienced. If physical and vocal behaviors are means rather than ends in speaking, a general standard for good delivery is easily found: *Good delivery helps the listener to concentrate upon what is said; it does not attract attention to itself.*

There are, as we have tried to show, general principles of bodily and vocal action which encourage free and full use of the human body in reinforcing thought and feeling. There are also specific behaviors to be learned if listeners are to empathize favorably with speakers' messages. In essence, however, it is a speaker's attitudes toward his ideas, himself, and his audience that govern the functional value of his delivery. We have offered suggestions concerning constructive use of body and voice, and on reading for public speaking. But our belief is that it is from knowing and reflecting upon the possibilities of communicative action and from private drill to achieve conventional and variable habits that effective delivery ultimately emerges on the platform.

Exercises

WRITTEN

1. Write a description of the bodily action used by one of the following:
   a. A professor during a lecture.
   b. A classmate delivering a speech.
   c. Your roommate as he goes about his daily activities.

2. Write an analysis of your voice after listening to a recording of it. Comment specifically upon volume, rate, pitch, and quality.

3. Listen to a live speech delivered in person or over television. Write a description of the speaker's delivery with these questions in mind: What did the speaker do to support his ideas visually and vocally? What did he do with his body and voice which detracted from what he was saying?

4. Observe one of your classmates as he delivers a speech and during an informal conversation. Write a comparative account of his use of body and voice in these two situations. Note the similarities and differences in vocal and visual elements.

ORAL

1. Deliver a short speech during which you read aloud from at least three different literary forms: news account, scientific report, fictional prose, sonnet, ballad, essay, or dramatic scene.

2. Prepare and deliver a speech three to six minutes long in which you explain some procedure requiring much action of the body: how to do a dance, how to perform artificial respiration, how to handle a fencing foil, how to execute wrestling holds, how to gesture on stage, how to direct calisthenics.

3. Prepare a two-minute speech requiring gesture for description, explanation, and emphasis. Practice the speech aloud outside of class, deciding which bodily actions to employ. Deliver the speech in class *without* words. Use only eye contact, movement, posture, and gesture to convey your ideas. Discuss what you have done with members of your class in order to determine how much of your intended meaning was conveyed.

4. Assign each of the following sentences to three or four members of your class. Ask each person to say or read his sentence with an emphasis different from that used by the person preceding him, changing the meaning of the sentence each time it is read. Following the readings, discuss the differences in volume, pitch, and rate employed to achieve the differences.

   a. Who do you suppose I saw in class today?
   b. Oh yes, I'd love to go.
   c. You aren't really sure of that are you?
   d. I've never seen such food.
   e. There are always a lot of men at the movies on Saturday night.
   f. It was the most spectacular yet peculiar race you ever saw.
   g. There was the book just where I'd left it rain-soaked and falling apart.
   h. No I simply can't believe that that is so.
   i. Whoever heard of a person doing such a thing.
   j. Oh my dear what have you done?

---◦⊰{ 12 }⊱◦---   *Judging*

the Speech

A liberally educated citizen ought to be able to explain what happens when he is addressed by a public speaker. He ought to be able to describe the speech he hears and to explain why and how it contributed to the results. If people could do these things expertly in all cases, judging speeches would be a science, and public speaking would be human engineering. None of us has achieved precision in observing and analyzing public speech, nor are we likely to achieve it soon; but we can do better than we are accustomed to do.

Even the highly educated find it difficult to perceive the components of speeches as they listen. They find it even more difficult to judge what effects speeches have on people other than themselves. Those who have carefully studied the theory and practice of speech-making judge qualities and effects more reliably than those who have not, though the experts are by no means infallible. Like reliable criticisms of fiction, poetry, or painting, reliable evaluation of speeches depends greatly on practical and theoretical knowledge about what is possible and impossible.

Criticism is both the way we tell ourselves what is going on and the way we learn how to practice the art with greater insight. We are not likely to reduce speaking or any other art to science, but we still have both need and responsibility to bring as much knowledge as possible to bear when we respond to discourse. To equip us for such informed responses is a general object of all liberal education and a special object of speech courses.

The broad aims of a liberal education are to stimulate you to think in a variety of ways, to increase your ability to judge, to enable you to choose among alternatives, and to prepare you to take a responsible place in the world. We have explored theories with you to enlarge your understanding and described procedures and methods to enable you to fill your roles as public speaker and listener to speeches. As a final matter we invite you to consider how to form useful critical judgments.

We know there are those who believe that students are too young and inexperienced to be critics. But we believe criticism of live speeches is an important and necessary aspect of your study of public speaking. You were not prepared to function as a critic during the first rounds of speaking, but with some theories at your command you are ready and able to evaluate speeches with regard to those principles at least. Most important, critical activity will benefit you both as a speaker and as a private person.

The audience reactions revealed to you in early speeches are valuable. By knowing what your audience thought of your first speeches, you can improve your adaptation to the group in your later efforts. We are not saying audiences ever remain the same. By living a day longer your classroom audience changes each time you meet. Nonetheless, there are some criteria by which they measure effective speaking which do not change from session to session. Their consistent standards and recurring judgments can teach you much about speech and yourself.

Criticism in the classroom is a reciprocal activity. By openly registering your responses to your peers, you will aid immensely in their improvement, just as their frank responses to your speech-making will provide you with directions for improvement and always with insights into how others judge speaking.

To exercise full responsibility as a critic, you need to develop powers of discrimination and to know the methods and standards for criticism. We believe that preparing oral and written criticisms of live speeches and written criticisms of the texts of outstanding speeches are constructive experiences. We say with Dean Everett L. Hunt that

> . . . we might be better satisfied with the returns from the money and energy spent on rhetorical training if we cared more about producing educated and critical audiences. . . . Critical and analytical study of rhetoric and oratory should not be limited to those who expect to become professional speakers or writers, or to those who expect to teach it; it should be offered to all students who desire to understand the significance of rhetoric in modern life.[1]

Whether or not you are invited to criticize spoken or written public speeches at any juncture in your public speaking course, you owe it to yourself as a part of liberal education to develop standards of judgment and critical acuity toward the speeches you will hear, read, or deliver in future days or years. For this you must understand criticism, the standards and methods commonly employed in evaluating speeches, and the tasks you can effectively undertake as a critic of the speeches you will find in the laboratory of the classroom and elsewhere.

The Nature of Speech
Criticism

Criticism of any kind is judgment and/or appreciation. To evaluate or criticize implies analysis and comparison, approval or disapproval, commendation or censure. All reactions to objects, ideas, actions, and persons are critical or noncritical. Assessments or evaluations are criticism. Descriptions, reviews, commentaries, and surveys, unless interpretative, are not.

Criticism is essentially a comparative activity involving discrimination. Whenever we make a judgment or register appreciation, we do so with some standards of perfection in mind.

---

[1] "Editorial: 'From Rhetoric Deliver Us,'" *The Quarterly Journal of Speech*, XIV (April 1928), 266–267.

Where we are subjective in our judgments, our standards are likely to be very personal. We may not even be conscious of them. Where we become objective, we tend to become consciously aware of our norms and to identify them in our minds or on paper. Whichever cast of mind characterizes our criticism, we have some standards and our judgments place what we judge somewhere along a continuum of excellence. The object of our appraisal is contrasted to norms, or measured by them, and found to correspond in some degree. Either the item corresponds closely to the standards or it does not.

The Critical Object

A focus upon some object is essential in any type of criticism. The object may be tangible or intangible. It may be a material or combination of materials, an action or an idea. In aesthetic criticism this object may be a specific painting such as Picasso's "The Lovers"; a pattern of sounds such as Beethoven's Fifth Symphony, interpreted by a great orchestra; or physical action performed by dancers, such as the *pas de deux* from *The Firebird*. Objects for literary criticism are novels, short stories, poems, or essays, usually in the tangible form of printed words on a page. Whatever the kind of criticism, some object exists to be appreciated and/or evaluated and perhaps to be praised or condemned.

The critic who assesses a live speech, the speech as it is delivered, deals with a distinctive critical object. What he examines, appreciates, and judges consists of a combination of sounds and actions symbolizing ideas, existing in time, and cutting through air. This object is in constant flight, not static, not arrested. It is unlike some other critical objects. It is not a statue which can be placed on a pedestal and viewed from all sides. It is not a musical score nor a play script which can be consulted. It is not a painting which can be gazed at for hours. It is not print which can be pored over. The critical object in speech-making cannot be taken in with either eye or ear alone. It must be seen and heard—all in the moments of its creation. Like the dance, it does not stand still for

357

examination, yet its verbal nature makes it seem analogous to objects of literary criticism. And while it is true that a critic viewing a painting takes in first one part, then another, and the critic of music hears sounds in sequence in time, the critic of a live speech faces a more exacting assignment. He must see and hear sequences. Often he will not even have the drama critic's advantage of being able to consult a script before or after seeing and hearing the object he is to criticize.

The speech critic deals with a critical object which usually exists once and only once. There may be no public preview of it, and there may be no subsequent record. Speeches may be on identical subjects and in identical words, but exact duplication is impossible. The components in the speech situation are constantly shifting; the critic can perceive a whole speech only once. He may record judgments and reactions, but he cannot depend upon repeated exposures to the critical object.

To complicate matters further, the speech critic cannot always be present when the speech he wishes to criticize takes place. For example, he may choose to criticize a speech delivered in the past. Or he may decide to criticize oral utterance only after finding that it was of some importance to society or exerted some particular influence. In these situations he is unable to experience the *real* speech. Nonetheless, several alternative critical objects are available to him.

The most advantageous of these alternatives rarely exists. It is conceivable, though not very likely, that our would-be critic could obtain a sound motion picture that made all possible observations of visual and audible elements. A film of this sort would come closest to reproducing the real speech, but it cannot reproduce the speech situation because it will lack three-dimensional factors. The film is obviously not as reliable as on-the-spot observation for assessing such factors as environment and audience reaction. And this alternative will seldom be open to the critic, for even where films are available they usually contain only portions of major speeches.

A second alternative critical object is some form of electrical transcription of the sounds of the speech. This form of the speech

The form and content of any criticism are largely determined by the creative purposes that brought the object of judgment into being. The purposes dominating the creation of most speeches, as we have seen, are utilitarian. Thus, effect is usually placed above such criteria as permanence or beauty in evaluations of speeches. Nonetheless, judgments that evaluate only effects are but partial. Ethical and artistic considerations, too, are relevant. We contend that criticism which focuses upon the artistic achievements of speakers—the degree to which they fully use the resources of their art in seeking utilitarian and ethical effects—is that which produces the most comprehensive and constructive judgments.

In the classroom or out of it the criticism of speeches requires method and wisdom. Criticism, we think, requires (1) concentration on the speech as a critical object, (2) conscious identification of relevant data and criteria, (3) constructive attitudes toward the critical process, (4) comparison of observed speeches with criteria that define the ideal, (5) formulation of judgments that are specific and cogent, and (6) documented expression of the criticism itself.

Exercises

WRITTEN

1. Identify in advance some speech which is going to be delivered on some future date in your community. The speech must be one which you can both see and hear. Prepare to criticize this speech by systematically writing down pertinent information about the speaker and his purpose, the audience, and the occasion. Attend the speech. Make notes during its delivery using a body of criteria which you have decided to make the basis of your criticism in consequence of preliminary analysis of speaker, audience, and occasion. Finally, write a balanced evaluation.

2. Select a famous speech from a past era. Obtain the best text of the speech available to you for analysis and criticism. Read background materials on the period, including writings on the prevalent culture, living habits, and beliefs. Also read autobiographical or biographical materials about the speaker. After

375

achieving an understanding of the total situation and of the total speech, choose one of the following topics for detailed, written analysis and criticism:

a. The speaker's rational justifications.
b. The speaker's use of amplifying materials such as example, narration, statistics, definition.
c. The structure of the speech as it relates to the subject matter, the audience, and the occasion.
d. The speaker's style.
e. The authenticity of the text of the speech studied.

ORAL

1. Listen intently to a particular classroom speech assigned to you for evaluation. Keep in mind the requirements set forth in the speaker's assignment or avowed purpose. Take written notes where appropriate. Structure your judgments on the various aspects of the speech as clearly as possible. During the oral criticism period reserved for the speech assigned, deliver a one- or two-minute extemporaneous speech working from your notes.

2. Prepare and deliver a speech in which you discuss one of the following:
   a. The essential considerations involved in appraising one of the canons of public speaking: invention, disposition, style, delivery, *memoria.*
   b. The differences between the procedures for criticizing a live speech and those to be used in criticizing the text of a speech.
   c. The distinctions between the critical object in speech criticism and in other arts.
   d. The problems involved in arriving at a set of criteria to be applied in judging a particular speech.

Special Index for the Study of Types of Speeches

This index is designed as an aid to students and teachers who wish to structure the study or preparation of speeches around purposes for which speeches are made. The general section of the index identifies treatments of topics pertinent to all or to several purposes. Subsequent sections indicate the portions of this book which relate directly or with special relevance to a specific type of speech.

II. Speeches to Inform

    A. Invention: 108–138; 170–183; 185–190.

    B. Disposition: 221–222; 204–205 (Chronological); 226–227 (Spatial); 227–228 (Topical); 228–229 (Ascending-Descending Orders); 229–332 (Causal Sequences); 232–234 (Problem-Solution); 236–238 (Open Proposal); 241–242 (Monroe's Motivated Sequence); 242–244 (Elimination Order); Sample Outline: 261–266.

III. Speeches to Induce Inquiry

    A. Invention: 108–138; 170–183; 190–194.

    B. Disposition: 221–222; 238–240 (Reflective Sequence).

IV. Speeches to Reinforce

    A. Invention: 109–110; 112–120; 147–183.

    B. Disposition: 221–222; 226 (Chronological); 226–227 (Spatial); 227–228 (Topical); 228–229 (Ascending-Descending Orders); 229–232 (Causal Sequences); 232–234 (Problem-Solution); 236–238 (Open Proposal); 241–242 (Monroe's Motivated Sequence); 242–244 (Elimination Order).

V. Speeches to Persuade

    A. Invention: 107–109; 112–120; 128–131; 147–170; 199–204.

    B. Disposition: 221–222; 227–228 (Topical); 228–229 (Ascending-Descending Orders); 229–232 (Causal Sequences); 232–234 (Problem-Solution); 234–236 (Withheld Sequence); 236–238 (Open Proposal); 241–242 (Monroe's Motivated Sequence); 242–244 (Elimination Order); Sample Outline: 266–271.

VI. Speeches to Entertain

    A. Invention: 112–120; 170–183; 204–208.

    B. Disposition: 221–222; 226 (Chronological); 226–227 (Spatial); 227–228 (Topical); 228–229 (Ascending-Descending Orders); 229–232 (Causal Sequences); 232–242 (Problem-Solution); 236–238 (Open Proposal); 241–242 (Monroe's Motivated Sequence); 242–244 (Elimination Order).

Index

(A figure in italics denotes a footnote.)